T0246809

THE
HEART
OF THE
WOODS

THE HEART OF THE WOODS

Wyl Menmuir

Aurum

First published in hardback in 2024 by Aurum,
an imprint of The Quarto Group
One Triptych Place, London, SE1 9SH
United Kingdom

www.Quarto.com/Aurum

ISBN: 978-0-7112-8924-6
E-book ISBN: 978-0-7112-8926-0
Audiobook ISBN: 978-0-7112-9091-4

1 2 3 4 5 6 7 8 9 10

Cover illustration and design by Holly Ovenden

Map by Martin Brown

MIX
Paper | Supporting
responsible forestry
FSC
www.fsc.org   FSC® C171272

Typeset in Adobe Caslon Pro by Typo•glyphix, Burton-on-Trent, DE14 3HE
Printed and bound by CPI Group (UK) Ltd, Croydon, CR0 4YY

For Dad

JAPAN

Takayama

Meiji Jingu

N

Munlochy Clootie Well

Abriachan
Forest Trust

SCOTLAND

GalGael
Trust

Sycamore Gap

Devil's Water

NORTHERN
IRELAND

IRELAND

Hometree

Burren National
Park

Tomnafinnoge
Wood

ENGLAND

Wyl's father's woodland

Llangadwaladr

Pennant Melangell

Wenlock Edge

Burwash
Manor

WALES

Wytham
Woods

Chalford

Globe
Theatre

Family Tree,
Bodmin Moor

Pentiddy Woods

Tehidy Woodland

Dendles
Wood

Penzance

Isles of Scilly

Falmouth
Harbour

Bodlon wyf i'r ganiadaeth,
Bedwlwyn o'r coed mwyn a'i maeth.

DAFYDD AP GWILYM, 'Offeren y Llwyn',

I am content with the music,
It was nurtured by a beech grove in the sweet woods.

DAFYDD AP GWILYM, 'The Woodland Mass'

CONTENTS

Woodland Planter

*A woodland in becoming on the border between
North Wales and England*

We sweep up into a white sky and the grey-blue sea opens wide before us, fringed white where it meets the dark cliffs. We attempt, through scratched, lozenge windows, to make out the seal heads of surfers, sitting frozen on their boards, though we do not see if they catch the incoming set as we are banking away from the coast now, inland, and they are lost in cloud. We climb until we become the white cloud for what seems like an age and when we glimpse the sea again it is a line in the far distance.

All sense of speed is lost at height and as we emerge from the clouds it is as though we now hang over a patchwork quilt, which is being moved slowly beneath us, a conveyor belt of patterned cloth. The patches that make up the quilt are uneven, irregular things. They are the light grey of village and town, the slate grey of reservoir and lake, the bright, unnatural green of sheep fields. They are the bare browns of moor, hillside and fell, huge industrial units and power plants, fabrics stitched together by road and motorway. In small islands, there are squares and rectangles of dark green-brown, patchworks within patchwork, silently preparing themselves for the year.

Had we managed, somehow, to look down through these same

lozenge windows some 10,000 years ago, these green-brown patches would have been the quilt almost in its entirety, huge swatches of it stitched together with silver rivers.

We lean our foreheads against the windows and try to imagine it as it was before we learnt to craft and sharpen spears and axes, before we felled the first trees, before we drove out the wolves and bears, the buffalo and bison, before we chased the eagles to the far north.

The Celts, they said, held woodland to be sacred. They imbued the forests with spirits, tended groves of yew and oak, ash and elm like children, like ancestors. Somewhere, deep down, we know we have inherited that legacy, though we are children of the enclosures too, and the clearances, the settlements and plantations. The great Greenwood is a myth now, and this patchwork is our inheritance, the boundried and fenced, the sharp-lined and sheep-grazed.

Far below, we are beginning to get busy, attempting to stand the trees up again, planting and planting, working from memory. This bit goes here, right? Willow and alder in the boggy ground, field maple on dry? And the oak? Where does the oak go?

One of these tiny patches, little more than a thumbnail from this height, is the woodland my father planted: two small rectangles that sit by the thinnest thread of blue; a river that marks the boundary between Wales and England.

It was early spring and branches that were bare just a week ago were beginning to show green. I was wandering between tall, spindly trunks, looking at the tips of the branches, at their becomings, on the first day of the year in which I could feel the sun's warmth on my face. Some of these young trees were holding tightly to their leaves in bunched buds, dark and smooth, while others had put out tentative tips and blades in the hope, perhaps, that the last of the hard frosts had passed. Even compared to the previous day, the trees were looking greener, as though they were impatient to become their summer selves.

The trees I was looking at were the ones my father planted nine years before, on the outskirts of a small village in north-east Wales, close to the Berwyn Mountains. He wanted to create something that would outlast him, a canopy beneath which his grandchildren and their children could find shade, a source of wood for the fire, a sustainable building material and, perhaps above all of that, a small contribution to addressing the loss of biodiversity in the landscape in which he lives.

Nearby, I could hear him talking to my ten-year-old son, Tom, about the galls, the spherical woody growths which sat, improbably bulbous, on the thin, bare branches of the oaks. Tom, leaning on my father's hazel walking stick with both hands, had his face up close to one of the galls as my father explained that the oak apples were the birthplace of tiny wasps, pointing out the minuscule hole in each of the galls where a wasp had emerged. When Tom was satisfied that they were now vacant properties, he and Dad picked some and stuffed them into their pockets.

They were roughly the same age, Tom and the trees. Just five months separated Tom's birth and their planting, though adjust that for the fact that Tom arrived almost nine weeks earlier than expected, and you could barely fit a cigarette paper between their ages. I have marked Tom's growth alongside theirs, from carrying him around them in a sling when the saplings were barely up to my waist, still wrapped in their plastic deer guards, to watching them tower over him in full leaf as he walked the patch of land with the confidence of someone who has known this place his whole life.

Later, when we returned home to Cornwall, I would find the dun brown oak galls rolling around in the washing machine drum after some had managed to remain concealed in Tom's trouser pockets on their journey through the laundry pile. The majority, though, made their way into his bedside drawer, where precious things are stored, among the Pokémon cards, LEGO mini figures and keyrings yet to find keys.

For a while, he would carry a couple of the galls around with him like little talismans. Was the draw to do that similar to mine, the one that leads me when walking beneath autumn trees, to pocket particularly fine acorns which I then forget about until some months later when I root around for change or a tissue, and experience the satisfaction of feeling that smooth shell, and the rough cup in which it sits? I will find somewhere to plant it, in the hope that it might take root on the edge of a field or a path, or somewhere out of the way where it might stand a chance of growing. As I watched my father and son, I realized I still had a couple on me from the last time I had visited the year before, when the road to Oswestry, the nearest town in Shropshire, was blanketed in acorns. And there it was, that familiar thrill, the realization that within the tiny shell in my pocket there was the potential for a massive oak, waiting for its chance – an acorn is like a benevolent hand grenade.

Just as Tom knew nothing about my habit of collecting and redistributing acorns, I did not realize, until I started to talk about it, how many other people do something similar yet keep it to themselves. There is an echo in that of the story of the most famous of acorn distributors, Admiral Cuthbert Collingwood, Nelson's second in command at the Battle of Trafalgar. When Collingwood was home from sea, on his estate in College Valley in Northumberland, he would set out walking with a pocket full of acorns and plant them wherever he thought would be a good place for oaks to grow. He had in mind the protection of Britain and the future of its navy, and in particular the nation's ability to build more ships which were constructed largely of oak. It took 2,000 to 3,000 oaks to build a ship like the 104-gun HMS *Victory*. While Collingwood knew he would never live to see his oaks grow to a size where they could be fashioned into the planks of a hull, and could not have foreseen that by that time the navy would be reliant on metal and steam rather than wooden sailing ships, his oaks were a thought experiment, a hope for the future.

Legacies are funny things, aren't they? Unpredictable. Uncertain. Our intentions yielding mixed results. Like my father, Collingwood wanted to be a good ancestor, channelling the phrase that appears in one form or another in cultures across the world: 'Blessed is he who plants trees under whose shade he will never sit.'

Oak galls.

Tom, satisfied now his pockets were full of oak apples, wandered down to the edge of one of the two large ponds. Dad wades into them twice yearly and, with a pitchfork, removes the pond weed, prolific due to silt runoff from the road and the hills above. My son looked down through the weed for signs of the newts that Dad had told him skirted the mudflats on the pond's floor. Dad joined him and fished out some weed with his walking stick. He placed it gently on the pond's edge and explained to Tom that anything living in the weed should be given the chance to get back into the water, before it was taken any further from the pond. He combed through the weed with his fingertips, and I watched as, with Tom, he picked out dragonfly and damselfly nymphs, those uncanny pond aliens that would, in a month or two, molt and transform from the grotesque to the ethereal as they assume their adult forms. Dad began to talk about the dragonfly's lifecycle, but Tom was glazing over again, though later in the morning they would search for videos of larvae transforming into dragonflies and damselflies on YouTube and his interest would be rekindled.

As they investigated the pond, I tried a version of the thought experiment I had conducted while looking out of a plane window some months before, this time attempting to project my father's woodland into some distant future, to imagine how it would be when these trees were fully grown, though many of them will not have reached their full size, even when Tom is approaching seventy, the age my father is now.

While attempting the thought experiment, my mind wandered off again, onto the subject of life's uncertainties, thoughts of the future my children and their children – if they choose to have them – will inherit. I found myself spiralling on the news of the day, of mass extinctions, extreme weather and made the conscious effort to bring myself back into the here and now. I tried to remind myself that the present is a healthier place in which to dwell by investigating the woodland in front of me, noting how it was on that particular day, at that particular time.

At just over a couple of acres, it is a small, roughly rectangular patch of land and contains just shy of a thousand trees which my father planted by hand and which he looks after like children. The woodland comprises sixteen species of native broadleaf trees: three species of willow; two of oak – sessile and pedunculate; field maple; silver birch; hornbeam; hawthorn; holly; wild cherry; rowan; wild service tree; small leaved lime; crab apple and alder. With the exception of the holly, which is an evergreen broadleaf, all the trees in this woodland are deciduous.

It is not, as my father reminded me later, a woodland. Not yet. It was and still is, for now, a gathering of trees. It would start to look a little more like a woodland when my father thinned the trees out where they were vying for headroom and light, a job he was to start in the coming days, breaking up the lines and opening space for others to grow, allowing them to spread their canopies, to become themselves in full.

But what will make it a woodland proper, the things that will make it worthy of the title, will not be how it looks from above. It will be the complex web of life that grows up around it, the beetles and butterflies that make this place home, the bats and birds that roost in the branches and the cracks and holes that open up in the trunks. It will become a woodland when the mycorrhizae spread out their blanket of mycelia between the roots, in the way the trees find and hold their space in the land, the delicate, shifting balance between the fast-growing willows and the slower growing oaks.

It will become a woodland when trees die and lie where they fall, when the leaf litter on the ground transforms a grass-rich pasture to a woodland mulch, supporting life there too, as the previously infertile soil – a casualty of the intensive farming that is damaging so much of this unseen, yet exceptionally important realm – regains some of its life-giving properties, and as woodland plants take root and begin to show themselves. It will become a woodland too in the relationship between the people who live here and the trees that grow here has been established and embedded, as they too find their equilibrium, as some areas are left to their own devices and others develop as worked coppice. It may not become a woodland in my father's lifetime, nor in mine, nor even Tom's perhaps, though my father is doing everything he can to give it a fighting chance.

When I asked my father if it bothered him that he would not get to know what this place would become, he replied, 'You do wonder sometimes, what's the point if you're not going to see the benefits? But then you realize you are seeing the benefits. You get the privilege of seeing these trees grow, and there's satisfaction in that, and in knowing you've left something behind, and the knowledge of the joy that someone else is going to get from being here at some point far in the future.'

This walking of the trees is a routine we have been doing since they were first planted, one of many routines and rituals here, like the feeding of the birds in the morning, the spotting of the sparrowhawk as it swoops down from its perch on the hill to pick off one of the garden birds, the feeding by hand of the tame pheasants.

Before Tom and I arrived, my father had been coppicing hazel and willow with a handsaw and there were piles of long sticks beneath the trees. Over the phone a week or so before, we had talked about this annual job. He had been avoiding work on some of the trees with branches brushing the power lines overhead. The year before, the power company had been out to lop some of the taller trees where the branches touched the lines. They had asked him if he could feel a humming in his bones when he walked under these trees. I had suggested he found help this year, though I knew he wouldn't listen. It's a trait that runs in the family – he has the same conversations with his ninety-six year-old father who, until his mid-eighties, could be found three storeys up, clearing the gutters of his house. Somewhat predictably, the next time we talked, my father told me he had rigged up a system of ropes to pull the branches away from the lines and he was still alive, which I ought to take as proof he was taking safety seriously.

The next job, once Tom and I had returned home, would be to grade the wood – what would be useful for fencing or for reinforcing the riverbank where it had started to undercut on the bend, stakes for use in the kitchen garden, all the way down to firewood. Every part would be used for something.

Coppicing is one of the more magical aspects of silviculture, or woodland management, a process of cutting back and rejuvenation that benefits everything around it, from the tree itself, its ability to lock away carbon, to allowing flowering plants and grasses to grow on the woodland floor and, by association, providing food and shelter for bees, spiders, moths and butterflies, voles and shrews, whitethroats and warblers. It is magical too in the knowledge that coppiced trees do not age in the same way as trees that are left to their own devices. They maintain their youth, and they can continue to be coppiced over centuries. The practice of coppicing is one of many that make silviculturalists druids, a term that most likely derives from the proto-Celtic, meaning one who knows the oak or, more broadly, one who knows the trees.

In England at least, the practice of coppicing reaches back to the Neolithic. The evidence for this comes from archaeological work done on the Somerset Levels, on an ancient causeway now known as the Sweet Track, which was built across boggy ground and was constructed almost entirely from coppiced wood. At an age of about 5,800 years, it is one of the oldest known roads.

By the middle of the thirteenth century, most of England's woodlands were managed as coppices, providing timber of a size that could be transported and worked easily. I like the link between the ways in which woods have been managed for millennia and this small patch of young trees. And seeing my father, with his beard and long, grey hair over a checked overshirt, he looks pretty druidic to me.

Tom, seeing the sawn, coppiced hazel, decided he wanted his own walking stick, so we combed the piles to find him a straight stem that would make a decent walking pole. It would be, for him,

another connection to this place and perhaps, I thought, a first step on his road to druidry. At the same time, we took out a few trees that needed to be thinned, sawing them by hand and easing them down to the ground, avoiding damage to the other trees nearby. I shouldn't have been surprised when I counted the rings on the cross-sections of the trunks that they corresponded to the number of years the woodland has been here, a record of the time that had passed since they were first planted, the good growing seasons and the poor. Each one of them marked a year of Tom's life too.

This is hard land on which to grow anything. For a start, sitting at 1,000 feet above sea level, winters finish late and arrive early here. The sun may have been out but only the day before we had woken to a thin covering of snow, and it was well into April. And year round, winds roar up the valley. It takes constant effort to grow things here.

On one edge of the fields of trees is the kitchen garden in which my father grows vegetables. A second edge runs alongside the road. The far end abuts the top field of a neighbour's farm, the fourth has for its boundary the River Cynllaith, marking the border between England and Wales. The narrow river, as far as we can see, is dead, a victim of agricultural runoff from the farms upstream.

Beyond the stream, the land rises sharply. When my father and stepmother first moved here, a large section of the hillside was a dark plantation of conifers. The plantation was harvested five years ago, after which the clear-felled hillside looked like a badly shaved head. The first time I saw it after the harvest, I was shocked. I have no love for serried, uniform rows of conifers but to see them stripped back like that was hard. This year, this hillside had started to show some small signs of recovery. Some thin larches had started to regrow in small patches, showing bright green on the upper slopes, and further down, a half-hearted scattering of broadleaf trees that were planted as part of the foresters' agreement for growing the crop of conifers were starting to show through too. But that was to see the hillside through generous eyes. The damage was clear. Many of the trees had been left where they were felled or simply left standing dead, stripped of leaves and bark, bonelike and monolithic on the hillside.

Even several years on, it had the look of a battlefield weeks after the conflict had finished, still reeling from events. Like many conifer plantations, it was a poorly thought through scheme and cannot have been particularly profitable. The land was too steep and, when the contractors arrived with heavy machinery, the tree harvester slipped off the thin path they cut through the trees: it took them days to work out how to recover it.

When my father first moved into the house, I thought the hillside looked forbidding in its dark, deep, regular and regulated coat of green. After the hillside was razed, it just looked sad and mangled.

Beyond the hill and for miles and miles beyond, much of the area is given over to sheep farming. It is, in miniature, a reflection of the decisions made in the twentieth century across Britain and Ireland to replace woodland with rolling monoculturally green hills of sheep, and to favour fast-growing crops of conifers over the slower, messier tangled web of broadleaf trees we are now trying to reinstate. It raises questions about what a woodland is 'for', what purpose it serves and the broader conversation going on across the country about our place in the landscape. About how we can be a part of the natural world here rather than pushing out all other comers.

Walking back up through the woodland, Dad pointed out those trees that were doing well and those that had died over winter. A few of the holly trees had, for reasons unknown, succumbed, and some of the hornbeams were growing at odd angles and had taken on the look of elaborate bonsai. It was something to do with the stock from which they came, he suggested, as they all seemed to be bending at the same point. Others had split off, not forming a leader or clear trunk, meaning they would grow out rather than up.

Nine years on from planting them, though, the majority of the original thousand trees are still alive, which is miraculous. Just after they finished planting, a drought hit and for weeks they had to water each by hand with water from the stream. For the first few years, Dad painstakingly hand scythed the grass between the trees to give them space and room to grow, until they began to drop enough leaf litter and branches in autumn to keep the grasses down. Now there is enough of a blanket to keep some of it down and he has less to do, though being a steward of the woodland, he spends much of his time out here.

He wages a constant, though good natured, battle against the flock of Torddu Badger Face Welsh Mountain Sheep which graze the adjoining fields and sometimes manage to navigate the fences, along with the grey squirrels and rabbits, my father's nemesis to which he is less good natured.

The rewards of woodlands are slow to arrive, and the care of the trees requires a rolling programme of care and attention. My father knows each of these trees intimately. As we wander, he identifies them by their bark or by the dried remains of last year's leaves, still clinging on in places – a phenomenon known as marcescence – or by the catkins or the configuration of their branches.

He has been known, along with a small group of people who live nearby, to sing to his trees – wassails and improvised song. It has something to do with belonging to this place specifically, being with it and knowing it. He and my stepmother, Alison, have thrown themselves into life here in the fifteen years since they arrived. They attend Welsh classes and Dad uses his newfound language at every opportunity. They take stints at the local shop, help to put on the pantomime, chop wood with their neighbours and engage in lengthy discussions over tea. They march and campaign, lobby their MP for better environmental policies. And they plant trees. These trees are a statement of intent. A statement of belonging. And perhaps they are a statement of resistance too.

Just as I had been unable to imagine the woodland in its mature state, I realized as I walk between the thin trunks and listen to my father talking about them that even in full leaf, I would be hard-pressed to identify a quarter of the species in this woodland, suddenly aware of my paucity of knowledge and lack of language about trees and woodlands. Like most people in the UK, I can name a small handful of species, though in winter, especially, they often blur into an indistinguishable mass. For someone who claims to love trees and woodlands, I find myself suddenly and shockingly wanting. After all, I have always thought of myself as a tree worshipper, deep down. It has never surprised me that before Christianity arrived on these shores, our ancestors worshipped trees. The green walls of the woods are more permeable than those of the cathedral and in the middle of a forest it is easy to feel a sense of the profound, the deeply spiritual. And in terms of choosing deities to worship, it has always felt to me that the deities who give us the air we breathe are a pretty good bet.

It is the nature of this love for trees, for woodlands and for wood as a material with which our pasts and futures are profoundly enmeshed, that I will explore in this book. In its pages, you will find the stories of those who have a deep connection to woodlands, the communities who care for them, who love them and know them intimately: tree planters and tree fellers, tree worshippers and tree bathers, ecologists, makers, crafters, bodgers, storytellers and artists, those who know the joys and frustrations of working with a living material, and those who find solace and inspiration simply by being among trees and, in so doing, find themselves a little closer to the heart of the woods.

2

Willow Weaver

Woodland burials and willow coffin-making in Cornwall

I have my feet up on the sill of the open door of an Aga, a mug of tea held between both hands. I am in the kitchen of Ele and Anthony Waters, whose house sits at the heart of the 27-acre woodland they have made their home, at Pentiddy, near the former Cornish mining village of Pensilva.

Ele is sitting next to me, her feet on the stove too, warming herself after a dip in the pond outside the house, the temperature of which is just a few degrees above freezing, on an early March morning. The morning plunge is a small ritual to start the day with the others who live and work here. Life at Pentiddy revolves around such small moments. Just before I arrived, the team had finished their second morning ritual, which involved talking about the little misunderstandings that may have taken place the day before, the things they might have said in haste that upset someone else. It is a chance to make things right before the new day begins, a performative starting again. These rituals are small, practical starting points for a small, practical community, a way of helping them to rub along together.

If the house feels as though it has sprung up from the ground it is because, to an extent, it has. It was built entirely by hand, with a roundwood timber-frame infilled with straw bale walls, by the couple and a team of volunteers some twenty years ago. Almost every part of it, from the trunks that form the structural beams to the hay bales, were sourced from the surrounding area. As neither of us wants to leave the warmth of the stove, Ele is giving me the armchair tour, which ends at the centrepiece of the kitchen table, where there is a small wreath of willow growing in a shallow bowl.

'We do this every Imbolc,' Ele tells me. 'Whoever is here at the time, we put our intentions into willow wands and then weave them together as a community. We speak them aloud and put the wreath into water and those intentions sprout. We can watch them grow. We've always done little rituals like that here.'

It is a few days past Imbolc which, on the Celtic Wheel of the Year, is the festival that takes place at the peak of winter, at its tipping point, after which spring will begin to make itself known.

Beyond Imbolc, Ostara will mark the spring equinox, Beltane spring's peak, Litha the summer solstice and Lughnasadh (Lammas) the summer's peak. Mabon comes at the autumn equinox, Samhain at the height of autumn, and Yule the high point of the winter

equinox. The calendar, a laminated version of which is pinned to the fridge at my father's house, marks time and season and, in many images of this wheel there is, for each festival, a picture of a tree. The tree, as depicted at Imbolc, is at its most stark, almost dead. Imbolc is the festival of the dark before the dawn and, as such, it is often celebrated with fire, similar to Samhain, nine months later, the fires lit again as the darkness takes hold once more.

It's a pieced together thing, the Wheel of the Year. The Anglo-Saxons celebrated the solstices and the equinoxes, the Celts four fire festivals that took place in February, May, August and November. And that is to vastly over-simplify. The many tribes who occupied the various corners of Britain and Ireland had their own takes on how the season's change should best be celebrated, how deities ought to be placated or importuned for a good harvest, or how they ought to be honoured for bounty from the seas and trees, and various invaders and travellers to and from these islands brought new influences, new festivals or simply new meaning to old ones.

Early Christians mapped their festivals of Christmas, Candlemas, Lady Day, May Day, Midsummer's Eve, Lammas, Michaelmas and All Hallow's Eve, over the ones that existed there and, within these, traces of the older celebrations remain. As always happens, things continue to evolve. Just a few generations ago, Victorian Celtic revivalists brought in new, sometimes somewhat romantic, fanciful interpretations of Brittonic and Gaelic Celtic cultures, which gained traction of their own and which continue to influence the popular view of these marker points in the year's turning. And so we end up with a mishmash of corn dollies, Morris dancing and maypoles, bonfires with effigies, wassails and be-robed gatherings in woodland glades and at Neolithic stone circles, the original meaning and use of which we can now only guess.

The wheel as it stands today – as archaically as it is often depicted – is largely a mid-twentieth-century reconstruction. It is the work of neo-druids and Wiccans, a mapping of various festivals from different places into a new framework – a bringing together of folklores and traditions. It is likely, though, that celebrations of one form or another have been held at around these times as far back into our distant past as we might care to reach and the widespread adoption of the Wheel of the Year speaks to our need for gatherings and rituals, for a connection with the seasons and the land. This is despite the fact few of us work directly on the land now, and the agricultural cycle is, for many of us, a concept rather than the structure that provides a framework for our lives.

To families such as the Waters', though, whose lives are linked to the land in a way many of ours are not, these structures are practical, the rituals in which they engage meaningful and present.

Everything has meaning here, Ele tells me. Every part of the land and the house, the different areas of woodland, each has family stories associated with it, from the associations they have with setting up the community woodland the same year their daughter was born, to establishing the coppice the year of their son's birth – life and the land intertwined.

'You can feel like you belong when you live like this,' she tells me as we abandon the warmth of the kitchen and make our way up past the family's various schemes – the community woodland, the recreation Navajo hogan roundhouse, and a new community farm venture they are in the process of setting up – heading towards the place we are here to discuss, the natural woodland burial ground the couple run.

Ele has been thinking a lot about death recently, she tells me. Just a few days earlier she drew up her own death plan, a detailed document about what she would like to happen.

Sitting at my desk later I almost write 'in the event of her death', as though it might not happen, an unconscious skirting around of the issue. As a still and increasingly secular society, we don't talk about death much, despite its inevitability. Although recent years have seen a rise in the number of places where death is openly discussed – in podcasts or in death cafés – we keep it at arm's length with euphemisms and allusions on the whole. Not for us el Día de los Muertos, in which the dead of Mexico are invited back into their former homes, nor the Obon (or Bon) festival in Japan, in which the souls of those who have died are invited into the houses of their relatives, and waved farewell again on floating lanterns that are released onto rivers and lakes. You could argue that we retain Halloween, though, aside from in pockets, it is an almost entirely secularized celebration, with masks and sweets and none of the philosophy.

Ele is facing death head on though, she says. Writing her death plan has allowed her to clarify her thinking about what would be right for her and her family. She hopes she will die here, in the house she and her husband built with their own hands. Even if she dies elsewhere, she wants to be brought back here before she is buried, to cross the threshold one final time with her family.

'A lot of people never ask themselves those questions about what is right for them,' she continues. 'But talking about death before you die is so important. Otherwise, we just spend the time we're dealing with death in shock. If we've talked about it – even if it happens twenty years later – we know it's going to happen, and we've accepted it. We can then get on and do the grieving and transforming, rather than simply being in shock and carrying on. We have a connection to every other part of our lives, and I want that to be maintained through death.

'I realized I wanted to do that in a timely way, having said the proper goodbyes. I hadn't realized, before I wrote it down, how important that was to me. We've aways done our own homespun rituals for all sorts of transitions in life and, if it feels right and possible for me to come home or to be at home when I die, I would like that, in the home in which we've lived closely together.'

When they bought the land at Pentiddy, Ele and Anthony had planned to make their living coppicing the woods for charcoal. They had never considered making their living running a burial ground, though it was only shortly after buying the land that Anthony received a call from a friend, a woodsman who had mentored him, with an out-of-the-blue request.

Mary, the woodsman's mother, had just died, he explained, and, though he realized this was a strange request, he wondered if Ele and Anthony would allow her to be buried on their land. She had always wanted to be a member of a woodland community and he wondered if she might be able to come and be part of their project in death.

'It was a curveball,' Ele says, 'but we went along with it.'

She called the council, who could not see any reason why the burial should not go ahead, and the funeral took place at the end of August, coinciding with the day the couple moved onto the land.

'We had a yurt in the garden, where the family was sitting around. Mary was in her coffin in the middle, all made up with flowers in her hair. Everyone sitting round, sharing stories about her and laughing: it was beautiful and natural.'

The funeral was a deeply personal affair too. One of Mary's sons had made her an oak coffin with a carving of a swan on the front and another played the Japanese flute as the coffin was taken from yurt to graveside, which the third son had dug by hand.

Later, after the funeral party had left, the police arrived, following up on reports of a dead body in the woods at Pentiddy. The misunderstanding was soon ironed out, though before they left one of the officers asked the Waters if they might be open to a second burial, a local woman who had died and whose body had been refused at the local graveyards on account of her being a witch. It was an unexpected start to their new business.

I was unsure what I had been expecting of the graveyard and if I had been out and come across it, I might have walked past it none-the-wiser. It is only on closer inspection that it reveals itself to be anything other than a field, as the graves here are unmarked, visible only as mounds, some of them sprouting snowdrops and molehills, set between saplings. When these trees are grown, Ele explains, they will turn this whole field into a shaded wood, the graves lying beneath the canopies of the oak, wild cherry, crab apple, alder, silver birch, hazel, holly, spindle and hawthorn.

Some people feel overwhelmed at the choices available to them when they first come across the idea of natural burial, Ele explains. It's not as formal or as structured as a traditional religious ceremony.

'As long as it's legal and respectful, you can do anything you like,' she continues. 'Those are the only two rules. You can create anything, you can bring any part of yourself here, anything that was important to the person who has died. We've had horses in full dressage at the graveside, a family who staged a Hawai'ian wake, because the person who had died had always wanted to go to Hawai'i but never had. What matters is that it feels like a useful and important transition into the new phase of your life – there's no one way of doing that.'

The approach echoes a Māori tradition that when a member of the community dies the family will spend some of the funeral doing things that person liked to do – they will sing the songs they enjoyed, eat the foods they liked, play that person's favourite games.

We stop at a grave plot for a funeral that is to take place the next day. There are duck boards over the freshly dug plot and, by the side, a crate full of earth and stones. The graves are all dug by hand, Ele explains, a process that takes about six hours. It's a personal business, intimate, as is the family's choice of where the body is buried.

Ele tells me a story about a woman whose husband had died unexpectedly, who chose a plot next to a sapling oak tree. She found comfort in the thought that he would be cradled within the roots of the oak as it grew. It meant they would both have a particular relationship to that tree. It's often that way. Being buried by a growing thing, a tree that will go on to have a long life of its own, helps people to feel that their life has not been small or insignificant or that, even when the person has been forgotten, the tree will continue to be appreciated.

The second burial at Pentiddy was that of Anthony's father, who is buried right in the centre of the field, beneath a birch tree.

It was a meaningful choice for the family on account that birches shed their leaves and bark, which helps to feed and nurture what is around it, echoing the way the family felt Anthony's father behaved towards others in life.

'We say your death is contributing to the woodland ecosystem, so that woodland will have a bit of all those people in it and therefore a connection to it.' Ele muses. 'You are grieving their loss and celebrating their life at the same time – one without the other is not healthy.

'I had an email just this morning from the daughter of a man who is planted here … *buried* here,' she smiles and corrects herself. 'She asked if I can send her cuttings of the willows we used for his coffin, so she can plant them in her garden, so that can be a connection.'

The walls of Jessie Carr's small studio in a wooded valley – just a mile or so, as the crow flies, from Ele and Anthony's burial ground – are covered in her delicate botanical illustrations, the shelves that run beneath the windows filled with intricate baskets she has woven. She was an artist long before she began to weave coffins.

'I often say all of my best work is in the ground. I spend days and days making something that is then buried or burnt, though that's something I really like about it, that ephemeral nature of what I do,' Jessie says, lacing a withy through a series of uprights.

Jessie is mid-weave, creating a casket which is bound for the woodland burial ground at Pentiddy the following week. The base is already in place, the sides of the coffin outlined by vertical rods of willow around which Jessie is weaving the wale, which will create the coffin's walls. It is a slow process, layering the tightly spaced willow, and the whole thing takes about five days from start to finish. Occasionally, she stops to tamp the willow down using a rapping iron, with hands that are strong and rough. It is hypnotic, watching her weave quietly, and for a moment I think she might have forgotten I am there.

They are striking things, Jessie's coffins, with their layers of different colours of willow. It takes more than 500 rods to make a full coffin and though she cannot get enough from the burial ground at Pentiddy to create entire coffins, she likes using the willow they grow there for the vibrancy of the colours and the pleasure of working with a living material.

'When you harvest willow locally, you can use it when it's still living. And it's still living when it goes back into the ground, so you're seeing it at its best.' She continues to weave, working her way round the coffin anticlockwise, and the circularity of the process rolls around my head, the living and the dead alongside each other.

'There's something pleasing about knowing that you're putting something living back into the ground.'

There's a circularity in the story of how Jessie first came to do this. She was taught to weave baskets by Ele Waters fifteen years ago and went on to learn how to make coffins on her own initiative, returning to take willow from the burial ground, weaving it into the caskets and returning it to the ground there before starting the whole process again. The set-up feels almost mythic – the practice certainly ancient – though by the way Jessie describes it, that is more practical than anything. She was always a crafter, and the point at which Ele taught her to make baskets coincided with her having her second child.

'I was doing botanical illustration at the time, which is really involved, sitting there for hours concentrating. With a small child, you can't do that, though I could weave in the garden with my little one there. When I started making coffins, I didn't know how I'd feel about it. I didn't know whether I'd find it difficult or uncomfortable, but I enjoy the contact with the families.'

The weaving of a coffin is usually a highly personal thing, she tells me. While some people want to commission a coffin and have it delivered, without being involved at any stage, many more want to be hands-on. Some people will decorate the coffins they have commissioned, while others want to see the weaving in process or

to be involved in it themselves. Others still want to take things into their own hands, to exert some control over their own death, and commission coffins for themselves. Sometimes it is because they know they are dying and they want to feel they have done all they can to prepare, while others, like Ele herself, want to have put thought in well ahead of time, despite hoping that death is still some way off. One man for whom she wove a coffin wanted it to have a dual purpose, she adds, firstly as a bookcase in his small house, and later, when needed, as his coffin. She had to leave instructions with his family on how to transform it when the time came, removing the shelves and lining it for its next use.

The story that struck me most, though, was of an elderly couple from Devon who wanted to weave each other's coffins. Jessie showed me a card they had written to her afterwards, thanking her for her care. And that is what it seemed to come down to, a deep act of love for each other. They had considered their lives; they were now considering their deaths. They had woven their coffins together and taken them home, where they were using them as extra storage until needed.

Sometimes, Jessie tells me, when she mentions what she does, people don't want to know. The people who want to be involved in weaving a coffin, whether their own or for someone else, don't seem so fearful of their deaths – or perhaps, she muses, it is after having been involved in preparations for death that some of this fear falls away? If you can prepare for it, you are facing it head on.

'I wove one coffin for a lady whose son had died very young.' Jessie's weaving as she talks. 'She came and wove alongside me for a day, which was an amazing experience for both of us, because I've lost people who are close to me, and I guess there's something special about that time. When you're grieving, you're quite open. She was able even to laugh a little while we were doing it.

'All the time you spend weaving, you're processing that grief. You're releasing emotions in a physical way too. Yes, there are a lot of tears as you're thinking about that person, but there's joy too. It was quiet sometimes, other times we talked. It ebbs and flows, but it's never uncomfortable because you're always doing. You allow emotions to rise up and flow out of you through your hands as you're weaving.'

Working with your hands is a meditation, she continues. It's something about moving away from your mind and being in your body.

'Some of the tasks involved are very repetitive, so your mind wanders around. Sometimes I'm not really thinking at all, because it's just happening and I know the process without any thought going into it. It's lovely when you know something that well.'

Driving back across the moors, I encounter a formal, black Saab hearse on a narrow road. The oversized car demands attention, like a punctuation mark in the road, and I pull over to give it space. The hearse's smartly dressed driver looks appropriately serious, the coffin in the back shrouded in a sombre covering. It feels a long way from the experience I've just left, of the hard physical work of weaving the container in which the body of the person you loved will take their final journey, of the therapy of grieving through our hands, of working with living material to support our relationship with the dead.

We have always reached for rituals to deal with the big things – births and deaths, the cycles of life – the comings and goings of the herring, the growth and maturation of the crop, the cycle of the seasons, the many things over which we have no control, even in a society that has moved far from these ties to the land. In an age in which we are uprooted from the land and from one another, in a time in which we have, for the most-part, disconnected from death, it is no wonder that ancient rituals take on new meaning, or new forms. And it makes sense too that we would look for those rituals that bring us closer to one another, that reaffirm our bonds, and that remind us of the cycles of our lives, our interconnectedness, rituals that are, at their heart, acts of care.

3

Woodlore Gatherer

*Science among the trees at Wytham Woods, Oxfordshire,
and beneath them at Chalford, Gloucestershire*

The day had started with a blazing red sunrise in the most crystalline of midwinter skies and never managed to rise much above freezing. I was walking in one of the most heavily studied woodlands in the world, at Wytham in Oxfordshire, breathing in the cold air, thankful that places like this exist in the world, and wondering what it was to really know a woodland. It was a question that had been bothering me increasingly and this seemed a particularly relevant place to ask it.

Most of us think we know woodlands and forests. Instinctively, perhaps – our ancestors came from the trees. We have known woodlands our whole lives, their shapes and textures, even if we cannot name the species of trees nor the birds we hear in their canopies. We walk our woods in the evenings or at weekends, in our spare moments of time, and they are familiar to us.

Walking along the paths of Wytham Woods in the winter sun, the signs of others' attempts to understand this place were everywhere. Affixed to trunks were boxes of different shapes and sizes, for bats, owls and birds. Trees were pinned with metal tags or spotted with paints – blue, red, pink – their trunks encircled with expanding dendrometer bands. Ribbons were tied to their branches and trunks, signifying one of the thousands of studies that have been conducted here. Wooden boxes lay on the woodland floor, probably housing microclimate stations measuring the specifics of one tiny patch of the woodland. And there were metal cages, fluted plastic cones, posts arranged in quadrants, posts that had rotted at the base and lay in the undergrowth, that spoke of decades of concentrated research, their findings long since committed to paper. Beneath one tree, a parachute was gathering falling leaves and insects and, in a clearing close by, an enormous scaffolding frame reached up into the canopy and was topped by a wooden walkway. Hanging from the branches of a stand of beech trees, hollow, woven globes spun in the wind, part of a collaboration between a group of researchers and artists, a sign that not all the investigations were purely scientific.

A fleece-clad, postdoctoral researcher, who had been described to me as having a brain the size of a planet, passed me on the track between the trees, heading out to check the sensors he had installed to detect and measure the moonlight that filters through the canopy to the forest floor.

Wytham is one of just seventy-seven Forest Global Earth Observatory health sites in the world, and the only one located in the UK. In some parts of the woods here, every tree has been studied from root to canopy, its birds' behaviour monitored, its beetles, small mammals, lichens and leaf litter. For almost eighty years, researchers have studied these trees from up in the canopy on ladders and cherry pickers, from the trunks of Wytham's trees, while crouching low to the forest floor, their faces inches from the ground.

The woods at Wytham are home to the longest running biological dataset in the world on blue tits and great tits, research which started in 1947 and continues today. In 1950, it was one of the first places in the country to be designated a Site of Special Scientific Interest. 'It is almost certainly unmatched anywhere in the world as a place of sustained, intensive ecological research,' wrote the zoologist, Lord John Krebs, who began his long career studying the behaviours of birds by investigating the great tits of Wytham.

One of the hundreds of bird boxes at Wytham, part of the longest running study into bird behaviours in the world.

In the distance, a sharp whining emerged sporadically from among the trees to one side of the path, like something in pain, though it turned out to be the sound of two researchers taking core samples from trees as part of an investigation into ash dieback disease, which is wiping out one of the most abundant broadleaf trees in the UK. The disease, caused by a fungus, is now present across Western Europe, and consensus in the scientific community is that it may kill up to 80 per cent of ash trees in the UK.

There was more invisible work going on here though. Far above satellites spun, taking measurements of the chlorophyll content in the canopy. Of the mice in the woods, a proportion of them were

running round with subcutaneous tags used to track their movements, the state of their gut biomes, who they socialized with and
how long they lived. And, secreted throughout the 1,000-acre site,
owned by Oxford University, researchers were going about their
patient business of measuring and gathering, compiling and concluding their studies on the trees and fungi, soil and leaves, owls,
bats and badgers.

Right now, towards the end of January, the earthworm scientists would be concluding their work for the year on the forest
floor – worms are more active in winter than summer – while the
pupping of Britain's largest land carnivore, which takes place around
Valentine's Day, would bring out the badger researchers, just as it
had done since they started to study the mammal's behaviour in
1987. The bird scientists would arrive in March and stay through
until the middle of June, as they had done each year for seventy-six
years, looking at each of the thousand or so nest boxes to investigate
the ways in which great tits and blue tits age and learn, their social
habits and acquisition of skills and the size of their territories.

I was in the woods to meet Keith Kirby, the Old Man of
Wytham, one of a small handful of people who may lay claim
to knowing this place better than anyone else alive. When Keith
retired, in 2012, as one of the country's leading woodland ecologists,
he returned to the woodlands of Wytham, which he first came to
know as a postgraduate in 1973 when he studied the growth of
brambles in the woodlands.

As we set out, Keith informed me that to know something of the
woods was to know something of their history. Before Wythham
passed into the keeping of the university in 1942, it had been owned
by Raymond ffennell, who bought it in 1920.

Halfway up the hill, Keith stopped and gestured to a long, brick-
lined pit, perhaps 32 by 14 feet, in the base of which several trees
had sprouted. It was not immediately obvious what the structure
was, the sense of context missing without water. Keith explained
it was a swimming pool: ffennell – a keen philanthropist as well as

The beech tree by Raymond ffennell's Bavarian chalet has had its genome sequenced for the Darwin Tree of Life project, the model for its species.

the very image of an English country squire – had it built, so that children from London's East End and the deprived parts of Oxford could learn to swim there. He believed that underprivileged children benefitted from having access to the countryside.

'The thing about woodlands is they're very much shaped by individuals,' Keith told me as we walked towards a line of trees at the top of the hill. 'So, Raymond ffennel built a swimming pool and a Bavarian chalet because of his Bavarian heritage and the rondavels modelled on the servants' quarters from where he had lived in South Africa. And these trees up ahead are Brogden's Belt, a remnant of one of Wytham's earlier owners.'

The owner in question, the 5th Earl of Abingdon, inherited the estate around 1800. The land over which we were now looking was his parkland, and the copse of beech trees that would become Brogden's Belt would, when fully grown, frame his house in line with the aesthetics of the time: the desire for symmetry in the landscape. From the hilltop, we looked down across a much older area of woodland, oak over hazel that was cut as coppice with standards in the Middle Ages, a worked woodland that had long since fallen out of use for coppicing, and, when we left Brogden's Belt, we walked down through newer areas of planting, through stands of conifers and younger broadleaf trees.

The coppicing in medieval times was one of the earliest ways in which the woodland here was worked. Yet there were signs of earlier use too, the presence of rare arable weeds and fragments of Roman pottery which suggest that at one time what is now woodland was open ground. Somewhere in this landscape, Keith felt it likely there were Iron Age remains too, at a high spot out of the flood plain, a position perfect for a fort from that time. And below it all was a layer of coral rag, limestone complete with fossilized sea creatures, that told a far older story of a time when this whole area was the floor of a shallow, tropical sea.

About 330 million years ago, this woodland floor was the bed of a warm, carboniferous sea on which the shells of dead sea creatures came to rest. Over time, compressed into layers of rock, they became the Corallian limestones of Wytham. And later, walking through the woods with ash dieback researcher Cecilia Dahlsjö, I saw evidence of this, when she suddenly knelt in the middle of the path and showed me her favourite part of the woods – a fossilized shell, a remnant of this hidden past.

When the university took over Wytham, the country was in the midst of the Second World War. Many of the trees here, as in woodlands across the country, were felled to support the war effort and when the UK emerged from the war there was a growing need to produce more timber, so the policy of the first foresters and conservators here was to plant up open space, to do it in a way that would produce tall, straight timber and to get rid of any gnarled

A fossilized shell in the heart of Wytham Woods, evidence that the whole area once lay at the bottom of a shallow sea.

and unsightly trees that would have no value – in terms of usable timber at least. This, in turn, Keith told me, started an argument between foresters and ecologists, the latter of whom were against the planting of fast-growing conifers, which they considered unsightly and bad for biodiversity.

Over the following decades, there were uneasy truces in the argument, the evidence of which we could see in the later plantations of mixed sitka and oak, beeches and larch, the idea being that when the conifers were harvested, the slower growing broadleaf trees would take their place.

Seeing Wytham though Keith's eyes, it became several woodlands rather than one, each a palimpsest of decisions that had taken place over thousands of years – a profoundly human landscape.

This rich human history was, he explained, one of the reasons it is difficult to work out what to do with it in terms of re-wilding.

'It's difficult to get a practical natural baseline for conservation, given we've been messing with trees and woodlands for millennia, at least since our Neolithic ancestors started grazing cattle,' Keith explained.

Our extensive entanglement with the land has made it difficult to decide how best to develop and conserve a woodland, or even *whether* to intervene. It was not even a case of letting the land revert to some previous state. Leave a woodland to itself now, he told me, and rhododendron might entirely dominate it, to the exclusion of virtually all other plant life, a result unlikely to be on the list of desired outcomes for anyone interested in the woodlands of the future.

'We're still in the middle of an argument about what a woodland is for.' Keith gestured towards a line between a conifer plantation and the broadleaf trees that had been planted in the next plot. 'There's still quite high polarization between commercial forestry and ecology.'

I had seen the evidence of this polarization during a talk given by a woodland ecologist in Falmouth a few weeks earlier, in which a local forester took issue with the idea for regenerating the few remaining patches of Atlantic rainforest clinging on in Britain simply by creating space in which trees could self-seed around these existing patches of ancient woodland. In his view, this was missing an opportunity to work the woodland, to create health and carbon capture through coppicing and pollarding, by growing trees that could be used for their timber as well as for their inherent values. Both were passionate about their point of view, both knowledgeable in their own areas, though I remember thinking at the time it was as if they were engaged in slightly different conversations that just happened to overlap.

The way in which these arguments have been framed over the past century has roughly been along the dividing lines of the planting of native broadleaf trees versus conifers, with ecologists favouring broadleaf trees like oak and ash, and the forestry industry preferring fast-growing crops of pine, spruce and larch.

Little is ever as simple as it seems, though, Keith commented as we walked through a block of trees that were mainly spruce. Even in the case of wood as a crop, it was not a matter of spruce bad, broadleaf good. There was an element of human decision in that too, biases that would be easy to overlook, including those of woodland ecologists.

'Why would you want to study a sitka spruce plantation when you could be studying a lovely oak wood?' he murmured. 'We've got this idea that we should be conserving things that are native and natural. But our woods aren't natural. The conifers that were introduced are not native in the same way that sheep or wheat aren't native – they were introduced and they're part of our cultural landscape too.'

We had come down into a valley where the tone of the woodland shifted yet again. This part of the woods was mostly ash, a large proportion of which was dying or already dead, and we stopped by a remnant of what had once been an enormous ash tree.

'In the fifties, planting ash seemed like a good idea. And until 2012 it was. It's the fastest growing broadleaf tree, the one that was regenerating most freely. This area here is trying very hard to be an ash wood. Then the disease arrived, and it was badly hit. About a third of the canopy is dead as of last summer. Ash dieback has been progressing over the years and I'd be surprised if more than 10 per cent survives.'

The fungus, *Hymenoscyphus fraxineus*, that causes ash dieback was previously only common across Asia, where the native ash trees developed tolerance to the disease. When it arrived in Europe – one of the side effects of globalization, in which timber and plant materials are moved around the world with ease – the ash trees native to Europe had no resilience and began to die in huge numbers. Although much of the research currently being undertaken is on the impact of ash dieback and the changes we are likely to see in woodlands across Europe, a lot of which is happening in the woods at Wytham, there are small signs of hope for the future of these trees. One scheme, the Living Ash Project, is currently working on identifying ash trees with resilience to the disease, in the hope of securing the future of the species by breeding trees that are found to have natural tolerance.

Beyond the ash trees, we came to Radbrook Common, where great excavations ran between the beech trees, channels that stretched out in different directions. They seemed to me intriguing at first, these channels, an unusual feature, though their meaning shifted as Keith explained they were the evidence of the First World War practice trenches dug by conscripts and recruits. They snaked back on themselves so as to minimize the damage that would be caused by a grenade landing in them. From here, we could make out through the trees another line of trenches, some 1,000 feet away, by a stand of conifers – the opposition lines, the same distance the practising soldiers would find themselves from their enemy when they were shipped over to the trenches in the Somme or Passchendaele.

There was a low sun in the sky and as twilight approached, the woods were flooded with a golden light that streamed in through the bare branches and trunks to us on the hillside and we both fell silent for a few moments in the afternoon winter sun. In spring, Keith, said, this whole woodland, trenches and all, would be a sea of bluebells.

With the intensity of study in sites like Wytham and all we know from our longstanding relationship with these woodlands, which stretches back thousands of years, it would seem realistic to believe we might understand something of their possible future. When I put this to Keith, and later to Nigel Fisher, the conservator of the woods, they were unified in their answers.

'In terms of what we understand, we're just skimming the surface,' Nigel told me as we warmed up in the kitchen of ffennell's Bavarian lodge, now used as a laboratory. 'We don't have precise enough models, or statistics to act on.'

In short, we're heading into completely unknown territory, the theory being that, as climate change speeds up, we will know less and less about the likely effects of our actions.

Nigel and Keith are rarities in terms of the length of their involvement with these woodlands and the depth of their scientific investigations, having studied them for decades rather than the few months or years allowed by the funded research that makes up most of the studies here, dependant on fluctuating trends and needs. Nigel, in contrast to this, is only the third conservator at Wytham since the university took ownership, appointed in 2000. He has watched the coming and going of thousands of researchers and, in that time, Wytham has changed a huge amount, yet it is the changes in the world around it that concern him. And the impact those changes are having, in turn, on our woodlands.

'In the past, as a woodland manager, I knew that if I did something, 85 per cent of the time it would work,' he comments as we look out of the windows at two trucks, laden with leaves, which are being shifted from one part of the woods to another, 'because you'd be following what everyone had always done. Now, the chance of it working here is below 50 per cent, because a disease will come in or there will be a drought, or gales, or even problematic deer numbers. The number of unknown variables has increased dramatically, which makes it difficult to know what to do with a thicket of trees, let alone a whole woodland habitat. On a good day, I will say I understand about 2 per cent of the woods. Though, later on, rationality strikes and I'll think no, I understand well under 1 per cent.'

And although the woods may look healthy at a glance, after the droughts of the previous year, the team here now considers Wytham to be a woodland in crisis.

'As conservationists, we've failed in so many ways to get our messages across.' As we talked, two researchers came in from the freezing woods to warm up with tea. 'There's a disconnect between society and what actually happens in the natural world. We get worried about things we shouldn't get worried about and we put too much emphasis on things which aren't going to make any difference at all.

'People walking through a wood like Wytham tend to see a healthy woodland. As long as there are trees here and places to walk, most people don't mind so much. They might see dead trees, but they don't know whether that's just part of the natural process or if it should worry them. As long as this landscape is about 70 per cent trees, people aren't going to care because it looks like the vision of the woodland that we have in our heads. I think we're getting used to degraded landscapes.'

The researchers, warming their hands on their teacups, agreed. These woods, rich though they seemed walking through them with Keith, are empty compared to what they were a generation ago, and the same was true for the generation before, and before still. It is perhaps one of our great weaknesses as humans that we become used to denuded landscapes, our loss that we are not able to experience woodlands as they were in earlier times, to see the richness of texture, the abundance of flora and fauna that once counted as normal here.

Instead, we normalize the woodlands we see. We assume this is how it has always been because we can imagine it no differently. This thought reminded me of an article I had read about the way in which we can no longer imagine the seas as they were before we decimated them. In the diaries and travel accounts of seventeenth-century pirates, buccaneers, naturalists and explorers, a common trope was tales of natural abundance, of innumerable whales, turtles filling whole bays, fish in such numbers that they could be taken from the sea by hand. In isolation, these reports could be dismissed as fanciful exaggerations, though together they point to a natural wealth that we cannot begin to imagine now, an example of shifting baseline syndrome, in which our idea of what is normal changes to suit our current experience.

Walking back to my car in the fading light, I looked around and found I was unable to imagine the woodlands through which I had walked as anything other than they were. The bare trunks of the trees in deepest winter looked to my eyes just as they did when I was a child. I recalled something Nigel said to me about losing texture. It's like going into a library and finding just one author's books covering 90 per cent of the shelves, he had said. We might have lost all the Shakespeares and Brontës, the Austins and Tolstoys, though we've forgotten we've lost them. The danger is that we are beginning to accept that as normal.

In the dusk, the temperature plummeted again and I walked through the woods one last time before the gates were closed for the night. The trees jangled with the artefacts of science. In the dying light, Wytham became mysterious and I tried to mentally replace some of that lost texture, the millions of birds, beetles, rodents and mammals that had called this place home over millennia. I tried to paint on the scene the people who had called this place home too – the Iron Age farmers, the Romans in their villas, the medieval peasants coppicing firewood, the young soldiers in the practice trenches, unaware, surely, of the scale of horror that awaited them, the landowners who had shaped the woods and made their mark on the land, the foresters and ecologists in their differing understandings of what a wood is there for, the walkers and artists, scientists and dreamers.

Fifty miles to the west and a year later, I walked with the tall, quietly expressive biologist Merlin Sheldrake, in a forest of beeches. As with those at Wytham, the woodlands on the edge of Chalford in Gloucestershire were profoundly shaped by their human history, a

legacy of the furniture makers and, later, the stick making industry of the Stroud valleys, where, in the early twentieth century, thousands of walking sticks and umbrellas were turned out daily.

I recounted to Merlin the rough statistic Nigel Fisher had given, about understanding far less than 1 per cent of what was happening in the woods at Wytham, and asked if the same would be true of what was going on beneath the surface. He thought on it as we walked and told me – taking into account all the studies in plant sciences over the past few centuries – it stood to reason that we would understand a great deal less about his area of study, the kingdom of fungi, which has been far more overlooked by the scientific community until recent years.

'There are millions of fungal species and we have described less than 10 per cent of them,' he told me as we criss-crossed through the woodland, weaving our way up and down the valley. 'And that's just species description – it's saying nothing about what they do, who they live with, how they behave, their life histories, their ecologies – it's just bald taxonomic description.'

This relative ignorance about fungi led Merlin to write the book, *Entangled Life*, introducing a fungally blind readership to the fungal networks that form both some of the largest organisms on the planet and tiny fungal networks that would fit on a speck of dust. Fungi represent a hugely diverse kingdom of life about which we know staggeringly little, yet which give rise to the conditions that allow for our existence – and may well hold at least some of the answers to our species' continued survival here.

Despite never having walked in these woods before, the beech-wood, interspersed by scatterings of ash trees and hazels, felt profoundly familiar. Comforting even. I often have this sensation among fully grown beeches. It is something to do with the height of the canopy and the quality of light that filters down through the leaves in spring and summer, the spaciousness of the forest floor, the heady tapestry of reds, yellows and browns formed of fallen leaves in early winter.

As we walked, we discussed a mutual appreciation of beech-woods, though it was when Merlin started to talk about the world of fungi that he became suddenly more animated. Ideas rolled out of him in quick succession, concepts he expressed as much with his hands as he did with description, forming structures with long pianist's fingers, as though words alone did not quite cut it when attempting to describe organisms whose lives are entirely dissimilar to our own.

'I'm interested in what fungi do, how they live and how they underwrite the regenerative capacity of the living world, and their mystery is part of that fascination,' he explained. 'In the fungal sciences you're never more than a half step away from a deep, unanswered question. It's an exhilarating feeling, when you're asking questions that make you feel dizzy and confused – it's part of what pulls me forward into enquiry.'

Arbuscular mycorrhizal fungi – those fungi symbiotic with about 80 per cent of plant species, which Merlin spends much of his time studying – do not produce mushrooms, the most recognizable sign of fungal life on the surface. Instead, as he puts it, they 'erupt into human life in the form of plants'. Plants are the visible outgrowth of mycorrhizal relationships, he told me. So, when we walk through a woodland, much of what we see is a result of processes taking place beneath the woodland floor, phenomena to which fungi give rise.

When we first entered the woods, we were not discussing plants and fungi but rather surfing and freediving – and when Merlin first described the way in which he approached woods, it was in oceanic terms.

If we look at the soil as being like the surface of the sea, he told me, plants are like snorkels sticking up above the ground into engagement with the light and the air. This perspective, one he often adopts when he is in a woodland or forest, he described as a kind of grounding one, sending the centre of his awareness downward, below the level of what can be seen, into an environment that is dizzyingly other, and astoundingly complex.

'When I think about life in the soil. I think of the environment there as a dense, three-dimensional obstacle course. Because there are no sightlines, nor much light, organisms in the soil orient and navigate and experience their environment using vibration and sound, and using chemicals, and gradients of chemicals. Imagine being able to navigate by using gradients of chemicals.'

The underground world he conjured up for me was as far from the familiar and comforting beeches as I could imagine, a landscape of chemical weather systems he populated eloquently with gyres and eddies of chemical transformations that guided the interactions of the creatures in the soil. These chemical transformations of bacteria, fungi and plants, he explained, take place on a microscopic scale, yet they spill out over vast areas. They comprise the systems that regulate our atmosphere, that break down dead matter and give us the space in which we live, systems and processes that are at the root of what makes life on the surface possible.

It was mid-January and we were walking across a blanket of fallen leaves that were beginning to decay, slowly becoming soil. Merlin gestured towards a pile of these leaves in the undergrowth. We perceive the leaves as rotting down, in a kind of passive process, he told me, though it is an active one, in which fungi and bacteria are the doers. And, in geological terms, this is happening not slowly at all, but incredibly quickly. If the fungi and bacteria did not turn the leaves into soil, they would pile up so deep we would not have a forest here, which makes the zone in which we live out our lives a kind of negative space that exists only by virtue of decomposition.

It might be useful to consider a concept developed by the German polymath Alexander von Humboldt, Merlin suggested. Humboldt evolved the idea that, as gases and liquids are both fluids – the only difference being that gases are compressible fluids and liquids are incompressible – we, humans live at the bottom of an ocean of air.

'I like to extend that idea down into the soil,' he said, as we reached a gate at the bottom of the valley, crossing a chalk stream on stepping stones into a patch of coppiced hazels where the ground underfoot was claggy and soaked.

'So, it's as though we're walking on the surface of this ocean of soil. That puts me in mind of the depths below me. Even if I can't know exactly what's going on in those little crevices in the soil below, even if I'm terrifyingly ignorant of what's going on underground, I'm aware that I'm walking on the surface of an ocean of life and that changes the way I experience the forest right away. Because I'm suddenly in this plane within the forest on a vertical level, and I can feel the depths, even in my ignorance. That kind of exercise is one way to acknowledge the life underground, while acknowledging our lack of knowledge of what's going on there.'

As he talked, a sudden, vertiginous feeling washed over me, similar to the one I get when swimming in very deep water, an expansiveness of mind the traces of which would stay with me long after we left the woods.

'There are so many different environments in just a cubic centimetre of soil, so many different kinds of cavity, so many different types of charged micropore,' he said, sketching them out with his hands as though conjuring them into being. 'Imagine if you were living on that kind of scale. Your engagement with water, for example, would be completely different, because surface tension would play a much bigger role. So, organisms that live there have to produce things like surfactants that change the way they interact with the skin of the water. A tiny, tiny area of soil is an inconceivably complex three-dimensional labyrinth. Then imagine scaling that up to a larger volume of soil, over metres and kilometres, across the whole globe.'

The question of scale comes up a lot in mycology. One moment Merlin might be focusing on what is happening at one particular branch in a tiny mycorrhizal network, the next trying to create a global map of fungal networks. Your mind, he told me, has to take all that on board and deal with it.

'We're looking at everything from individual branchpoints to a level of quadrillions of branchpoints on a global scale. Just in terms of what you're asking of your mind and your imagination it's overwhelming, but I find that overwhelm helpful. It deepens the enquiry because I feel drawn into it. If it feels like an exhilarating, wild, imaginative adventure, then I'm in.'

The sensation of being overwhelmed was a common feature of many of my conversations in woodlands throughout the year. At the scale of the challenges ahead. At the changes we need to make in order to avert the worst of climate breakdown and ecological collapse. At all the unknown unknowns of the situation in which we find ourselves. At the complexity and scale of the problems we face as the earth heats and our weather systems become increasingly volatile. There are those who face being overwhelmed with panic and those, like Merlin, who face it by leaning into it, by being brought into the enquiry, whether scientist or artist. And in looking towards fungi and their seemingly alien lives, I felt Merlin was pointing towards a future in which the boundaries of academia would need to become, by necessity, permeable and porous.

'The living world is a story of wild collaborations, and intimacies between very different creatures,' he observed, as we discussed the benefits of collaborations between scientists and artists to explore possibilities for deep learning. 'So much of the story of life is what happens when very different creatures get together and do something that none of them could do alone.'

Lichens – not a single organism but the symbiotic relationship between a fungus and an alga, like the dusty, rust-coloured ones on the trunks of the beeches past which we were walking – are a perfect example, embodied relationships rather than two separate organisms. Merlin argued that they give us a useful metaphor or analogy for how we might face some of our biggest challenges, by bringing together people from different disciplines to address problems in ways that have not been considered before.

'This is a basic recurring principle that we see in the long history of life and I think it applies to humans as well, so in this time of unprecedented crisis and opportunity, perhaps we need to respond like organisms have responded to analogous moments in the past, by forming new relationships.

'Can we think of relationships between artists and scientists as a kind of lichenizing? What about projects with three different artists and three different scientists from different fields? Why not throw in lawyers and philosophers and supreme court judges and see what happens when we try to address these phenomenally complex questions together as a kind of lichen?'

The important questions that need our attention might require a network approach rather than an individualistic one. And in lichenizing relationships we may be able to formulate answers for questions we might not even be able to articulate alone, let alone solve.

The complexity of woodlands makes them difficult to understand. The reasons that a tree may flourish in one area and not in another just several feet away may take a researcher years to understand. Or the reasons why an orchid may flower on the edge of one stand of trees but not the next, similarly so. The needs of one species may clash with those of the others. A sudden change or the appearance of a disease may alter a woodland beyond recognition. And so much of what affects the woodlands we see is the product of networks about which we have only begun to scratch the surface in terms of what we might know, as Merlin's work indicates.

It may be that to know a woodland is the work of lifetimes far beyond the span of those available to us, yet approaching woodlands with wonder and awe, in collaborative enquiries that enable us to see what we cannot alone – in a kind of lichenization – seems to me like a good point at which to start.

4

Heartwood Carver

Among the bodgers in a field outside Cambridge

When I was nine or ten, I filled in a form on the last page of my copy of Richmal Crompton's *Just William* which suggested, for a small fee, I could join the Outlaws. The book was maybe second- or third-hand by the time it got to me, and I had no idea if the offer to join William's gang still stood, but I had hope. I sellotaped the requested 50 pence piece to the short application form and spent every afternoon over the next few weeks sitting at the bottom of the stairs when I returned from school, staring down the hallway at the back door, as if my desperate expectation would encourage the post to come. By the time it arrived, I had all but given up hope, but I still recall the excitement of opening the envelope to find the red, plastic wallet with Thomas Henry's illustration of William staring up from it, opening it to find my membership pack, oath an' all, to be sealed by spitting on my palm and shaking hands with another Outlaw. I did not know anyone else who shared my enthusiasm for them at the time though and I've still not sealed the deal with a spit and shake. Having the card, though, I felt like I belonged. I was a William too and about the same age as as the evergreen William Brown who appeared in the books.

I joined the Outlaws in the hope of making my life more like that of Crompton's anarchic William. This was at my peak of interest in the Outlaw stories, when I sided with him on his brother, Robert, who is always falling in and out of love but, more than that, the desire to be away from prying parental eyes – as William puts it, to go to the woods, live on blackberries and roots, shoot bows and arrows and, more or less, live as an outlaw.

I grew up in a small village on the outskirts of Stockport. It was certainly not as gentrified as the one in which the Browns lived, but I overlaid the two places, one on top of the other. Romiley contained many of the same stock elements – a church with grumpy parishioners, a fishing tackle shop that sold catapults we would eye on the way back from school, a sweet shop in the centre, where we bought bulls' eyes and sherbet. Outlaw-like, we would pool the snacks we bought and those we had filched from cupboards and – less Outlaw-like, perhaps – herbs stolen from our parents' spice racks which we would attempt to smoke at our meeting place in the woods.

Like William Brown, all I wanted to do was to get out of the village to climb the taller trees, swing from the rope some of the older kids had slung over one of the high branches and pretend the outside world did not exist.

Thirty-three years later, when I filled out my application to become a member of the Association of Pole-lathe Turners & Green Woodworkers – sometimes shortened to the even less catchy APTGW, but more commonly known as the Bodgers – the memory of joining the Outlaws came back to me. When my membership pack arrived through the post, I got that same thrill as when my long-awaited membership to the Outlaws finally dropped through the letterbox. Emma declared she wanted to know nothing about it, and I barely dared to tell her that, by default, my family membership meant that she and our two children were also signed-up Bodgers now.

While the desire to be part of a club may have started with William's Outlaws, the direct chain of events that led me to a field in Cambridge, discussing the finer points of pole-lathes, *kuksas*, spoon shanks and scorps had started on Valentine's Day three years earlier.

In the February of the first year of the Covid lockdown in the UK, Emma bought me two whittling knives, one straight and one curved, and a box of wood samples. I opened the box and, intending to spend a few minutes with it, began to whittle away at the first piece. I was still sitting at the kitchen table in my dressing gown with an empty breakfast bowl in front of me two hours later, only now the table and floor were covered in wood shavings and in my hands was a spoon. It was a plain thing, yet it pleased me in a way I had not expected. More than that, I experienced the release of having been absorbed in something completely, something I had not been able to do since the pandemic was first announced.

I had made the spoon myself. With my own hands. I had spent most of the morning in a state of complete flow, absorbed in the task. It was satisfying in so many ways. First, the simple pleasure of having made something with my own hands. Second, the object I had made had a use. And third, despite a lack of any sort of finesse, it was beautiful, especially in the last stage of the process when I had applied oil, watching as the hidden patterns within the wood emerged.

I've made perhaps sixty spoons since then. Each, slightly wonky and uneven, tells a story of a particular tree that grew in a particular place, a story told in its patterns, in the patches where I had to rout out rot, or when I discovered a knot or beautiful whorl that was not visible before, the presence of a fungus that led to a beautiful spalting. Each one represents a kind of meditation too, a memory of a period of complete enthralment. And, more than that, in giving the majority of these spoons away – after all there is a limit to the number of wooden spoons any one person really needs – I found they connected me to the people to whom I gave them.

I have kept a record of the spoons I've carved, from ones for measuring out coffee or for eating, stirring spoons and spatulas, and the people to whom I've given them. Occasionally, I still receive a message from someone using one of my coffee scoops, or another item, to let me know that they think of me while using it.

I began to exchange these spoons for other handcrafted things. A pair of salad spoons for a painting of a wave with a farmer on Bryher on the Isles of Scilly. A set for a friend on Twitter who was stuck for what to buy her dad for Father's Day, a chance to repay a favour after she had gifted me a copy of *The Oxford Companion to Ships and the Sea*, a couple of years earlier. An eating spoon for a hand-turned eating bowl made from pittosporum with a musician friend who lives on the island of St Agnes – I now eat my porridge from it, using an eating spoon I carved from cherry wood.

The act of giving and receiving of wooden spoons has long been a sign of respect or love. The Welsh love spoon was traditionally given by the working classes as a declaration of love and affection. The earliest surviving examples date from the mid-1600s. Highly decorated and often intricate, love spoons are encoded with a whole language. Hearts – unsurprisingly – represent love. Wheels are a sign that the giver will work for his love, and chains demonstrate that the object of affection has taken the giver's heart captive. Many feature an anchor and were carved by sailors during long sea voyages.

My spoons are nothing like these. They are plain and utilitarian, meant for stirring porridge, scraping a frying pan or scooping coffee – everyday things that I hope someone will use over and again and, once in a while, remember they were given by me in affection.

My children – rightly – laugh at my attempts at carving. They treat my woodworking with the sort of gentle contempt with which they treat most of my endeavours. Yet, I notice that the things I give them that are made from wood – the small carved animals and spoons – are kept in drawers or on shelves in their rooms, and have not been thrown out in the regular purges of their earlier childhoods. I'd like to think that, in the future, when they are stirring soup or a sauce with it in their first flat, when they leave home, they will recall the love with which I made it.

An oak burl pen pot.

The pleasure of these things, though, is more than the care that has gone into them – there is something about the material itself that is inherently satisfying. There are few things in life more pleasing than wood made useful and beautiful. An axe handle, a wooden bowl, a beautifully crafted chair, a clinker-built boat – the simple pleasure of having created something with one's own hands, and that secondary pleasure of knowing that process has minimal impact on the world around you. As Hugh Johnson remarks in his introduction to the imaginatively titled *International Book of Wood*, it has the unique value of being the one material we use that we can also renew. When we take a tree, as long as we plant more in its place and care for them as they grow, we can maintain the resource from which we have created fuel, tools, shelter, food, for longer than our cultural memory stretches back.

As I tell people that I am now making things from wood, logs and branches begin to appear at the gate, dropped off by a local woodcutter. I receive messages from people in the village asking if I might like some of the timber to play with from a tree they have felled. A friend messages me on Facebook to let me know he has a whole apple tree on the roof of his shed, waiting for me to collect it. One of Emma's cousins brings me a lump of olive wood from a tree they had to fell at her house in Italy. And then, one day, in a dark car park close to home, a friend opens the boot of his transit van and beckons me over. It feels to all intent and purposes like a drug deal and I half expect, as happened once in a similar such place in my teenage years, suddenly to be blinded by the headlights of a police car – but there is no one else there to witness when Alex hands over some knotty, gnarled chunks of a cherry tree he had taken down earlier in the week, and which he'd been carrying around in the back of his van until he saw me. The shelves in my shed become dense with wood, a physical reminder of other people's kindness.

In stolen hours, like bodgers across the country, I will lose myself for a while making this gifted wood into more spoons and bowls, objects that might be used and passed on, perhaps treasured as I treasure the wooden objects others have given me.

The first woodworkers worked beneath the trees, it being more practical to work the wood where it fell rather than dragging it out of the forest. The trees beneath which they worked provided shelter as well as the materials of their trade, fuel for the fires to keep them warm and materials for a simple hut. These woodworkers shaped the forests in which they worked, coppicing and pollarding, favouring certain trees for particular properties – ash for the shafts of spears, yew for longbows, oak and elm for ships, hazel for hurdles and hoops, willow for cricket bats and basketry, walnut for a gunstock. They came to know the woods and their properties intimately, their durability, flexibility, resistance to shrinkage or to damage by water, their workability, the kind of grain they knew they would find locked within a trunk. They grew to recognize how the wood felled from a tree in winter differed from one felled in summer. They specialized and perfected their crafts.

In his preface to *Woodland Crafts in Britain*, Herbert L. Edlin stated that his purpose in writing the book was to preserve a first-hand record of the skills of the traditional woodworker. Edlin had been a forester in the 1940s and was concerned that as the UK's forests dwindled, so the sound of the axe-like adze and the saw would fade in the heart of the woods, and that traditional wood-crafts would be remembered only in surnames, in Bowyers, Colliers, Cleavers, Hoopers, Wrights, Sawyers, Turners and Carpenters, those who now might know little of the woods.

And there are the Bodgers, of course. Bodger is the term now used for anyone who does green woodwork, though originally it came from Buckinghamshire dialect and referred to the small community of woodworkers who turned chair legs in High Wycombe in the Chilterns, specifically those who worked in the woods with a portable pole-lathe, which they set up in situ and turn legs from the wood all around them. Like charcoal burners, they established camps where they worked, as it was easier to go to the materials than to take a tree trunk to a workshop. In recent years, the term 'bodger' has been reclaimed by workers of green wood, from pole-lathe turners to whittlers and basket-makers.

I was not alone in discovering woodcarving during the pandemic. The membership of groups like the Bodgers has expanded rapidly in recent years. Festivals with names like Northern Bowl Gathering, Spoonfest and Spoontown have cropped up across the country, brought on, in part, by the explosion of interest in spoon carving and *sloyd* – the Swedish craft system that incorporates woodwork – during the lockdowns.

On approach, the Bodgers' Ball could have been any summer festival. It had the same temporary town feel of marquees and stalls sprung up like field mushrooms. Walking through the site, past people with spills of beech in their hair and spoons on their belts, their hats or strung on necklaces, the differences became apparent fairly quickly. Aside from conversations going on outside camper vans and caravans, the site was quieter than most other summer festivals. There was no music and no loudspeakers, no stage nor sponsors and advertisers, though there were knives and axes to be bought, woven baskets and hand-carved wooden objects.

Walking the field and queuing for the tea urn, it seemed to me the markers of belonging here, more so than the spoons in hats, were wooden cups – many of which were in the Finnish *kuksa*-style. Driven, perhaps, by the desire to be part of the gang, I had signed up to a workshop to learn how to carve a *kuksa* for myself.

Originally a Nordic craft, *kuksas* (or *guksi*) are best known as the cups of the Sami reindeer herders in Finland, a form of *duodji*, the traditional craft of the Sami which takes in needlework, carpentry, traditional costume and knife-making. Among walkers, hikers and bushcrafters in Scandinavia, *kuksas* have a certain mystique, and to create a traditional *kuksa*, several conditions must be met. Firstly, that it should be carved from birch, and, in particular, from a burl, the scar material that forms on the trunk or roots of a tree, which results in a strong, beautiful cup. I had read somewhere that carving a *kuksa* was a rite of passage across Scandinavia, and had fallen for the whole thing hook, line and sinker.

A few months before, I had attempted to carve my own *kuksa*, from a gnarled chunk of wood I had liberated from a branch that had fallen in a local woodland. It had taken weeks of chipping out a bowl and shaping. I blunted all my knives and impaled myself several times in the process but persisted, ending up with a cup that looked as though it had been hewn out of rock, a rough, uneven thing. Still, I was proud enough of it to set it in the cupboard alongside the other mugs.

I read a statistic a few years ago – I can't recall where, nor can I track down the source and, even if I could, I am aware the story may be apocryphal – that the last time we, as humans, could truly understand the complexities of the things we, as a species, made, was sometime around the height of the great age of sail between the mid-sixteenth and mid-nineteenth centuries. At that point in history, it was possible for someone to understand all aspects of something as complex as a wooden sailing ship, from its design, construction and build, through to navigating and sailing it. Beyond that point, as industrialization led to the development of increasingly complex machines – so the story went – we were only able to understand in part. The production line put paid to any chance of understanding most machines in full, with each worker focusing on one element that would later combine with others to form the whole.

I tried to verify the story about the sailing ships and understanding on the browser on my mobile phone, a machine that, while I can operate it, I understand almost nothing of the technologies that underpin it, the ways in which it magically brings back the answer – or, rather, *usually* brings back the answer as my search for the statistic about the age of sail returns no hits. Bearing in mind the complexity of the machine itself, and the software on which it runs, the countless connections it has to other machines worldwide, it is almost impossible to imagine that any one person could truly understand what is going on in the slim rectangular box that allows us access to infinite knowledge. Add in AI, and the whole thing becomes dizzying. Any idea that we might control this aspect of our lives is fantastical at best, and the more one unpicks that thought, the clearer it becomes why we might be beset by anxieties in the modern world. So, it makes sense that one antidote for that anxiety is to step away and, in my case, work with my hands, even if it is only at the weekends and evenings, creating things I understand.

We all want to feel we have some sort of understanding of the world around us, a way in which to make it make sense, a sense of control over some small parts of it and, with that in mind, it is understandable that people might want to engage in something simple, something understandable and tangible, like the making of a spoon or bowl. And perhaps there is something empowering about being able to look up into the branches of a tree and see within it the things we need for life.

It was in this spirit that I had signed up to create a *kuksa* with one of England's most talented cup carvers, Paul Adamson. Five of us gathered beneath a tarpaulin on a day in which a storm rolled clockwise around the bowl in which the Bodgers' field sat, occasionally pelting the tents.

Paul had prepared blocks of alder and laid out our tools – axe, straight knife, push knife, gouges, and a spoon horse or clave on which to carve – and he walked us through the process.

'Where I grew up was mainly urban,' he told me as we carved, 'though there were three fields in the middle of it that hadn't been developed and we lived on the edge of that. When everyone else was getting into computer games, I'd do whatever it took to stay out in woods and fields, building dens, making traps, collecting frogspawn and building dams, all those things you read about in books. I was completely feral. We'd spend all summer there, but I'd still be there in winter too, when everyone else had headed inside.'

So far, so William Brown, though, as happens to everyone aside from William, life got in the way. Paul ended up taking an apprenticeship with Rolls-Royce and went on to work in engineering, though, he said, it made him miserable. He ended up returning home where, after seeing a careers programme on the BBC, he resigned from his job and returned to the trees, this time as a tree surgeon, first in woodland management and then in conservation, his role now with the National Trust where he is a Ranger. While being paid to climb trees and play with chainsaws, to spend his days in the woods again, he began to carve spoons.

'I realized spoons were the tip of the iceberg of green woodworking and then that was it, it took over.' He grinned broadly, 'You know, the way one thing leads to another?'

I heard other bodgers saying the same thing over that weekend. Many people come to green woodworking through spoons, one carver told me. It's a gateway drug that leads to pole-lathe turning and then to the crack cocaine of the bodging world, bowl turning.

'*Kuksas* were the hardest thing I'd tried to make,' Paul continued, 'so I worked out all the problems and eventually started to make some successful ones. I remember the first time I drank out of a *kuksa* I'd made myself and it felt like such an achievement. You haven't had to buy it. You haven't had to rely on anybody else. And the best thing was I didn't even use anybody else's advice, because there wasn't anyone out there making them.' Paul added, 'I don't really like asking for help.'

He shared his progress on Instagram and people began to get in touch with questions about the process and the pitfalls they themselves had encountered – and not just green woodworkers but people interested in the adjacent field of bushcraft. Eventually, Paul started to teach people how to make *kuksas*.

Wandering around the field after I had finished the course, an unfinished *kuksa* in my backpack, I listened to various bodgers talking about the rabbit holes down which they had fallen. In one tent, a man in his fifties, wearing a doublet and hose, was giving demonstrations on his pole-lathe. His outfit, he was explaining, was an attempt at making garments that were as close to authentic sixteenth-century clothing as possible. The only concession, he told me later in hushed tones, was a small square of rubber on the underside of his leather shoes to better grip the pedal of the lathe, though he supposed that was okay in the grand scheme of things.

Another man, pointed out to me almost as though he was a drug pusher, I was told, would show me the highly specialized scorp blades he had been working on, for hollowing out cups and *kuksas*.

In a huddle beneath a tarpaulin, there was an argument going on about what it takes to make something truly handmade. Most of the group were arguing that it was okay to use some machinery – a bandsaw, for example, to do some of the work of cutting a billet of wood down to size, made some of the drudge work quicker. On the other side of the discussion, a man, carving out the bowl of a spoon, was insisting that the log had to be split with an axe or hand saw to qualify.

'It's about the hand and the heart,' he was saying, insistently. 'The hand and the heart, that's what makes it handmade.'

I left the tent with the argument still in full flow and ducked, instead, beneath another large tarpaulin shelter as the rain came in again, to admire the work of a woman who was creating intricate flowers from stems of hazel with a draw knife. They originated from gypsy flowers, Maz told me when I asked her about the woodshave flowers, though she refers to them as 'folk' or 'hazel flowers'. Carved in one piece, the flower emerges from the stem in thin, curled strips of wood that create the flower's petals.

'I find it quite hard to unplug and the nature of my role means that I need to pretty much be on call. I have my phone with me most of the time.' Maz's day job was in corporate finance, a busy, high stress role with long hours spent in front of the screen. 'It means I'm always at work really, so I struggle to switch off from it and enjoy my own time. When I'm doing this, though, I'm sitting alongside other people and I can hear what's going on around me, but I have to focus on what I'm doing, so I'm not thinking about work. I'm just enjoying the process.'

She got into woodwork through her partner, Fuzz, who, like me, spent much of lockdown carving spoons. The couple were away from home, working in Toronto when the pandemic hit and when they returned to the UK, as things started to open up again, he joined a local bodgers' group and encouraged Maz to come along. One of the group lent Maz a drawknife and gave her a piece of willow, and it took off from there. Now, when she gets home from work, she carves a couple of flowers in the kitchen while Fuzz cooks the dinner. She told me she had made around 650 flowers.

'I have to focus on the process of making the flower to avoid cutting off the petals and also to get the shape and the curl that I want.' She was drawing a flower marvellously out of the thin stick. 'Concentrating on that enables me to stop thinking about whatever has been going on during my workday and to manage the pressures I'm under there. It is a craft but it's absolutely mindfulness too.'

On Saturdays, when she and Fuzz make things alongside their green woodworking group, she said, they become part of a community too.

'I'm focused, I'm producing something that I think is pretty and it gives me enormous pleasure to make something that other people enjoy having in their homes. It's something to do with the process of having something in your hands, applying a tool and having a tangible product at the end of the day. You can feel that progress. With a lot of computer-based jobs, I think it's difficult to recognize what you've achieved over the day, and that can be hard.'

Maz's hazel flowers.

Maz explained that some of the appeal of the bodgers' groups to which she and Fuzz belong in East Anglia, lies in how they help people to step outside their everyday lives, the amount it means to the people involved and how the community of woodworkers values neurodiversity. There's an almost obsessive quality to much of the work here, an intensity of focus and a collecting of information and skills. Looking around the field the common factor was the pursuit of finding perfection in a beautiful spoon with a beautiful form, or making something beautifully decorated, while other people were allowing the wood to speak simply for itself and to dictate whichever form the spoon should be.

'I mean, how many wooden spoons does the world need? There's a lot of neurodiversity and mental health support going on here,'

Maz commented on green woodworking, where the wood is still soft enough to be worked with hand tools. 'Whether it's spoon carving or green woodworking, we're quite precise in what we're doing and we channel a lot of energy into it. We're present in the here and now. There are people here trying to perfect a particular form of spoon or bowl, that one niche that's really important to them. I think that in this community, we recognize this in each other and we support each other.'

It's a conversation, she continues, that is also taking place in the world of corporate finance, where more and more people are opening up about the things that help them to self-regulate or decompress after the stresses of the office. Maz thinks the reason why green woodworking is becoming much more popular is, in part, because it is an opportunity to sit alongside other people and talk while concentrating on that activity. In part, it is about the wood, but much of it is about the community the practice of woodwork enables. Unlike other forms of carpentry, green woodworking is a particularly quiet activity. Working just with the heart and hand, it is possible to sit around in a circle or semi-circle and have a conversation while everyone works on their individual craft.

'You're not talking about the spoon you're carving or the knife you're carving it with, often it's a conversation about life that happens,' she proves this, talking to me while working. A small semicircle of admirers have gathered, watching Maz carve, the hazel flower now at full spread, the final twists falling into place. 'And there are few opportunities for that in much of the rest of our lives.'

I left her as the admirers started to ask questions about the beautiful, delicate flowers. As I passed Paul's tent canopy, he called me over.

'I've been thinking about what you asked earlier,' he said. 'About the attraction of all of this, about what draws me to it.'

He waved in the direction of his van and the tarp he had rigged up, beneath which were his bowl horses and tools, his spoons and *kuksas*, and across at the field of earnest woodworkers with their spoons and beech spills, axes and adzes.

'It's about being accepted. You know, being good enough or worthy or respected or whatever it is. You know, being part of something.'

Kuksas and spoons might be a symbol of self-reliance – if you're able to make both in the unlikely scenario you are stranded in the wilderness with little to hand, it might make life a lot easier – but the real value of the Bodgers is the community. These events, the Bodgers Balls and Spoonfests, the Bowl Gatherings and woodlore festivals, are like magnets to people who otherwise spend much of the year on their own, in small workshops or in clearings in woodlands, in living rooms and the backyards of terraced houses. Here, they can share something of what they love and understand.

A pole-lathe turner at the Bodgers' Ball.

Once the storm had passed, the sky cleared and a full moon rose over the camp. The pub tent, all real ale, tankards and bar billiards, drew in half of the bodgers, and the other half made their way to the far end of the field where a fire had been built. It was Beltane eve, known in Irish mythology as *Cétshamhain*, the eve of summer. Several people had brought wood from their own small camps to build up a communal bonfire, and as the fire got going, someone passed around a bottle of whisky. In ancient Irish texts, the smoke and ash from the Beltane bonfire was deemed protective of people and cattle. Someone called for a song and an elderly lady sang a reedy lament. As no one offered anything in the space that followed, I put forward a sea shanty from Cornwall, which was taken up around the circle. One of the pole-lathe turners sang a song of revolutionaries overthrowing a corrupt regime and a young Irish man sang a drinking song that involved him taking off all his clothes.

A full moon rose behind a stand of poplars and low mist drifted in over the flat land. In the light of two sharp shafts of moonlight between the trees, I saw misty figures and it would have been easy enough to believe they were *aos sí*, the fairylike people of Danu to whom offerings were made by the Irish and the Scottish on Beltane. It may have been the full moon that caused it, the fire, the singing or the effects of the bottle of whisky that was still doing the rounds, but people begin to dance in the shafts of misty moonlight that shone between the tall poplars on the field's edge, spinning silently, their arms wide and their heads thrown back.

After the dancing and the singing had stopped and the fire had begun to die down, I watched the moon and the glowing embers for a while before returning to my van, where I picked up the *kuksa* I had started earlier that day. I worked on it for half an hour before turning in, experiencing some of that satisfaction that Paul talked about earlier, carving a wooden cup with a knife I had forged while, in the tents and vans across the site, others were doing the same before sleep. And whether it was that or the Beltane wildness I couldn't tell you, but for a few moments before slept I felt the profound peace of working with my hands, and for the first time in weeks, I slept with the abandon of the Outlaws. I suspect had William known about the Bodgers, he would have wanted to be part of their gang too.

5

Boat Builder

A Scillonian pilot cutter in the waters off Cornwall's south coast, and a Highland birlinn in a green hollow in Glasgow's former docklands

The sea heaved and I steadied myself on the rigging, not yet used to the boat's movement on the water.

Although in the harbour all was calm, there was movement in the flags above the National Maritime Museum, and when I had walked down the hill towards the harbour, I had seen the invisible line across which the flat, dark blue sea gave way to waves tipped with white.

Surrounded by the industrial derricks and the high-sided walls of ships, in waters protected by the outstretched arms of Falmouth on one side and the Roseland on the other, the sea had been entirely flat, the air calm as the tender carried me across from the pontoon to the boat that was to be home for the next few days.

Among the sleek super yachts, tourers, fishing boats and naval vessels, *Agnes* was an outlier, a distinctly analogue, wooden shape among hulls of steel, aluminium and fibre reinforced plastic. She looked for all the world as though she had slipped through a gap in time and found herself propelled 200 years forward.

One of Colin Macleod's carvings from the Pollok Free State camp, many of which depicted animals that once roamed Scotland.

Coming aboard, I had run my hands along her gunwales, to enjoy the sheer tactile joy of being on a boat I had watched from afar and dreamt of sailing for several years. I have always had a thing for wooden boats and when I daydream – which is often – it is usually about being under sail on boats constructed of beautiful woods. It is something to do with the knowledge that the material from which the boat is constructed is organic, that it is almost a living thing, that I connect to it in a way that I do not to boats constructed of metals or plastics.

When we go out on the water in boats, we put our faith in them, that they will be seaworthy and will hold us safe in an environment that can become hostile with little warning, and the knowledge that our ancestors put their faith in wood may have something to do with it. Our collective histories with wood as a material of construction makes it almost like an extension of ourselves and, for me at least, there is something intensely comforting about hearing the sound of water against a wooden hull, or halyards against a wooden mast, the feeling of connection to the sea through a rudder, the sensation of being propelled by the world's winds, of having harnessed, or connected to, some small part of that elemental energy. At their best, they feel as though they are almost alive, as the wind fills the sails and the boat heels, gaining speed and you brace yourself against the transom, the warmth of the wood reassuring, comforting.

These wonderings are a combination of the profound – memories of small moments of feeling in harmony with the world – and somewhat more ridiculous dreams of being a pirate or a smuggler, dreams I indulge when I am sailing too. There are no engines in these memories and imaginings, no electronics or motors, just wood, rope and canvas, and a sense of expansive freedom. Perhaps this is natural since, from the earliest moments of human history, we have built boats and rafts, canoes and kayaks from the trees around us, and for most of that time they were powered by wind and by hand. It is in our lineage.

No one knows when we first developed boats and much of the discussion around the first ones centres around the earliest human remains found on islands such as Australia, Crete and Flores in Indonesia, which suggest we were able to cross seas tens, if not hundreds of thousands of years ago. The earliest watercrafts are thought to have been wooden rafts, though the development of the first boats, which may have been dugout canoes, papyrus reed boats or sewn hide boats with a wooden frame, allowed us to travel further afield. The earliest known examples of these date back some 8,000 years. In the Neolithic and Bronze Ages, we developed the tools and techniques to create plank-built boats, allowing us to build them lighter, broader and more stable, and marked the beginning of a history of building with wooden boats that was only interrupted some 150 years ago by the advent of the steamboat. For tens of millennia, wood was used for the combination of properties that made it perfect for creating boats. It is light and stiff, though with some flexibility. It is hydrodynamic and floats well. For most of our history, the materials for building were abundant and, when damaged, a wooden boat is easily repaired if there are more trees to hand. So, for most of the boat's history, we kept the material the same and simply refined the designs, developing specific boats to use on specific waters.

Agnes could have been built specifically to inspire the daydreams of the sort I often have. A faithful replica of the Scillonian pilot cutter of the same name, that was built in 1841, she is the past resurrected. None of the original pilot cutters of Scilly exist now, though at one time each of the inhabited islands of this tiny archipelago at the far south-west of England had at least two or three of these boats working their waters. Like most working boats, pilot cutters were born of geography, designed to sail in a particular place for a particular purpose, wood made useful for our ventures and shaped to the seas in which they would be put to work.

Lying 35 miles off the coast of Cornwall, the Isles of Scilly had long been a key staging post for ships crossing the Atlantic from, what was in the mid-nineteenth century, a sprawling empire. Scilly was a logical place for ships carrying the produce of empire to pause before finding the right wind with which to travel on to their destination port, though the islands were not entirely the haven they appeared. The waters around Scilly are among the most treacherous in the United Kingdom and Ireland. To the east and west lie rocks around which countless ships lie wrecked in the shallow waters, among the reefs and submerged ledges, rocks that are invisible to an approaching ship and that might go unnoticed in a storm on a dark night.

There is a saying on Scilly that there is no rock among these that has not taken down a boat. Approaching the islands in heavy weather, as violent squalls blew through and made a chaos of the shallow seas around the islands, fighting waves that had started out as ripples hundreds of miles offshore and that had built to huge size as they met the islands, powerful tides that raced the gaps, it is understandable that a ship's captain might be happy to pay local fishermen and sailors to come out to them as they approached the archipelago. These local sailors put a man aboard the incoming ship to guide it safely through the treacherous maze of shallow waters and hidden ledges into shelter.

The higher the seas and the more powerful the wind, the greater the need a ship's captain had of the expertise of a local pilot. It makes sense that ships' owners would pay well for this service and that in time a fleet of such pilot cutters would be built, designed specifically for the purpose of carrying pilots out to incoming ships. Naturally, competition for this business was fierce, with the first boat out to an incoming ship earning the commission for bringing it in safely (or possibly to take on board some of the goods on which the crew had no intention of paying duties) and, therefore, that these boats would be built for speed, able to handle the heaviest seas, to be raced out against others vying for the same commission. And, human nature being what it is, it makes sense too that the same boat might have to be able to make the journey across to Roscoff in France with a consignment of imported contraband, to evade the authorities on the lookout for smugglers or race against the other pilot boats for sport when there were no ships incoming. So the boats became powerful beasts, seaworthy in the worst weather and sailed in all conditions.

'It'll be bumpy,' Gabe, the captain of *Agnes*, had said as we brought up the mainsail and weighed anchor, two of us working the windlass by hand. And once we crossed the invisible line that marked the end of the land's shelter, the wind and the waves were upon us, and we knew it. The forecast had been for strong easterlies, the most uncomfortable of wind directions for leaving Falmouth, pushing blocky waves up in our path. The easterly wind would limit our choices. It would mean, by necessity, we would have to head up along the coast of Cornwall's Roseland towards Fowey, a journey during which there would be no protection from the wind and waves.

Out of the shelter of the harbour, we hove to, *Agnes* lurching in an uncomfortable swell as Gabe ordered us to raise more sails, the topsail above the huge mainsail and the two foresails that provide the power.

Once raised, we came off the wind and *Agnes* heeled. Although I know boats are not living things, it is difficult in moments like that to see them any other way, to feel a boat come alive in the wind, surging forward, cutting through the waves rather than being buffeted and knocked about. Each wooden boat feels different and distinct, as though they are possessed of personalities, instilled by those who designed, built and sailed them. Under full sail, *Agnes* felt muscular, solid – as though she was at home in a big sea which, as the performance boat of her time, she was – happy even. Or, rather, it was me who was happy to be there, overlaying my emotions onto a wooden boat that has been designed to sail well in a strong breeze. Shortly after, one of the new crew began to heave his guts over the side, emerging occasionally to give us the thumbs up. We ploughed on, through waves that would have swamped a less seaworthy boat, spray flying.

Away from the more modern ships and boats of the harbour, with only glimpses of land, it was easy to indulge in the daydream that we were pilots racing out to a ship sailing towards Cornwall after a long Atlantic crossing, though the pilots of Scilly may have had something to say about our qualifications to do so.

Some months later, I tracked down Luke Powell, who built *Agnes*. I found him in his attic study at the top of a labyrinthine cottage in Penryn, an office that was crammed with boats that hung on the walls, every inch of which were covered in paintings and photographs of topsail schooners, steamers, square riggers, brigs, brigantines and plans of boats he had built or planned to build. A large painted piece of wood from the transom of an elegant naval clipper, a boat that wrecked in Plymouth Sound in 1808, hung from one beam, and from others half models of boats were suspended, including the one on which Luke had based *Agnes*, a lucky find in a back room of the museum on St Mary's, Scilly's largest island.

As much as boatbuilding, what Luke was engaged in, he told me, bringing extinct boats back onto the water, was experimental archaeology. It was something he had been building up to for years, ever since the late 1960s, when he had travelled to Greece as a young boy with his parents in an old fishing boat. There, he had become obsessed with the old sailing cargo boats that worked between the islands.

'Even at the age of nine or ten, I was aware I was witnessing the end of an era,' he said.

Their arrival coincided with the moment more modern boats were being introduced. The next generation had little in common with the cargo boats that had been sailed between the islands for hundreds of years previously.

'This was the end of the line for an evolution that had been happening since Jason and the Argonauts. It was an incredible piece of linear history, and whatever came after that would break that continuity. When I started building boats, I realized I didn't want to build new designs, I wanted to resurrect something from the past. I wanted to bring alive, in some way, a period of history that I'm particularly interested in, and boats seemed the perfect way to do that.'

It was a fascination that led Luke to work restoring old wooden cargo and sailing boats on the east coast of England and, eventually, to build his own when he settled in Cornwall. He described coming across a photograph of a pilot cutter lying derelict on a beach on the island of St Martin's during his honeymoon on Scilly, in 1986, and the immediate interest it generated. There was little information available about the boats then.

By the time Luke came to the islands, the wreck of the original pilot boat, *Agnes*, was buried deep on a beach on St Martin's, a wreck uncovered only after particularly heavy storms at the lowest tides. In the twentieth century, he said, the trend had been to jettison ideas of the past, as the islanders embraced the modern age, so any plans that existed for the boats were long gone and there was little to go on, though Luke, his new wife and local historian Alf Jenkins started to research the history of the pilot cutters.

Many modern boat designers, Luke explained, think we make boats better today than anything that was built in the past, though, he said, for his money, the apex of maritime design was in the 1790s, the era of sleek sailing ships with tall masts and powerful sails, and ever since then all that had really changed was fashion and technology moving materials along. The tail end of the eighteenth century was an era of boats designed by craftspeople who were also sailors, people who knew the sea intimately and put that knowledge into the boats they designed. That too was the end of a lineage that stretched much further back.

'Even today, if you rebuilt a modern Viking boat, there wouldn't be many yachts that could keep up with it,' he went on. 'It's incredible

Agnes *under construction.*

to think that something over a thousand years old in design could out-perform a lot of modern boats.' And what made building a boat that had last sailed some 200 years before from scratch interesting was the sense of being part of that lineage.

'This boat sits on the shoulders of all these generations that went before it. With *Agnes*, yes there had been a gap in the continuity of those boats, but when we launched her, Alf Jenkins, who was in his eighties by then, got up and told stories of his great grandfather, who used to skipper the original *Agnes*. He told us stories about his family on the islands, and going through the Second World War, his childhood on Scilly and the boats he knew. By doing that, he was lighting the fire of life within the boat, he was resurrecting his family story and connecting the boat that was there with his family, with his heritage, and giving it the blessing of being part of that.'

It is a fundamentally romantic thing to bring a boat back from the past, to put it on the water and to sail it as it would have been sailed in the time before the age of steam and steel, a work of the imagination as much as one of practicality.

On the water off Dodman Point, the towering headland at Penare, *Agnes* under full sail, was now powering through the heavy sea. Sitting at the long wooden tiller, feeling the steady power of the cutter as she scythed the waves, it was easy to feel we were sailing a piece of history, part of the lineage that Luke described. To the west, the next point of land, some 2,300 miles away, was Newfoundland. I watched gannets dive, bullet-like, into the dark water, emerging with silver flashes of fish, guillemots and Manx shearwaters as they skimmed the waves. To the landward side, the coastline of the Roseland Peninsula looked almost entirely untouched, and I indulged in the fantasy that we were smugglers outpacing the revenue.

As Luke was to tell me later, the rougher the weather, the more this design of boat comes into its own. 'When we launched the boat, we found she sails like a dream. It's like when a foal is born and within a few minutes, it's up on its feet, galloping around. All of that is programmed into the creature. It's the same with a boat. Put a boat in the water and it knows how to sail. You've embedded in it the ability to do everything you ask of it. It becomes like a living creature when it goes out across the waves.'

It was a matter of having faith in the people who designed and built the original pilot cutters, that they knew what they were doing. Modern sailing can often look like anything but, the controls operated by on-board computers, digital chart screens giving read-outs about wind and tide, information about safe passage and obstacles. It was a case of not assuming that because we have more technology today that we are better informed. On a traditional wooden boat like *Agnes*, which does not use most of that technology, the experience of sailing is a whole body one, reliant on being able to read the wind and the waves, feelings that would have been familiar to those who sailed the original pilot cutters. And, as Luke said, it is difficult, when sailing a beautifully designed boat, not to feel it is in some way sentient, an extension of the sailor, a coming together of wood and consciousness.

'The people who sailed *Agnes* were born to the sea, and they came from people who were born to the sea too,' Luke commented. 'Their fathers and grandfathers for generations and generations had spent all their lives on the water, and their children would go to sea as soon as they were strong enough to haul ropes. They sailed in all weathers, especially in weather in which you wouldn't want to be going out, the weather in which those ships were in most danger from the hazards. To guide ships safely through those hazards, they had to be able to deal with anything the sea could throw at them.'

Agnes *moored by Ferryside, the former home of Daphne du Maurier.*

After the uncomfortable sea swell and the flying spray, the calm waters of Fowey were welcome and we moored beneath the blue-and-white frontage of Ferryside, the house where novelist Daphne du Maurier lived in the late 1920s. As I sat on deck in the evening calm, a heron flew across the water and landed silently in the shallows between where we sat on the pontoon and du Maurier's house. I listened to owls hooting at one another in the woods above the water, as a hectic day gave way to a quiet night.

By the time du Maurier arrived in Cornwall, *Agnes* and the Scillonian pilot cutters were already a thing of the past, pushed out by the more powerful Falmouth versions that muscled in on their territory, superseded by the steamships that replaced sailing ships, vessels that did not need to stop at the Isles of Scilly before reaching the mainland. Wood gave way to iron, sails to engines and the pilot cutters were abandoned on beaches, or simply not repaired, and sank out of sight, casualties of the conveniences of modernity.

In a nook in a dark corner of my bedroom at home, there is a small, framed woodcut print. It shows the outline of a Cornish working boat, distinguishable by its huge sail area and bowsprit and above the boat are the words: 'We cannot control the wind, but we can adjust the sails.' It's a phrase that is so often used in self-help circles that it might be considered meaningless, if it were not so true.

Although it is a metaphor for life, the literal meaning of that phrase may be the reason I love being on wooden boats under sail, as opposed to being powered by an engine. It is the simultaneous realization that you are at once at the mercy of the world's capricious currents and winds, in control of so little, yet there are still choices to make, sails that can be set to make best use of that wind, skill to be employed in navigating, speed to be coaxed out of a boat where the alternative might be to rock aimlessly on a pitching sea, or to sit helplessly as she is swamped by the waves. To sit at the helm of a boat like *Agnes* as she surges through the water is to feel connected to the wind and the waves, and to know you are riding those winds rather than being buffeted by them, and to know as well that, in some small way, you have tamed some of nature's forces to propel yourself forward.

I ran my hands along *Agnes's* gunwales once more before I stepped off the boat, back in the marina at Falmouth three days later. The small, temporary community that had formed on board dissipated and, as I walked back up the hill, I attempted to hoard the specifics, memories that would fortify or reconnect me in times of disconnection. I stored the feeling of connectedness with the world's energies through the tiller, the sensation of wood meeting water in a way that our ancestors, going back hundreds of years, thousands even, would have recognized.

'With a boat like this, you're building something that isn't like a sculpture or a house – you're building something that has to go out there and fight for its life,' Luke told me before I left his sail-crowded attic.

'You know people's lives are going to be enhanced and changed by being on that boat. You're creating something that is vastly more than the sum of its parts: you're creating a time machine, a beast that will fight the elements. You're creating something that will look after you, something that is made by hand, built using the skills our forefathers developed. You're not building an object, you're making poetry. A boat like this makes it a pleasure to be alive.'

A birlinn on the 1528 funerary stone of Alasdair Crotach MacLeod, 8th Chief of the MacLeods of Harris and Dunvegan. In the churchyard at St Clement's at Rodel, on Harris.

Carved in relief on a 1528 funerary stone in the churchyard at St Clement's at Rodel on Harris is an image of a double-prowed, striking, Viking-looking sailing boat. The boat is under full sail, running with the wind and the carving is so detailed that the stitching on the sails, the oar ports and the individual planks of the hull are visible. The grave is that of Alasdair Crotach MacLeod, the 8th Chief of the MacLeods of Harris and Dunvegan, and the carving represents a birlinn, or Hebridean galley, another boat that went extinct, though for vastly different reasons.

Derived from Norse *knaar* longboats, birlinns were adapted by the clan chiefs of the Hebrides from the design of the powerful Viking ships that arrived in Scotland in 850 CE. They were fast, powerful and manoeuvrable, clinker-built boats, in which the wooden planks that made up the hull overlapped, a feature the Vikings developed to give their boats strength for sea crossings. These birlinns, or galleys, could be sailed or rowed, and they were key to the power and independence of the Highland clans, enabling communication, trade and travel between islands. They facilitated raiding and war too, though, more importantly, they allowed the clans to travel further afield and, for almost 500 years, they were instrumental in the spread of the Gaelic language and culture from Ireland to Scotland.

It would be difficult to find a stronger image associated with the people known as the Gall-Ghàidheil, whose name translates as 'strange, or foreign gaels' or, more poetically, 'strangers of the heartland' and who were formed of the native gaelic peoples and assimilated settlers who lived in Scotland at the time. The Gall-Ghàidheil had become so settled that by the ninth century they were known as a single people. The birlinn was a symbol of their strength and it is unsurprising that the image can be found on the gravestones of many of the clan chieftains who relied on their speed and stability, their manoeuvrability and seaworthiness.

Yet just ninety years after Alasdair MacLeod died, the boats of the clan chiefs were erased from the waters of the Hebrides. For the next 500 years, no birlinns sailed Scotland's coasts having been, effectively, outlawed early in the seventeenth century by Stuart king James VI of Scotland (James I of England) at the time he proclaimed the Statutes of Iona – which many historians and Scots consider a sustained attack on Highland culture. The birlinns, so much a part of the culture of the Gall-Ghàidheil that they were engraved in stone when the clan chiefs sailed on to the next life, were destroyed, the Gaelic language going into rapid decline too. And, as there were no examples to follow, nor plans to copy, replica birlinns, such as the one beneath which I was standing in a workshop in Govan on the outskirts of Glasgow, were built using sources such as MacLeod's gravestone and the funerary stones of other prominent clan chiefs on the Hebridean islands.

Picture a birlinn on the waters of the Irish Sea. This boat is not the grey of stone but instead its hull is dark on the water, its crew beginning to get a sense of the journey they are about to undertake. *Orcuan*, as it is named, has been waved off, sung out by a piper standing on the shore. Picture her powerful surge through a winter sea as sixteen oars pull in time away from Irvine Harbour on the Firth of Clyde on Scotland's west coast, as this crew of ten leaves the land behind. They pass the uninhabited island of Ailsa Craig, with her cacophony of gannets and her barking seals, and look out to the open ocean, where clouds are brewing. Some of the crew are hungover, having drunk the whisky as they waited for a weather window to make the crossing. As one of the crew notes, waiting and whisky is a bad combination. It is the end of August, though the weather is more like late autumn. There is a head wind and the boat's square sail, which only works downwind, will be no good to them: they will be rowing against this wind the whole way. The atmosphere on board is tense – they are still working out how to do this, how to pull in time, how to work with the skipper and he to work with them. They got off on the wrong foot, a clash of culture around what it means to lead a crew - though they will bond before they have completed this three-day crossing. The skipper is an experienced sailor and rower. He has circumnavigated the globe several times, captain of his own boat, though this crew feels, perhaps, that he has not yet cultivated their respect.

Orcuan's crew is engaged in a journey from the Mull of Kintyre across the Irish Sea where the distance between these two islands narrows here, to Strangford Lough in County Down, Ireland, ploughing across the sea roads in which these boats were once commonplace. This is a form of pilgrimage rather than a raiding party, a journey designed to enlighten.

The men and women now sailing and rowing this resurrected boat are the descendants of the Highland clans for whom these boats represented power and freedom. Some of the crew on board were involved in building this very boat. They shaped her planks, drove rivets into her hull, made her seaworthy and safe. Others have repaired and cared for her, patched her up after the last long season on the water. Some of them are long-term volunteers of the Govan-based charity which built that boat, others have been helped by that charity's work. And one is undergoing what might now be called an intervention.

What will unite this disparate group of people is not just that they live in Govan, on the banks of the River Clyde, but their affinity with this boat. It is unity that comes of a sense of ownership having built her with their own hands, of connecting to their ancestry, of having recreated a vessel that was extinct, a cultural memory, and floated it on the Clyde where countless ships were once launched. Soon, when they have rowed until they hit the wall and pushed through it, they will feel affinity for one another too. They will go from being rowers to a community, a crew. On the boat, they are all sailors, all rowers. On the water, they are all Gall-Ghàidheil, following the wake of their forebears who sailed and rowed across this same stretch of water, hundreds of years before.

On land, it is another matter. In their lives, some of this crew have been appointed other labels. Alcoholic. Addict. Homeless. Reductive epithets that have a habit of sticking. They are the inheritors of unemployment, the children and grandchildren of the decline and closure of Govan's once-famed shipyards, where the ships of empire were built and launched. They are numbers on indices of social deprivation, inheritors of the grind and of the poverty endemic in this outpost of Glasgow.

It is difficult to square the two things: the elemental nature of sailing a wooden boat in wild Scottish seas with the terraces of shuttered and boarded Victorian buildings, the latticework of industrial units with graffitied shutters, the low rise and the high-rise housing overlooked by the Ibrox football stadium, the bookmakers', fish and chip shops, sports pubs, vacant lots and car yards. The signs of social deprivation apparent when you walk through Govan, some two-and-a-half miles south of Glasgow's centre.

If, 100 miles south and 250 years earlier, Admiral Collingwood's dream of a future navy built of planks from the oaks he planted was never realized, it was, in part at least, because Govan benefited from the new technologies of the mid-nineteenth century and industrialization, when Robert Napier opened his iron shipbuilding works on the banks of the Clyde. In total, about 3,000 ships were built at the Govan shipyards before the collapse of the industry in the 1970s, precipitating its sharp decline from one of Govan's two short-lived periods of prosperity.

'In Govan, we're famous for building boats,' Dorothy Graham told me as I admired the lines of the recreated birlinn, which was out of the water for repairs. '*Orcuan* was the first of ours. Boats are our heritage. But it's more than that. They're a metaphor for the journey through life, of hitting storms, violent, horrible storms. And what happens when you're on a boat? You can't have a diva in a boat. Not in a rowing boat. And in Scotland, when you're in a storm, you can't have a diva having a fit; you have to row together. So there's something about the collective there, about everybody having their role and working together. It's to do with everyone knowing their place, which isn't just about hierarchy, but as in what is your function in that boat? The boat is a metaphor for life and how we get through it together. How do we row in time?'

Orcuan *in for repairs at the workshop at GalGael.*

Dorothy is employed by the charity, GalGael, which took its name from that of the native Scots and its logo from the boat of the clan chiefs. The 32-foot birlinn *Orcuan* was the first of twenty boats built in GalGael's workshops. When people walk through the doors of the workshop, she tells me, they shed, for a while at least, the labels that follow them round, and become a member of this community.

'Rather than saying you're injecting heroin because you've got deficits, what we say here is Scotland's got a drug problem,' she explained. 'We say Scotland has a heroin problem, Scotland's got a mental health problem. There are structural reasons why you're injecting heroin now. As long as you can be safe in this workshop, you might still have a drink problem. You might still have a drug problem. Your mental health might not be good but, if you can be safe, you can work alongside us. And we're not going to be talking about drinking and drugs, we're gonna talk about wood and the environment, and boats. When you're here, you're a community member and all we ask is that you respect the place and that you are safe and don't harm people.'

It takes a community to build a boat, so it might stand that in building a boat you might start to rebuild a community suffering the effects of decades, centuries perhaps, of intergenerational trauma brought on by the Highland Clearances in the eighteenth and nineteenth centuries, people often forcibly removed from their homes to make way for lucrative sheep. Along the way, those engaged would learn skills they could use to rebuild a career, build one from scratch or help them to steer themselves back onto a more stable path. They would learn how to work alongside one another, and engage with some of their shared heritage through the laying of a keel and the setting of planks, in much the way the community would have done in the time of the clans. They would learn self-respect, respect for one another and for wood as a material. And they would then sail the boats which they had often had a hand in building, a waterborne community, and, in doing so, reconnect with the land and waterways of the River Clyde and Scotland's west coast and the vastness of the sea, beyond.

Orcuan, en route to Strangford Lough, is in that vastness of sea now. Guillemots and petrels ride up alongside the rowers, eyeing them before wheeling off, leaving the crew grinning and energized. There is still a long way to go, and exhaustion is never far off.

One of the rowers on the 5-ton boat is the charity's founder Colin Macleod, another is Alan Torrance who has been with the charity since it first started. Alan tells me the thing he learnt most from that trip, midway between Scotland and Ireland, in the dark and torrential rain, was that he was not a sailor.

'When we left the Mull of Kintyre, we were into open sea then and the Atlantic is coming right into that wee bit of water between the island of Ireland and Scotland. It's like a funnel. We were heading due south in a south-westerly wind and there were big waves hitting us diagonally on, almost flooding the boat,' he said, the memory still fresh. 'It's the ultimate leap of faith to go on a boat like that.'

As rowers flag, they are rotated out by one of the five on the accompanying safety boat and, for periods, the birlinn is towed. They are not an experienced crew by any means, and the prospect of nine hours solid rowing is enough to daunt even those with the most experience, though many of the crew had never really rowed before, aside from short trips out on the Clyde – as Alan put it, messing about on the river. Some have rarely been this far from Glasgow.

The trip to Ireland came about, ostensibly, after an invitation to take part in a Viking festival on Strangford Lough that celebrates Magnus Barelegs, the eleventh-century Viking King of Norway, and the last of the Viking kings to raid up and down the Irish and Scottish coasts. At the festival, held at the place where Magnus was buried, after being ambushed, there would be other recreated Viking boats, races and challenges, mock battles and boat burning. But it is more than this for *Orcuan's* crew. One crew member on this three-day row to Ireland is a young man who Alan described to me as being at a crossroads in his life.

'He was going to court, in the hands of the criminal justice system, so it was a kind of rescue attempt for this one young guy who we wanted to save from going down that road,' Alan told me. 'We wanted to give him a different perspective. We wanted to show him you could have adventures without going down the wrong road. A lot of the guys in the boat had been down that wrong road and they wanted to influence him'.

It was Colin Macleod, whose parents were from Ireland and the Isle of Lewis respectively, and whose ancestors were among the

clans who used the birlinns, who saw the connection between the
boats his ancestors sailed to navigate their islands and the problems
he saw all around him in Govan.

The roots of GalGael date back to a woodland protest in
neighbouring Pollok, at the time the largest housing estate in
Europe. The protest built up around the charity's charismatic
leader Colin, with his mass of springy dark hair in dreadlocks,
who became a spokesman for a movement, incensed that a proposed motorway would cut off access for deprived communities
to the biggest green space in Glasgow.

When Glasgow City Council announced plans in the early
1990s for a spur of the M77 motorway to cut through Pollok
Country Park, the only one in Glasgow, Colin, who attributed his
love of trees to spending so much time there as a child, reacted
by climbing a large beech tree in Barrhead Woods on the estate,
in the path of the planned motorway, and refusing to come down.

Colin stayed nine days and nights in the branches and the
story of the 'bird man of Pollok' got out. As it did, a community
built up around the tree in which Colin had made his camp. The
protest was unsuccessful in the end, though it brought to light
many of the area's social problems. As well as environmentalists
and campaigners, the camp attracted people from the housing
projects of Pollok and Govan who saw the campfire, Dorothy told
me. They would sit around it and discuss the environment and
the importance of trees, though it was not always an easy ride.

'Lots of guys appeared, injecting heroin, drinking Buckfast
or whatever. There was drink, drugs and partying around the
campfire in the woods,' she adds.

It was perhaps unsurprising, given the area's rates of violence and substance abuse, its grim record as an area with one
of the country's highest rates of drug deaths. It was only natural that these problems would find their way in as the camp
became a place where people felt safer than they did in the
housing schemes.

Eventually, despite the protest and the marches on Glasgow's seats of power, the motorway developers won. Two years after the camp opened, in February 1996, police, security firms and contractors moved in to forcibly clear the camp.

Though the trees in the park were cleared for the motorway, what happened there during the protests underpinned the thinking for what became GalGael, a movement dedicated to social, ecological, spiritual and cultural renewal, a place for the strangers of the heartland to rediscover themselves. They built a workshop in central Govan to support the people living there, regardless of their background and the problems they had encountered in life.

It was Colin, Alan said, who made the connection between the huge trees the city council were felling and the people of Govan.

'Those trees had to come down, but the trunks were going to landfill,' he said. 'And Colin's like, "Why would you do that?" All the glory that tree represents having lived the many years it did to eventually end up in landfill beside the other household rubbish. He's seen the comparison between that resource getting flung in landfill and the people here being made redundant. They were just getting flung on the scrap heap. So that's two great resources being wasted by us. When we bring people in here, we help them understand that from that going from a tree to being a bit of wood on the bench, there's a journey involved. There's a lot of love and energy dedicated to get that bit of wood onto a bench, with which you can then create something beautiful, like a box or a boat, which will let it survive and live on.'

When *Orcuan* finally arrives at Strangford Lough, there is a rip tide running at 10 or 12 knots against a boat that rows at perhaps 4 or 5 knots. The crew's forebearers would have faced the same. Alan looks over the gunwales at houses on the shore and sees they are making no progress against them. Locals turn out to greet them in yachts and shout over that they will never make it through, that the rip will spit them back out. The skipper guides them through the eddies and currents and they make land. The tense atmosphere has long since lifted and the crew are all camaraderie. The boat has been a great leveller and they have found respect for the skipper, and the skipper for them.

The sea crossing complete, the crew from GalGael expect to rest, though the following day there are to be races of Viking boats on the lough. There are teams from Oxford and Cambridge, the Royal Ulster Constabulary, the British military, a crew who have travelled over from Fiji, serious racers. Some of these crew are less than polite about the 'wee scrag tags' from Glasgow and Govan's chances in the race, though if anything, this gives them determination to give it a go.

'They were serious rowers and they wanted to annihilate us,' is how Alan describes the well-trained crews they met. 'When you looked at them rowing, they were magnificent. It was like poetry on water. And then someone showed us footage of our boat and there were oars everywhere. It was like watching a spider on acid. Though in the end we won. We won because we were determined to win. Some of the other teams were a bit snooty and aloof. We didn't like that, so it motivated us to try harder. We didn't look like them rowing, but we were faster than them.'

After *Orcuan* crosses the finish line, Colin insists that it is Craig, the boy they hoped would be influenced by this trip, who should collect the trophy, which is in the shape of a Viking boat, complete with carved Viking warriors. There is a photograph of him in the charity's archives, which shows a bemused-looking young man holding aloft a trophy that looks too large for him.

When it is time to return to Scotland, the crew of *Orcuan* raises the mainsail and, with the wind behind them, the journey that had taken them three days on the way out, takes them just one on the return leg.

I asked Alan about Craig and where he was now.

'He was a clever guy and he realized there was a different world out there,' Alan returns. 'We still hear from his family, who tell us he's doing well. He has a family of his own now, and a job.'

I suggest it must feel good, but a self-deprecating Alan says that's the way at GalGael. 'If someone's waning, you step in to help them. We weren't great bright shining examples. There was lots of stupidness on the boat and people not behaving right because drink got involved. Young Craig saw we weren't righteous, we had flaws as well as being a collective. We made mistakes, and that's what we say at GalGael, that mistakes are there to be looked at.'

Sailing *Orcuan* is a rite of passage, he told me. Many of the people he works with have had negative experiences of rites of passage – the first can of Buckfast, the first crazy thing they did that got them respect from their peers, the first needle. Sailing as part of GalGael's waterborne community is another rite of passage. It's about heritage, identity, a sense of reconnection to their own stories, a sense of reclamation. In the charity's wood workshops or on the birlinn, they can be more than drug addict, unemployed or alkie. They are part of a community and, through working with their hands, through working with wood and sailing on the boats they have had a hand in crafting and caring for, look to their own possibilities, the shapes their futures might take.

The highland birlinn, Orcuan.

Luke Powell's Scillonian pilot cutter, Agnes.

6

Landscape Roamer

Dendles Wood, Dartmoor, and a community forest in the Scottish Highlands

'The first time I saw this wood, I was completely blown away,' Guy Shrubsole told me as we entered the shade of the lush green canopy of Dendles Wood. We walked up through old growth oak and beech where he pointed out epiphytes and bryophytes – the plants and mosses that grow on the surface of other plants – that are the markers of one of the rarest habitats in Britain and Ireland, Atlantic temperate rainforest. Guy has an infectious enthusiasm for the liverworts and mosses that coat the trunks here in thick blankets, for the ferns and lichens growing on the branches of old oaks and, as we walked, he stopped regularly to point out plants that are found in few other places on these islands.

One of the things that makes this place particularly special, he explained, is there is no nearby car park or road, so it takes a willingness to go out of your way to get here, meaning it is often quieter than many other public access woods.

Originally, we had planned to take this walk alone, though Guy had mentioned it to a few members of the South Devon Right to Roam group of which he is part, and he had warned me ahead of

Dendles Wood.

time that we might be joined by a few others. The few others ended up numbering about twenty-five, a diverse group of parents with young children, students, ecologists and campaigners, the recently retired and not so recently retired, who were now spread out along the path running up into Dendles Wood. One, a young girl of about four, dressed as Wonder Woman, was engaged in a game of running ahead of her parents, her cape flying out behind her.

There are certain activities that can almost be guaranteed when someone walks into a wood. If there are piles of leaves by the path someone will kick them up or be compelled to drive their hands into the leaves and throw them into the air. If there are fallen branches, children will inevitably want to pick them up to use as a wand or a sword. And, in close proximity to trees of a certain stature, almost everyone passing will want to lay their hands on the trunk. Some, if no one else is around, me included, will put their arms around that tree, out of some instinctive drive, perhaps for the sense of stability they provide, perhaps for the textures of the bark or the sensation of being so close to a life that is so familiar to us, yet so strange and different to our own. Whatever the reason, I suspect this instinct is deeply rooted in us. The old growth trees of Dendles Wood inspired this as much as any ancient woodland in which I've walked, and I watched as the walkers made contact with the trees. Others were kneeling to watch Comma butterflies in the undergrowth, bright orange and brown, while others still were staring up into the canopy, marvelling at the density of greens.

Atlantic, or temperate, rainforest is mostly confined to coastal areas along the west coasts of Britain and Ireland, the regions where the conditions are suitable, close to the wet Atlantic Sea air, and open to the storms that bring with them the downpours necessary to keep these forests permanently wet. Where temperate rainforest once stretched up and down these coastlines, we have pushed it back into small pockets through deforestation, by the pressure on the land to be productive, by the practices of the mid-twentieth century to replace old growth, deciduous woodland with spruce plantations.

At several points in its history, Dendles Wood has been brought to the brink of not being at all. In the late 1950s, this patch of ancient woodland was privately owned and, in line with what had been taking place across the country in what leading historian and ecologist Oliver Rackham called the 'locust years', the owners put in a proposal to raze it to make way for more productive conifer woodland. The plan was only abandoned after extensive protests and an anonymous donation with which the woodland was bought in order to preserve it as it was. Now, these fragments of rainforest woodlands are under renewed threat from climate change, especially from prolonged droughts and our behaviours which continue to threaten them.

While Dendles Wood is home to the Comma butterfly, one of the few species whose numbers are on the rise, most likely due to climate change, it also houses several rare creatures, including the barbastelle bat, named for its star-like beard, and the blue ground beetle, which is found in just thirteen sites across the country and only ever in mature oaks and beech woodlands like Dendles. Within Devon and Cornwall alone, this beetle had once been found in twelve sites. These beetles, Guy explained, are under threat from another source, pheasants released for the shoots that take place locally, which are believed to eat them.

We paused on the path and Guy took out from his bag maps and a copy of the woodland management plans, which he had obtained through a freedom of information request to Natural England. As the author of books on the temperate rainforests of Britain and land ownership, he has form in this area. These woodlands, he explained, should have some of the strictest protections available, and the woodland management plan he had obtained identified the importance of the blue ground beetles as well as the threat to them posed by high numbers of pheasants. Dendles Wood is a National Nature Reserve, an SSSI (a Site of Special Scientific Interest), under the protection of Natural England, as well as forming part of Dartmoor Special Area of Conservation.

Although SSSIs were designed to protect valuable habitats, a recent report by the group Wild Justice found that fewer than two-thirds had been assessed in the last decade, and that many of those were in a poor state.

'There's very little regulation around the release of these pheasants,' Guy explained, 'though in recent years some regulations have been put in place about their release so close to national nature reserves, sites of scientific special interest, and European designated sites, all of which applies to Dendles Wood.'

According to Natural England's rules, if a landowner releases large numbers of pheasants within some 1,600 feet of a site of special scientific interest, they must inform the relevant people. We looked at the maps and Guy pointed out the location of the large pheasant release pens on neighbouring, privately owned land.

'Some landowners are careful stewards, others are not, and often they don't get scrutinized,' Guy observed. 'It's usually the public who have the finger pointed at them for dropping the odd crisp packet or letting their dog foul a path, so we thought it would be worth having a poke around, and lo and behold, Natural England are quite concerned about the number of pheasants being released into the wood.'

The walkers – the activists and students, parents and retirees – had begun, noticeably, to relax beneath the protective canopy of Dendles Wood. Earlier, we had passed through another beautiful woodland,

though this one had felt entirely different, a result of being owned by someone who had erected fences to keep walkers out.

The walk had started cheerfully enough. We gathered in the village square, formed a polite circle and introduced ourselves. Many of those who turned up already knew one another, veterans of the Right to Roam campaign. Many had been involved in organizing the protests that had taken place earlier in the year against the ban on wild camping on Dartmoor.

'It's unlikely that we'll meet the landowner,' one of the organizers said, as he outlined the route for the walk.

As we set off, we continued to talk about the idea of trespass and the protests on Dartmoor, the organizers' surprise when their small call to action on a Facebook group began to gather steam, and the 3,000 or so people who had arrived in coaches and busses from across the country to make their voices heard.

The atmosphere only shifted as we crossed a line on a map in a beautiful woodland from land in which we were free to go where we wanted onto the estate where we had no right to be. Across this invisible line, the woodland was just as stunning, and we walked down into a steep wooded valley of beautifully inosculated beeches and old holly trees, the branches of which, twining round themselves had grown to form a single branch. I am able to offer little in the way of knowledge of woodland ecology, though I was pleased to be able to use one of my favourite words, 'inosculation', which is the process by which two branches or tree trunks fuse into one another.

At the bottom of the valley, a stream ran noisily across stones and we watched small fish and dragonflies in the dappled light. Beyond the stream, we skirted the large pheasant pens from which young birds would be released in a few weeks, in advance of the shoots later in the year. Although the woodland was, in many ways, idyllic, there was now a palpable sense of tension across the group. Some were discussing what would happen if we were to meet the landowner, their experiences of previous trespasses, how concerned or unconcerned they felt, though the only members of the group who seemed genuinely unconcerned were the children. Miniature Wonder Woman was blissfully unaware that we were trespassing on someone else's land, and she seemed entirely unaware too that we were now being observed through the trees by one of the estate's gamekeepers, who had been keeping track of us from a quad bike.

'Land ownership is a very powerful story,' one of the group said to me as he pulled aside a curtain of holly for the group to pass through. 'It's something we're socialized into. Our culture is shaped by the stories we inherit and Keep Out signs are part of our collective story. It's a powerful story too, about where we are welcome and where we belong, about our place within the landscape. And it's the story which is the biggest barrier, more than the fences and the threat of an interaction with a landowner.'

For him, like many of the other people on the organized trespass, the Covid pandemic had brought the lack of access into sharper focus. Confined to a small area for his daily walks, he had found much of the land around him blocked off, even those permissive paths that had been open before the lockdowns came into force. And even after the restrictions of Covid were lifted, he said, many of these paths remained blocked off by landowners who had decided they preferred to keep the land they owned to themselves.

'We have a deferential approach to landowners that has been ingrained in us for centuries,' he continued. 'It goes all the way back to the enclosures. When you think about it, it's ridiculous that someone should have access to all this land and that no one else should even be able to walk on it.'

It has always surprised me how little access we have to the land in which we live, in England in any case, the way in which we accept that we must keep to the paths, that we must not step on the grass. Perhaps it is, in part, a result of having grown up in view of both Kinder Scout and Winter Hill, the sites of two of the most famous trespasses. But more than that, it has always surprised me how little, in my lifetime, we have questioned our obedience to fences and cordons, to the signs marking private property that keep the overwhelming majority of the country away from vast swathes of its woodlands and rivers, and that we accept the monopolies of major landowners. In England, at least, we are brought up with the idea of land ownership as something sacred, though when the few rights that remain are challenged, the protests are often loud and vocal. Many of these rights, such as that of estovers (a tenant's allowance of firewood or timber afforded from an estate or from the commons) and pannage (the privilege granted to local pig farmers to graze livestock pigs in a forest on Common Land to feed on fallen acorns) have fallen out of use in much of England, though the tradition of camping freely on the Dartmoor commons is one that many campers hold as particularly important. Dartmoor represents, for many, a symbolic freedom that is lacking across most of the country.

When the Right to Roam group put out the call earlier in the year for people to march on Dartmoor in protest against a High Court ruling that prevented wild camping on the commons there, what had started as a small protest resulted in some 3,000 protesters descending on the tiny village of Cornwood, catalysed by the threat to the long-established right to camp freely in this small, beautiful pocket of England. They arrived by bus and coach from across the country in one of the largest land rights protests in the UK since the Winter Hill protests at the end of the nineteenth century. They carried with them an effigy of Old Crockern, the guardian spirit of the moor who, legend has it, 'grey as granite . . . his eyebrows hanging down over his glimmering eyes like sedge, and his eyes as deep as peat water pools', rides out at night on a skeleton horse and keeps his terrifying wisht hounds in Wistman's Wood, the most well-known of Dartmoor's iconic woodlands. Old Crockern was a carefully chosen symbol for the Right to Roam group. The nineteenth-century Devonian priest and scholar

Sabine Baring-Gould, wrote of a rich Mancunian who bought the land around Crockern Tor in Dartmoor and enclosed it to farm. Depending on the telling, the terrifying figure of Old Crockern appeared either to one of the landowner's men or to one of the infuriated locals, and declared of the landowner, 'if he scratches my back, I'll tear out his pocket'. The rich man turned farmer found the land he had enclosed entirely unworkable and, though he sank all his money into trying to prove his venture, he ended up returning to Manchester, penniless and broken.

Just as Baring-Gould's story said much about the hubris of wealth, the story of the wild camping protest says much about where England is as a country. The landowners' lawyers argued there was no specific right to camp freely on Dartmoor and, further, that campers were damaging the environment. By removing the right to camp, they said, they were working to 'improve conservation of the Dartmoor Commons'. While the High Court ruling was overturned, reinstating the right to wild camp on the Dartmoor Commons, just a month after our far smaller trespass, the bigger picture remains that only about 8 per cent of England is covered by open access rules, available for the public to walk on freely without having to ask permission of a landowner. Dartmoor, where 37 per cent of the land is covered by these open access rules, is very much an outlier.

On the other side of the private woodland, in the shade of the oaks that marked the boundary of the estate through which we had passed, the group stopped to drink from their flasks. They sat and chatted among themselves and watched the house martins and swifts that were performing acrobatics across the valley on the other side of which was the woodland through which we had just passed. One passed round a Tupperware of flapjacks and, from across the field, a figure in a floral shirt and brown flannel trousers marched towards the impromptu picnickers.

'I would appreciate it if you would get off my land,' he said. 'Right now.'

The group's allotted spokesman stood and approached the irate man, explaining that we would be on our way once we had finished our tea, that we were a peaceful group out for a walk, enjoying a midsummer day. There was a brief discussion among the group, though the majority opted to finish their drinks before moving on.

'You don't have any right to be here,' the landowner was saying to the spokesman, who was attempting, politely, to engage him in discussion about land access. 'And I want you to leave now.'

'I'm feeling very tense right at this moment,' the woman who was sitting next to me said. 'Though this is a very gentle statement to be making at the same time. It's one of those little profound moments – it's not going to change the world but it's psychologically significant.'

She was not the sort of person who ever broke the law, she told me. She had never been that sort of person though it felt important to stand her ground for a while here, in the midst of these feelings of discomfort and conflict.

The landowner was now alternating between filming the group and making calls, perhaps to his lawyers or the police, or to members of his estate staff, anyone who might be willing to forcibly evict the picnickers.

'It's deeply engrained in us that these are the borders,' she continued, waving a hand at the line of trees behind us. 'We stay off this land because it "belongs" to someone else. It's a weird feeling to fall in love with a place and to know you can only be there at someone else's behest. Follow the trail of what these boundaries do to us psychologically and to our internal landscapes, and how it reflects on our autonomy at all levels of life and it's hard to imagine what kind of person would I be if I lived in a world where no one owned any land. What kind of relationship would I have with this place?'

Now off the phone, the landowner was standing at a distance, taking photographs of the picnickers, tea and sandwiches finished. The group was now in the process of packing and scouring the area for anything they might have dropped, before leaving by the gate.

'It's responsible trespass,' Guy explained to me, a small act of protest, yet largely symbolic, an important action for those who wanted to explore their relationship with the land and perhaps to challenge our lack of access.

Back in Dendles Wood, we were preparing to leave, though it was a slow sort of parting. Most of the walkers were still wandering in the lush green, and it seemed to me they were drinking it in, this protected, vivid place, storing it up in memory for when it would be needed again in the grey of winter. I listened in to the conversations going on among the walkers spread out along the path. Tiny Wonder Woman was tired now and was falling asleep on her father's back. Others were talking about the earlier trespass, the sights and sounds of it, and it seemed to me they were writing themselves new stories about the ways in which they related to the land. Later, we gathered in Cornwood, where the wild camping protests had begun, and the group presented the landlady of the local pub with a large, framed photograph of the protesters carrying the effigy of Old Crockern to thank her for catering for and accommodating the thousands of marchers who arrived for the protest. I expect that next time I visit, the photograph will be on display in the bar, part of the story of the village, a reminder of a small victory and another movement towards removing the barriers between the people and the land.

When I left the house in which I was staying at Moniack Mhor, just after six in the morning, I could see clear across to the Cairngorms. Huge clouds scudded across the mountains, whose colours shifted constantly beneath them. I was alone in the house and the landscape over which I looked showed no sign of people at all. The top road, when I reached it, was quiet too, occupied only by hares and their leverets, which brought my focus away from the expanse of the far-distant Monadhliath Hills to what was going on right in front of me. The hares, alert to my presence, disappeared through the juniper scrub into the conifer plantation that ran alongside the road, where they have their forms, though their young continued to dance on the asphalt. As I came closer, to walk by, they too scattered, only to regroup on the road behind me.

In Scottish Gaelic, the old term for hares was *geàrr-fhiadh*, a literal translation of which might be 'short deer', though the name is most often shortened to *geàrr*. The Gaelic word *fiadh*, though, refers to both the animal, deer and to the wild more generally, so perhaps the hares might be better translated as 'short, wild ones'. In the folklore of the highlands, and across much of Celtic Britain and Ireland, both hares and deer were said to shapeshift into human form and at this time in the morning, with no one else around, in a landscape that is often, and rightly, described in hyperbolic terms, I could believe they might, that out of our sight they would be capable of becoming all manner of things.

Quarter of a mile down the valley, I saw deer proper through the gaps in a fence that separated the road from the pines, though it was only after I had been looking through the trees for some time that I became aware I was being watched. Even then, it took a while to discern the deer from the mottled grey trunks. When they emerged into my vision it was like seeing the pattern in a magic eye puzzle rise out of the page. I saw their eyes first, wide and alert, their heads and then their bodies which, until then, had been indistinguishable from the forest around them. Once I had made out a single deer, I found I could now see at least five more in my peripheral vision, all standing stock still. I had assumed, until the day before, that the high fences were there to keep the deer out of the woodland, but a walker I had passed explained to me they were there to keep the deer in. This woodland was part of a deer farm, which seemed somehow perverse in a country where deer numbers have rocketed and, in many woodlands, they are culled regularly to avoid them causing catastrophic damage.

The forests of Scotland's highlands are to be listened to as much as looked at. Down by the loch, a pair of whooper swans seemed to have missed the memo that the time to move on had passed, though it had been a strange year for weather. Two cuckoos called to one another across the teardrop shaped water of Loch Laide in uncanny, un-echoing voices, louder by far than the willow warblers and skylarks, the snipe and siskins, goldcrests and treecreepers, pipits and stonechats, redpolls and crows I had noted on my slow walk down the valley, an abundance of birds that made my heart soar. Just inside a block of conifers, a curlew churred invisibly. I had seen her out of the corner of my eye earlier, flying just below the cloud line, her curved beak dipping just beneath the grey. Looking for her again, I saw instead a silent hen harrier, which emerged briefly from the tree line below the small peak Carn na Leitire before ducking back in.

I felt watched by two red kites that were there each time I looked up, circling high above in huge overlapping ellipses, throughout the six-mile walk to Reelig Glen. I lost them when I left the road and found myself among the giant conifers of the place known locally as the Faery Glen on account of its seclusion and the sense of otherworldliness one gets walking among the moss-covered boulders and the ruined remains of nineteenth-century buildings and bridges in the valley. I climbed down the gorge through redwoods whose trunks shot straight up to dizzying heights, and where I felt over and again the sense of awe I often get when walking among living things that dwarf me. Walking at the feet of huge trees is an experience not unlike encountering whales close-up, unexpected and breathtaking.

Reelig Glen is home to a Douglas Fir known as Dùghall Mòr, the big dark stranger, once thought to be the tallest tree in the UK, until it was overtopped by a tree in Perthshire. To walk beneath these trees is to be put in our place and to be reminded of our own smallness in the order of life on Earth, though if I walked by Dùghall Mòr I was unaware of it. For a while, I walked alongside a burn which was heavy and brown with the recent rainfall to where it fell off in a waterfall to the floor of the gorge far below, before I turned back up the hill to where the conifers gave way to beech, birch and sweet chestnut. An area of the woods here is known as The Cathedral, and by the time I reached it, I was prepared to believe all manner of holy things, not least the stories of the *sìth*, the sometimes benevolent, sometimes malicious fairies of Gaelic folklore, who could shape shift into animals and cause humans to be changed into animal form too.

Of all the stories told about the woods of Scotland, those of the *sìthichean* are among the most engaging, though few survive in full. Perhaps the best known is 'Tam Lin', a ballad from the Scottish borders and Northern Ireland, a version of which was written down in 1549, and which has roots in a much earlier oral folktale. As with most folktales, there are different tellings and the details vary, though in most, the story tells of the *sithichean* Tam Lin, who was said to live in the forest at Carterhaugh. The women there were warned not to go into the woods, for Tam Lin took payment of all who passed through, in the form of a belonging or their virginity. Janet, daughter of the Laird of Carterhaugh, ignored the warnings, claiming the woods as her own. When she picked a rose deep in the woods, Tam Lin appeared to her and she found she was pregnant by him later. Returning to the woods, she found him again and discovered that he had once been human but had been kidnapped by the Queen of the Fairies as a child and brought up as *sith*. More than this, he was to be given in sacrifice to the realms of hell that night, hallowe'en, as a tithe paid by the Fairy Queen of the woods. The only way he could be saved, and become the father of her child, he told her, was if Janet could wrestle him to the floor as he passed by that evening in the fairies' procession. If she could hold onto him through the transformations the fairies put him through – as an adder and an eel, and perhaps as a deer and hare, and eventually as a hot coal, which she was to throw into the well to quench him – he could return to his human form and she could take him out of the woods and away from the power of the fairies. Janet, whose uncommon bravery seems to warrant her name as being worthy of taking the tale's title character, risks the ire of the Queen of the Fairies and succeeds in keeping Tam Lin from the sacrifice.

Leaving Reelig Glen, I found I had not had enough of the shade of trees. I wanted to stick to the woods and chose a route that avoided the road almost entirely. The legislation that allowed me to do this, the Scottish Land Reform Act of 2003, made the hills and valleys, the lochs and rivers, open to anyone who wanted to access them. It stands in stark contrast to England's trespass laws, though even before the adoption of the act, custom and tradition allowed for access to most land this side of the border. Having grown up in England though, I spent much of the walk back across land that was clearly owned by other people, with one eye out for irate landowners. Old habits die hard, and it took some doing to keep in mind that it was unlikely I would have a farmer set their dogs loose or brandish a shotgun in my direction, as has happened to me on occasion when I have strayed across a fence line closer to home.

Early the next morning, I returned to Loch Laide and turned off the road into the woodland signposted as Abriachan Forest Trust, across the burn though which brown trout swim, fish that are picked off occasionally by the otters which call this burn home too. I was early, so I waited and watched for otters by the river and for pine

Reelig Glen.

martens in the woods, though the closest I came to seeing either was a brief flash of dark brown beneath two of the woodland's buildings, there and gone. It could have been a pine marten or maybe just a product of my hope that I might see one. The flash of brown, seen out of the corner of my eye, brought me back to thinking about the shapeshifters in the woods, the uncertain things that occur at the edge of our vision, a movement on the periphery that might be a person or might be a hare, a deer or one of the *sìth*. Our minds are adept at filling in the blanks and woodlands are full of things half seen or barely glimpsed, part-sightings that invite speculation: hares that might be witches, deer that might be fairy queens, snakes that might be kidnapped children, forced to join the ranks of the *sìth*.

A sudden screaming and whooping crashed across the valley floor, startling me. I must have been thinking too much about the *sìthichean* because it took me a while to work out they were the shouts of children rather than anything supernatural. When I met with Suzann Barr, who manages the woodlands here, half an hour later, she told me the screams and shouts from the woods were definitely not from the fairies but from the scouts camping there, letting loose in the forest in some of the 1,300 acres of woodland to the west of Loch Ness, which had been owned by Forest Enterprise until the scattered community at Abriachan bought it twenty-five years ago.

They were unlikely trailblazers, Suzann told me as we bounced across the rough tracks that crisscross the woodland in her battered Landrover. When the land came up for sale in the local paper in the early 1990s, all the community wanted was to ensure there were access rights in place for the people who lived there. It was before the Scottish land access rights had come into effect and they were concerned about being kept out of the woods. They had never planned to become foresters or woodland managers, though the land coming up for sale brought about a conversation among the people who lived at Abriachan, about what the woodlands here could become. They realized they wanted to improve access to the land, to improve the biodiversity of the mostly monocultural woodlands around them, to create jobs for local people and provide opportunities for their children to learn from the woods. In short, they wanted some control over the land where they lived, so put in a bid.

'We all had kids and we wanted this to be their back yard to play in. We weren't foresters, though. No way did we want to be landowners,' Suzann stated.

Few of the people involved had experience of managing woodlands. One was a retired forester, though most came from other industries. There were car salesmen, oil workers, crofters, accountants, architects and teachers, and one of their number was the popular memoirist and fiction writer Katharine Stewart, who was instrumental in galvanizing the community to take charge of the land on their doorsteps.

Suzann's story reminded me of something I had read in Margaret Wheatley's book, *Turning to One Another*, about there being no power for change greater than a community discovering what it cares about as, twenty-five years on, the woodlands at Abriachan are almost unrecognizable from the ones the community bought, though there are still stands of lodgepole pine, which are harvested and the timber sold. The money made is then ploughed back into improving the paths and tracks, and the biodiversity of the woods, shifting it from a bleak mono-crop to a mix of Scots pine, downy birch, rowan, oak, aspen, alder and larch.

Where there was a relatively lifeless conifer crop, there are now ponds and hides for watching birds on the loch, dragonflies among the bogweed and newts beneath the duckboards. As well as the managed woodlands, the forest is now home to a school, attended by, among others, the grandchildren of the group who bought the woodland. There are classrooms and wood workshops, bike and walking trails, sensory walks and playgrounds, all aimed at bringing the community into the woods. It was a case of engaging people with the land or, rather, re-engaging them, Suzann told me.

The history of the relationship between the people of Scotland and their woodlands is a fraught one. It is a story of a diminishment of Scotland's woodlands that has its roots in pre-history, and continued though centuries of disenfranchisement which many argue continues today.

Scotland's moment of peak forest occurred about 6,000 years ago, at a time when lynx and wolves still prowled the dense woodlands of the Highlands. It was the time of bears and the giant cattle, aurochs, of damming beavers and wild boar. When humans started farming the land, shortly after this peak, large areas of the land were burnt and cleared. In his book, *People and Woods in Scotland*, T.C. Smout refers to it as a long retreat, precipitated by human interference, along with climate changes that encouraged the growth of peat bogs and the retreat of woodland even further, some 3,000 years ago.

The Romans wrote of a great Caledonian forest, though many historians believe this was a myth, perhaps brought on by the fact that this was the only area of the island in which Scots pine grew. Like the mythical Greenwood of England, the story of the great Caledonian forest has persisted, fuelled much more recently by what the author John Fowler described as overheated nineteenth-century romanticism. This romanticism was, perhaps, driven by the fact that at the turn of the nineteenth century, just 5 per cent of Scotland was wooded, having been over-exploited for charcoal, timber and tanbark from the Middle Ages onwards.

While demand for timber for housing and ships increased the pressure on the woodlands of Scotland, the biggest blows in human terms came in the eighteenth century during the Highland Clearances, when large numbers of Highlanders were forcibly evicted from their land or found they were now tenants of often absent English landlords who demanded huge rents and taxes. Large areas of woodland were deforested to make way for sheep farming, ushering in an era of over-grazing and depopulation. The violence wrought during the Clearances was also brought onto trees that held significance for the people of the Highlands as part of a campaign against the Gaels. In

1746, following the battle at Culloden, British forces burnt down a huge ash tree by the church at Kilmallie, said to have been 58 feet around and which was revered by the Jacobite chief Cameron of Lochiel, and which some commentators believe was an object of worship well before the arrival of the church there.

Alexander Mather argues that the legacy of this long retreat, along with the fallout of the Clearances of a landlord–tenant relationship in which the people living in the Highlands were disenfranchised from the land, represented a disconnect between people and trees in Scotland. Even into the late twentieth and early twenty-first centuries, many of the decisions being made about Scotland's forests and the increasingly ambitious plans for afforestation were taking place from afar, with little input from local communities, though there have been moves in recent years to buck the trend, with charities like Trees for Life, who plan to restore the Caledonian forest, bringing back Scots pine to areas in which it had been lost, returning red squirrels and beavers to the landscape, and providing habitats for the rare capercaillie, a bird that was believed extinct in the eighteenth century.

In Suzann's jeep, as we bounced along the Newfoundlanders' Road, known locally as the corrugated road, she picked up the story. The two world wars of the twentieth century made huge demands on Scotland's woodlands, claiming entire forests at a time. The road over which we were driving was laid by the Newfoundland loggers, brought across to the Highlands during the Second World War in the absence of local men, who had been drafted to fight. The Newfoundlanders laid logs down to create the road, over which to pull out the timber they harvested and over time the road had sunk onto those trunks. In the aftermath of the wars, as happened in England, there was a revival of woodlands, one dominated by monocultures of conifers and tax breaks offered to those investing in plantations.

'In the sixties and seventies,' Suzann explained, 'you would have people with lots of money buying up huge areas of low country as a tax break. They were gated off and made private. "Keep off" signs went up and it wasn't even as though they were being put aside for hunting and fishing. They were just fenced off and North American lodgepole pine was planted.'

When Abriachan Forest came up for sale, it was an example of one of these forests that had not been managed in the intervening time, an unloved, uncared for plantation that had been left to its own devices.

Land in the Highlands is hot property again. Just as land in New Zealand is being bought at record rates by millionaires and billionaires hoping to ride out the climate crisis in a stable haven as and when the worst happens, land in the north of Scotland is being bought by investors wanting to offset their carbon emissions. It is the latest in a centuries-long argument about the way in which land is used here, whether for sheep grazing, deer hunting, or sitka plantations used as tax dodges.

Abriachan, despite having turned a quarter of a century, is still an outlier. Communities own just 3 per cent of land in Scotland and the price of land on which planting is possible is rising fast in what some papers have called a 'carbonanza', land that is being fragmented by so-called green lairds. It is a process that land reformer Alastair McIntosh describes as having 'weel-kent roots. Roots of historical oppression. Roots of sustained inequality.' This land hoarding by the green lairds, buying areas of forest or planting up new forests, may be, at its worst, just the latest in a long line of alienation of people from the land, and the commodification of nature.

Before I left the woods, Suzann drove me up to an area where they had cleared the lodgepole pine and replanted early on, mostly with broadleaf trees, one of her favourite spots in the forest.

'It has changed so much over the years up here. When I first came, this was all lodgepole, though we thinned it out and with the extra light coming in, you have ferns, you have wood sorrel coming up.' The community, she explained, had bought the land really for the right to determine and control the future of the land on their doorstep, and there was power in that, a sense of belonging to it.

In the afternoon, the temperature dropped suddenly as the *haar* from the Moray Firth rolled up the valley. Many of the birds stopped calling and I saw a lone curlew flying silently ahead of the mist, skimming above the high fenced fields where farmed deer were grazing and into the dense block of woodland by which I had seen the leverets that morning. In the fields at the edges of the spruce plantations were the remains of prehistoric houses some 3,000 years old. The people who lived in these houses were here when the Caledonian forest was still more truth than myth. All that remains of these people now are the circular outlines of their huts, which suggest the homes were thatched with a central fireplace, the smoke filtering up through the reeds, heather and turf, keeping them dry and preventing them from rotting.

As I passed the hut circles in the thick mist, I wondered if the people who lived in this place had concepts of land ownership, what boundaries they recognized, if any, and how they would have reacted to someone who claimed to own the land, fencing it off and putting up 'keep out' signs.

7

Wish Wearer

The clootie well at Munlochy on the Black Isle, Scottish Highlands, a family tree on Bodmin Moor, Cornwall, and the tree at Sycamore Gap, Northumbria

You had to look for them, but they were there if you were prepared to spend the time. Coins on the bed of the stream. Dull bronze among the stones. Silver that caught what sunlight made it to the floor of the woods. And carvings on tree trunks.

> *A for J*
> *The Boys*
> *X. Emil*
> *Frankie*
> *Christine waz ear*
> *Oaky and Buck*
> *Loved*

Names, symbols and short messages that the trees had begun to reclaim as bark closed in over them.

Look up and there was a whole wardrobe hanging in the branches. A pair of Nike trainers nailed high up the trunk of an

Clooties at Munlochy.

old beech tree. The underwire of a bra, the material of which was long gone, leaving just a few strands of silk hanging loose over the frame. A baseball cap advertising a construction firm. Tatty boxer shorts and a pair of socks that looked as though they were fresh from the packet, some 20 feet above the ground. A leopard print coat. Woven bracelets. A hoodie and a pair of tracksuit trousers. A child's cup tied on with string, with a faded picture of Winnie-the-Pooh and Piglet with their paws in a honey pot on its side.

And ribbons. Ribbons everywhere. Some new and unfrayed, some so old they had started to rot into the branches on which they were tied, barely distinguishable from the bark. Ribbons on saplings at knee level, on branches the width of a wrist and ribbons the width of a pinky finger. Ribbons tied in neat bows and tight knots against the wind, in pinks and reds, blues and oranges. Plastic strips and foil like chaff, catching the 'shivelight'.

At first, I had only seen the socks, which were visible as I peeled off the road, the only sign that this was anything other than another path into the woods. The stream running out of the hillside and the scars on the trees from years of people carving their names into the trunks were clues too, though there was little else to suggest this was the site of one of the most famous of Britain's clootie wells.

Until a few months ago, this whole glade, a few feet from the B9161, just outside the village of Munlochy on Scotland's Black Isle, was crammed with these mementos. When I arrived, though, they were thin on the ground or, rather, thin in the trees, a mixture of beeches and pines. It was only when I ventured into the woods around the well that I noticed the offerings spread out over a thousand or so square feet.

It was a few weeks past Beltane, the Gaelic May Day festival that marks the summer's beginning, and I had expected, I think, to see the well 'tapestried with rags', as Thomas Pennant on his 1769 tour of Scotland described when he came across the wells in

the Highlands, though the clooties were not, as one report in *The Times* from 1957 had it – 'far too many for one tree alone . . . tied indiscriminately to the branches of fir, and spruce, and beech'. In January 2022, the well was cleared overnight and, though no one took responsibility, it would have taken some doing to strip the festooned branches, the trunks dressed in tracksuit tops. Given the number of offerings left at the well, damp with the smell of rotting and mouldering fabrics, the clooties – clouties in England, clotties in Ireland – that give the well its name, it must have taken some doing, some determination. From photos taken just prior to the scouring of the well, near on a ton of material was removed.

Sitting by the well, I found it a difficult one to square. On one hand, many of the items I could see were clearly meaningful to the people who left them. A tatty pair of boxers, the remains of a peaked cap, a tea towel – all of these things memorials to loved ones both living and dead. Many of them would have been placed with a memory or a wish, though their proliferation made it hard not to see them as litter, too. I feel the same about the carvings on the tree trunks. I can understand the drive, to declare love in writing and to display it for all to see, the trees here are scarred with hearts, but there's a thin line between sacred place and dumping ground, between timeless love and graffiti. It brought to mind the scenes of the Everest base camp, all those mountaineers, hell bent on making an ascent of the sacred mountain, leaving ton upon ton of tent fabric and oxygen tanks, clothing and excrement in their wake. Sitting by the well as my eyes adjusted to the light, I was able to pick out more and more clooties in the branches, each one presumably attached to a wish or a prayer.

Tradition has it that a clootie is a small piece of cloth belonging to someone who is afflicted, in the hope that the protective spirit of place – what the Romans called *genius loci* – would cure the person of their illness. At the well, the clootie would be soaked in the stream and rubbed on the afflicted area, before being tied to a branch close by. The belief was that as the cloth rotted away, so the illness would leave too. Most of the items left, though, were synthetics, a point in favour of those clearing the well. By the time most of these socks and caps break down, the person involved would most likely be long dead.

I was lost in these thoughts, trying to work out on which side of the argument I came down, when two lanky whippets appeared, loping along the path, followed by a woman with a walking pole. She asked me if this was the well. I said yes, although I was no expert. The woman looked around for a moment and declared herself underwhelmed. She had been meaning to visit for years, she told me, but now she was here, she was not sure why she had bothered making the journey. The woman whistled to her dogs, which had disappeared into the undergrowth and strode on. The small stream tumbled out of the well, undisturbed by her passing, down a gulley and into a pipe that took it under the road.

I sat for half an hour and listened to the well and the stream, to the wind in the newly opened leaves, the chaffinches and siskins in the canopy, the blackbird and the showboating wren, which seemed to be in competition with one another. Aside from the woman with the whippets, no one else turned up to leave a clootie or declare themselves unimpressed. I was alone.

Walking up the hillside away from the well and seeking out the hidden clooties, I became aware of the layers of memory here, represented by cloth streamers and clothes. Some new, still shining, others rotting into the branches, high out of reach of those who cleared the well. The well here is a place of memory upon memory. It was dedicated to a seventh-century bishop, St Curitan or St Boniface depending on who you talk to, and almost all accounts agree it was originally previously dedicated to a much older goddess. It is ironic that St Boniface should be associated with the well at all: Boniface was the leader of the Carolingian mission strategies of 743 CE, which regulated against pagan customs, in particular those related to trees and wells. A few years later, in 769 CE, the cult of

wells and trees was explicitly forbidden in the text *Capitulatio de partibus Saxoniae,* a legal code issued by Charlemagne; however, these traditions are slow to die out, if they ever do.

In the following century, Rudolph of Fulda noted that the Saxons continued, despite censure, to worship wells and green groves, as well as a sacred tree trunk they called *Irminsul,* Latin for 'world-pillar'. Animism, it seems, is hard to expunge, so it comes as little surprise that it may instead be absorbed, or vestiges of those beliefs embraced, perhaps in the knowledge that banning a thing doesn't mean it no longer exists.

There is another celebrated clootie well on the other side of the Firth at Culloden Moor, where the annual pilgrimages at Beltane – which went on well into the twentieth century – saw thousands trekking up to the well and hanging cloths on the trees, leaving money that would later be collected and divided between local charities.

Although they can be found across the islands, the greatest density of clootie wells are found around the Celtic fringe – across Scotland, in Wales and in Cornwall, where I live, and further afield in Brittany. The one just half a mile from my house is much smaller than the well I explored on the Black Isle, and for as long as anyone can remember, people have hung trinkets, baubles, dummies and small items of children's clothes protected in plastic wrapping from the branches of the tree that overhangs the well. This well, too, was cleared earlier this year, and there was an equal amount of ire mouthed on local Facebook groups, some from people who had hung things there, who considered the clearance to be desecration, others who felt the decorated well itself was a desecration.

It is by no means just a Celtic observation, though, and similar forms of tree worship stretch across the globe. Many native American traditions include prayer ties of cloth and tobacco that are left in sacred places, often in the branches of trees. In parts of South America, *milagros*, charms in the shape of body parts afflicted by illness, are attached to or embedded in trees, and tree shrines are common across India and Nepal, with statues of deities placed at the base of the trunk, flowers and incense. The medieval German chronicler Adam of Bremen, writing in the eleventh century, describes the sacred grove at the Temple of Uppsala in Sweden, in which each of the trees was considered, by worshippers there, to be divine. He recalls the corpses of men, horses and dogs that hung from the trees as sacrifices, and at the centre of the grove, a huge evergreen tree at the foot of which was a well to which sacrifices were also offered.

In Japan, *goshinboku* are sacred trees, shrines for Shintō spirits or *kami*, and across Japan there are examples of forbidden forests, deep in the mountains where people did not enter and where ancestor spirits and deities were said to live. In Shintō, prayers tied to a tree branch are transported to the spiritual realm, and *shimenawa*, ropes festooned with paper streamers, are strung around the trunks of sacred trees. One of these shrines, the sacred tree of Takeo no Okusu, which stands just outside the Mifuneyama Rakuen garden, is a camphor tree over 3,000 years old. It is almost 100 feet tall and has a root circumference of about 65 feet; the shrine itself sits within the trunk's huge hollow.

A few years ago, in a narrow strip of woodland close to home, tiny doors started appearing in the boles of trees along a path that runs alongside a stream. These were followed by more intricate and brightly coloured elf houses that were affixed to trunks or to posts in the ground, with roofs of tiny shingles or pebbles, and decorated on the outside walls with paintings of trout, seaside scenes, owls, and foliage. The doors of these small houses open, and inside they are decorated with tiny furniture; some even have lighting. In recent months, people have started to leave small items in them, messages, jokes, facts. They are the work of John Rowe, who began to install the houses after the first UK Covid lockdown, in 2020, after he realized how fascinated his grandchildren were in the small houses he had made for them in his shed. There are more than seventy fairy doors in the woods now, along with bat, bird and owl boxes. My children are beyond the age of believing in fairies, though they open the doors as we pass to see what each house holds. My children and I have seen John walking in the woods, undertaking small works of maintenance on the houses and he has pointed out things he has hidden in the trees. He tells me he likes to hear children as they discover the doors and make a connection with something outside their homes, to see them looking up into the canopy rather than down at screens.

The names on many of the doors, he told us the first time our paths crossed, commemorate friends and family members – a young man who killed himself, an artist, some of whose slate paintings hang high up on the trunks, a local soldier who was killed on what was supposed to be the last job of his final tour in Afghanistan, while defusing a roadside bomb. Each of the houses has the numbers 12 5 5 painted on them somewhere, on a wall or the inside of a door. The numbers correspond to the letters L E E, a memory of John's son who died of cancer six years ago and make each one of them a small shrine. I had been unsure about the fairy houses before hearing John talk about them. After all, what was wrong with the trees as they were? Now, listening to the woods after our paths had diverged, I could hear children opening the doors of the tiny houses, the sounds of their delight and wonder, and I understand.

On the noticeboard in the small car park for the clootie well there was a Gaelic proverb – *Dèan math an aghaidh an uilc* – do good against the ill. It can be difficult to see what good and ill are from close up. Leave synthetic fibres on the trees for long enough, pile them on year upon year and you may end up with a landfill site. Take them away and you are removing something meaningful, sacred even, to many.

The clootie well sits at the top of a valley and, as the bus back to Inverness was not due for another two hours, I walked the long way back to the village through the Douglas firs and western hemlocks. The grass was high among the bluebells that had already faded by the time I left Cornwall at the other end of the island. Fiddlehead ferns were in the process of uncoiling themselves and the greens of the woodland seemed to shift as I walked, a rich, complex tapestry. I lost my concentration and the path at about the same time, though it being a valley, I headed in a vague direction of the burn on the valley floor where it was hot and still, walked among the butterflies and bees and pushed through thick spring undergrowth until I emerged in the village again.

A fairy door at Coosebean.

I suspect that each of us has – or at one point had, before we started to take life too seriously – a favourite tree, one to which we would nod as we passed it or to whom we would give silent thanks as we crossed the threshold of its canopy from full sun to shade. A tree we saw on the way to school each morning or one we made an otherwise unnecessary detour to visit. A tree that felt protective, into whose branches we climbed or among which we hid, whose apples we scrumped or cherries we filched in that narrowest of openings between ripening and being picked off by the birds. I suspect, too, that as adults many of us make pilgrimages to these trees for which we have such fondness. They are touchstones, living symbols that are at once familiar and unknowable, mysteries with whom we share our lives.

In the garden of the house in which I lived for the first few years of my life there were two trees – an apple and a cherry that stood side by side, perhaps 2.5 metres apart. According to family legend, a story that still gets wheeled out at Christmases, as a child I used to talk to these trees when I returned home from school and, on occasion, would hug them like family members. I have vague memories of doing this, though whether they are true memories or those that are formed by the retelling of the story I'm not sure. I vaguely remember one-sided conversations with the cherry tree, though I have far more visceral memories of the sap that used to cling to my hands and my school jumper when I hugged it. I remember the blossom too, the annual transformation of the garden by the pink–white flowers. I have changed a little since then, yet, faced with a beautiful tree, I will still rest my head against its trunk for the comfort it gives.

I'm not alone.

In 2015, the city of Melbourne, in Australia, gave each of its 70,000 trees an identification number and an email address, so people could report problems connected to individual trees. However, as Arron Wood, one of the city's councillor's told the *Guardian* newspaper, one of the unintended but positive consequences of the scheme was that, as well as reporting problems, people began to write letters to the trees themselves, sharing memories and thoughts, posing questions, or simply showing appreciation. And in other parts of the world, Kerala on India's tropical Malabar coast for example, there is a long tradition of women in particular being caretakers of trees in *kavus*, the sacred groves that form part of many villages in the state, as responsible for the trees as the trees are for them.

I had my cherry and apple trees, and yet, in the manner of childhood loves, when I left home, I fell in love with new trees in other parts of the world and would declare those to be my favourites. I still maintained, and maintain, affection for those early trees, though. As I talk to people about trees, I have found so many have one or two that hold a particular place in heart and mind, trees the roots of which disappear deep in memory. As we grow, so do the trees of our childhoods. They become more idyllic, more perfect. The hours we spent high in their branches, on a platform or treehouse, stretch out in our imaginations. We forget the pain of a broken arm or ankle, caused by jumping from a far-too-high branch to the ground, recalling instead the joy of climbing into its embrace.

And among the trees of the woodlands of our childhoods, we interpolate our memories of actual trees with those from the books we read, *The Magic Faraway Tree*, the trees of A.A. Milne's Hundred Acre Wood. My overriding memory of trees in books is from the forest Susan Cooper conjured up in *The Dark Is Rising*, in which Will Stanton wakes on Midwinter's Day to find time stopped and his Buckinghamshire house surrounded by an endless, snow-covered forest from a time before towns and cities existed. It is an image so powerful that in the thirty-five or so years since I was first read that book by my father, I have dreamt the scene over and again. It is, for me, a true forest of the imagination.

There are other trees that have made the jump into our collective memories. In the hallway of the house with the apple and cherry trees in the garden, there were two black-and-white framed prints. In the first, a young couple are standing at the foot of a great oak. The young man, dressed in an officer's uniform, is carving their initials onto the trunk of the tree. In the second, the same woman stands alone under the same tree, her hand held up to the carving. I could never work out whether it was a hopeful scene in which she awaited news of her lover, or one of devastation, the woman having received the dreaded telegram. I always felt uncomfortable about the carving in the bark. The point at which this image was made, just following the Second World War, was one in which Britain's landscape was about to change rapidly, the onset of Rackham's 'locust years' in which the forestry sector trashed wholesale many of Britain's native woodlands.

Hundreds of copycat versions of this scene were produced, and thousands upon thousands of similar images framed and hung on walls. It is testament to the ways we often idealize woodlands, overlaying onto them ideas of nativism or prelapsarian longing. We have created all sorts of myths about these places, of the wildwood, of the unblemished and ever-summer Greenwood.

Another tree that has made the leap from memory into popular consciousness is the Hardy Tree, which made the national news when it was a casualty of a storm in 2022. The ash tree, in Old St Pancras Churchyard in London, became famous for the hundreds of gravestones that were stacked on edge around its base, the story being that this arrangement was the work of a young Thomas Hardy. Pre-writing fame and apprenticed to a Covent Garden architect at the time, Hardy had been given the job of exhuming the remains of people buried in the graveyard as part of an expansion of London's rail system in the mid-1860s. After the bodies were exhumed, Hardy reportedly stacked the gravestones in circles around the tree, and the tree took on his name. Only there is no evidence Hardy had anything to do with the tree and the story is, most likely, apocryphal. Amateur historian David Bingham, unearthed photographs taken in 1926 which showed the headstones in their current formation though no tree, suggesting the Hardy Tree was less than a century old at the time it fell, a result of being infected with *Perenniporia fraxinea*, a parasitic fungus that affects ash trees. What is more, Bingham's research suggested that Hardy may have had nothing to do with the arrangement of the gravestones. What seems clear though is that trees accumulate myth.

Some, like the Tolpuddle Martyrs' Tree in Dorset, the huge sycamore tree beneath which a group of farm workers met in 1833 to discuss their low wages and poor living conditions, sowing the seeds for the trade union movement, have a clear association with events we mark. In other trees, however, the association is more hazy, if no less compelling. The glorious Ankerwycke Yew, in Berkshire, is well-placed to have witnessed King John's signing of the Magna Carta in 1215, as well as some of Henry VIII's extra-marital assignations with soon-to-be second wife Anne Boleyn, though there is no firm evidence for either. And it is unlikely the Wallace Oak in Port Glasgow had any actual connection to Scottish independence leader William Wallace, nor that Irish king Brian Boru had any particular connection to the famed thousand-year-old Brian Boru oak in Raheen Woods in East Clare, Ireland. And the famous pollarded Royal Oak in which King Charles II hid from Oliver Cromwell's Parliamentary soldiers, which you can see if you visit Boscobel House in Shropshire, is not the same tree of the story, and nor does it stand in the same place as the tree in which the king hid. The original was the victim of souvenir hunters in the sixteen and seventeen hundreds, who came for branches and chunks of trunk, eventually leading to its demise.

So why attach the story to the tree in the first place?

Perhaps because they outlive us, perhaps because their longevity can hold our stories. Perhaps because they are markers of our time here, markers of seasons too, and markers of memory that stretches far beyond our time, and will stretch far into the future. We attach the story of the signing of the Magna Carta to the Ankerwycke Yew because it is one of the few living things we know was alive when this turning point in England's history took place, and because its trunks and twisting branches seem to gather story to it. Such trees, such emblems, bring us a little closer to events and people who have shaped the world around us. They are living memorials.

The same happens across the world. The Bodhi Tree that stands in the temple at Mahabodhi, in Bihar, India, is said to be a direct descendant of the tree that was growing there around the time of the Buddha, 2,600 years ago, where he is believed to have attained Enlightenment. Similarly, the enormous Plane Tree of Hippocrates, which stands on the island of Kos, is one which the philosopher is said to have planted, and beneath which he is said to have taught.

We are, and probably always have been, drawn to old and spectacular trees: the Major Oak in Sherwood Forest, the Fortingall Yew in Perthshire in Scotland, which is between 2,000 and 9,000-years old. We are drawn to trees that predate any concept of modern society: trees now gnarled and split and held up in places by crutches, improbably tall redwoods and ancient oaks, the centre of which have long since rotted away. Trees that hold mystery, history and cultural memory. Trees that attract and hold our imagination, that help us to tell the stories of who we are and the places and times from which we came.

The twisting oak at Tehidy Woods, Cornwall.

Standing beneath the outstretched arms of a sprawling sessile oak that stands dead centre in an ancient stone circle, a man lifts a small child, still a babe in arms, and passes him up and over the thick, crooked arm of one of the branches where it stoops down to head height. He brings the child out the other side and passes him back to his father. He is unsure what propelled him to act this way: it is

unfathomable, though he will explain later that he felt compelled
to do so. The moment, he will say, seemed to call for it.

This compulsion is perhaps not dissimilar to that of coming
across a tree and feeling the strong desire to throw one's arms
around it, or the sudden knowledge that the only way to really
experience it is to climb into its branches, to sit inside its canopy
and know it from there. It is, perhaps, the same drive that led to the
Irish tradition of splitting an ash sapling on the birth of a child and
passing the child from mother to father through the riven trunk.

The baby being passed through the curled branches of the oak
was the grandson of Nick Hart, whose family have lived in this
smallholding, not far from the village of St Neot on Cornwall's
Bodmin Moor, for over fifty years. The stone circle in which the
tree sits has been there for somewhat longer, and the stones were
set here at some point in the Neolithic Age.

The Celts might have called this a 'thin place', and the Romans
would have almost certainly considered it has having a *genius loci*.
Nick tells me that quite often, visitors to their family tree will stand
in silence, absorbing the atmosphere of the place. It is unsurprising.
The stones are thick with mosses, the twisting arm-like branches of
the sessile oak too. They seem to embody movement. The branches
are decked with lichens, and dripping old man's beard, and a shifting blanket of dappled patterns play across the long grass and ferns
beneath the tree from light that filters through the layers of the canopy.

There is also, to one side of the circle, an unexcavated pile of
boulders, which may or may not be a Neolithic burial mound,
although Nick told me that anything in it would have long ago
been eaten away by the acidic waters on the hillside.

We could play a guessing game about the rituals and rites that
took place here several thousand years ago, wonder what purpose
these stones had and whether they are echoed by the family rituals
that take place here now. It is unlikely there was a tree here then.
The oak is only a 150 or so years old, and whether it was planted or
self-seeded is a matter of debate. When I asked Nick his thoughts

on it, he said he favoured the latter explanation, that it self-seeded sometime in the 1800s, though the mine houses in the neighbouring fields would still have been in use at the time the tree started its life, and it seemed to me conceivable that a 'sacred' oak was planted here by a bored miner, or a mine owner in thrall to the Victorian Celtic Revival, or someone with forethought and a sense of place. It's possible, Nick replied, when I put this to him. There were traditions up on the moor of holding certain trees and woodlands in reverence, of never staying in certain woodlands beyond dark. There are a thousand possible reasons why this tree grew where it is, in the centre of a ring that may have been of spiritual significance to the people who set the stones there or which may stand where they had their hearth.

Regardless, he explained, it is a deeply important place to their family, and in recent years the site has seen naming ceremonies for

The Hart's family tree.

Nick's children, the exchanging of wedding vows, storytellings and poetry readings, jazz concerts and times of quiet contemplation.

In some ways, Nick's family oak is kind of inversion of the most ancient yews that sit in churchyards and graveyards, which predate the churches by which they stand, some by a considerable age. There, the trees came first in all likelihood, with settlements built up around them later. At Northwood, the stone circle came first by millennia. The oak was an afterthought. There was none of the severe solemnity found in yew groves in the oak circle, nothing of the scorched earth beneath and the rooks chattering above. Here, all was green, and late bluebells hung heavy among the thick grasses.

The tree's pleasing centrality – whether or not it was purpose-ful – makes the tree noteworthy, to the human eye at least. We like trees that are well-placed, that seem significant for the way in which they hold space in the landscape. We make pilgrimages to stand by them and photograph them.

A few weeks later, I would make a pilgrimage of my own, to view a tree the fame of which is entirely based on the way it stands within the landscape, a tree that may be the most photographed in the UK, the sycamore at Hadrian's Wall at the point known as Sycamore Gap.

While the Roman wall was built about 2,000 years ago, the sycamore, which stands in one of several dips caused by melting glacial waters, pleasingly centrally in the landscape, is a few hundred years old at best. It was already well-known by the time it upstaged Kevin Costner and Morgan Freeman in the 1991 film *Robin Hood: Prince of Thieves*, at the point where Kevin/Robin declares himself to be home. It seems strange that a tree that is considered across the country to be little more than a weed might end up being among the most celebrated, the most revered. There's a certain irony in the wall being overtopped by a tree that is considered to be an invader, too, a species that arrived in the country sometime in the 1500s making it, technically, a non-native species; native species in England being considered those that were there at the point the island separated from the mainland of Europe.

There was no one else around when I arrived, and though I had only planned to stay ten minutes, when I next looked at my watch two hours had passed, and I had done little else than watch the tree and listen to the cuckoo on the hillside to the right and the curlews in the fields behind me.

The famous sycamore at Hadrian's Wall does not link us to the Romans (nor to Robin Hood for that matter) any more than Nick Hart's oak links us to our Neolithic ancestors, though our perception and understanding of time is such that we might imagine it does. I sat and watched the sun set in the dip adjacent to the sycamore and for a good while after, until the heat of the day was all gone and the calls of the cuckoo and curlews had been replaced by the sound of rooks coming in to roost, and in the evening dimness, for a few minutes, with the tree in silhouette, it could have been any point at any time in history.

So, we find significance in pleasing symmetry, in a tree growing in the centre of an ancient stone circle or in the middle of a dip in an ancient stone wall. We pass a child through a looped branch in a tree planted 150 years ago, within a stone circle that has been there since the Neolithic Age, without quite knowing why we do so, only that it feels meaningful. We tie a rag on a branch that overhangs a well in the hope that it will do some good to someone for whom we care, that we might be able to tap into some of the vitality of this place. We talk about 'thin places' as being ones in which the gap between this place and some otherland is almost tangible. And sometimes, the thin place to which we are connected is our past.

On our way back down through the fields, Nick points out some of the other trees that are meaningful to his family. In one field there is what Nick refers to as a bee garden, with a tree in flower

every month for bees to take advantage of throughout the year. Nick's wife, Jenny, planted a copper beech on the birth of their first grandchild, an oak for their second – and a third, a horse chestnut planted from seed is still in its deer guard.

His youngest grandson, the one to whom the horse chestnut is dedicated, has declared himself unimpressed that it is still so small, especially in comparison to the copper beech. However, horse chestnuts grow quickly and it will soon top his siblings' and cousins'. I like this idea: that Nick's grandchildren will always have these trees keeping age with them. It makes the trees significant to the family, and to each child, markers of their belonging here.

This sense of belonging reminded me of a story I was told by Aruna Vasudevan, one of my editors, concerning her mother, who grew up on her family rubber estate in central Kerala where trees also hold meaning. That these trees – among them towering teaks and banyans – through the sharing of memories and love after her mother's death became for Aruna 'touchstones' that resonated between the living and the dead. They represented, she told me, both 'comfort and sanctuary'.

Nick suggests that on my drive back home, I should look up at the bell tower of the church in the village. St Neot is notable as one of a few remaining villages to celebrate Oak Apple Day, held at the end of May, which celebrates the return of King Charles II to the throne after eleven years' Puritan rule. The date of the king's return to London was marked with a public holiday, though the custom died out in most places over the following 200 years. As I drive through the village, I see the oak bough fixed to the top of the church tower. In the annual ceremony, the vicar carries a cross, the tower captain an oak bough. The old bough is ceremonially thrown from the tower and the new hauled up in its place after a blessing.

These traditions, the ones held around the family tree, and the ones in the village, with the ceremonial hauling up of an oak bough, are to do with belonging. They are statements of intent, a rootedness in the landscape. It is echoed in traditions around the world, notably the Scandinavian tradition of planting special trees. In Sweden, *Vårdträd* (a caring or guardian tree) and, in Norway, *Tuntre* (centre trees) are planted in the centre of a farmyard. It is a tradition that stretches back to the Vikings. Whether they demonstrated respect for the spirits that were believed to live in the tree, or were a reminder to care for the place in which one lives, they were markers of belonging and care. They are echoes of *Yggdrasil*, the guardian tree, cared for and often offered beer and milk by farmers, revered increasingly as they grow. They are, in Swedish, *guda-anknytning*, a connection to God.

Just a few weeks after I spent an evening with the tree at Sycamore Gap, it was felled overnight, at the end of September. The following day, as photographs of the toppled tree emerged, there was, across the airwaves and internet, a public outpouring of grief for the tree's loss, along with a torrent of stories of love expressed beneath its boughs. Vows exchanged. Pilgrimages made. Proposals and promises. Memories of times spent with people who had since died or parted ways. Ashes scattered. Prayers offered.

The tree, as iconic an image of the north-east as the Angel of the North and the bridges of the Tyne – though, unlike these others, living and therefore more vulnerable – was felled the night before a landmark paper on the state of nature was published, a damning report that found one in six species are in danger of extinction in the UK.

Framed in its gap between two hillocks, alone in a landscape, the Sycamore Gap tree drew the eye in a way that trees within a woodland, most of the time, do not. We often fail to see the trees for the forest.

As the day wore on, the National Trust appealed for people not to flock to the site, though many still did, leaving memorial stones and messages. In the days after, one man took a sapling sycamore and planted it close to the site of the felled tree, though it was later removed. People were asked to leave their messages at a specially created 'celebration room' at the nearby Sill visitors' centre. One wrote of his sorrow at the knowledge he would not be able to revisit the tree with his children as they grew, the tree as a living touchstone. The Bishop of Northumberland, left, for her message, the words invoked in Māori funerals, '*Kua hinga he totara i te wao nuia tane*', a mighty tree has fallen in the forest, the image of the tree as an admired and trusted friend. I have heard several people refer to trees as 'old friends', as things we look in on as we might a neighbour.

My friend, Sarah, tweeted: 'The older I get, the more I think that, besides books and a few people, trees are the love of my life.'

Sarah has a tree she addresses as buddy, a term she does not use for anyone or anything else. This tall oak has a hummock at elbow height which she shakes hands with when she passes, a kind of daily checking in. The wall to either side is broken, an accommodation to the tree, its roots running into the wall on either side.

My father has favourite trees too, ones he visits regularly in the woods by Chirk Castle, near Wrexham, in Wales, sweet chestnuts that were around during the reign of Henry VIII, the largest of which is more than 25 feet around.

A detail of one of the ancient sweet chestnut trees in Chirk Woods.

Take a step back and it seems, in some ways, strange for the tree at Sycamore Gap to be afforded this level of public adoration, loyalty that was captured in countless photographs and in outrage on social media. Strange, too, that a tree considered little more than a weed in most of the country had entered legend – there was notably more outcry about the felling of the tree at Sycamore Gap than there was when whole groves of ancient trees were being felled, and ancient woodlands bulldozed for the now-abandoned new high speed rail lines of HS2, which has already cut through huge swathes of countryside. Much as we may miss the tree, it is its association with myth and with our own stories – our identities, cultural heritage and the fragility of the symbols that connect us – for which its downfall is mourned. Like the clootie wells of the Highlands, the tree at Sycamore Gap acted as a shrine, a place of pilgrimage and familiarity.

I suspect that many people weren't even sure what was at the root of their collective cry of eco-anxiety, just that they were upset by the tree's felling, the gap it left. I suspect too that we over-estimate the strength of trees and underestimate our own capacity to damage, mistaking our soft skin for weakness and tree's bark for strength. We don't like to think of ourselves as destroyers, yet acts like this show us that we can wreck what we claim to hold dear, and all too easily.

We hang our wishes on the wishing tree and when it is felled, we mourn it as much for the things we have pinned there, as the tree itself. And when we encounter trees as friends, we mourn their loss deeply.

8

Forest Bather

*Swimming in the woods at Devil's Water, Northumberland,
and walking in Tomnafinnoge Woods, County Wicklow, Ireland*

B y nine in the morning, it is already hot. It is early June, and
by July the month will have been announced as the hottest
on record. It is a record that will be broken again and again
over the coming months.

I am already lost in the woods, having zoned out when receiving instructions on how to get to Devil's Water from another
motorist, though, after spending a while compounding my mistakes, I meet a dog walker who points me back towards the right
path. I should continue until I meet a series of fallen trees, she
says, climb over or under them, and take a series of right or left
turns which, even as I listen, I know I will not remember. I nod
as though I am listening and thank her. As we head in opposite
directions, she calls out that the last part of the walk is a scramble,
though I should not be put off by the steepness of the slope.
I congratulate myself on finding the first of the fallen trees but
lose my way again after the first turning. I am keen to reach the
Devil's Water, so I push on.

I had chosen my destination by name alone: Devil's Water. I am
fond of places named after the devil as they are often particularly

Devil's Water, Northumberland.

beautiful. A Devil's Gap or Devil's Gorge is, I figure, usually going to have dramatically high-sided walls; a Devil's Bridge, Ridge, Backbone or Pulpit is likely to be the point in the landscape that offers the most spectacular of views.

One of my favourites of these spots is close to Locunolé in Brittany, a woodland called *Les Roches du Diable*, the Devil's Rocks. Another gorge in the woods, at the bottom of which are huge boulders among the water, giant stones that it is easy to see might be seen as a devilish playground, or the site of a giant's throwing stones, the line between awe and fear paper thin. I had hoped to find something similar at Devil's Water, a beautiful place to cool off: promontories with sheer drops, high-sided gorges liable to flood, dark caves into which it would be possible to disappear. It ties in with philosopher Edmund Burke's description of places that are incomprehensibly beautiful, or which raise within us deep emotion, places that leave us unnerved and in a state of 'delightful horror'. 'Whatever is in any sort terrible or is conversant about terrible objects or operates in a manner analogous to terror,' Burke wrote in his *Philosophical Enquiry into the Origin of Our Ideas of the Sublime and Beautiful*, 'is a source of the sublime.'

I often experience a sense of the sublime deep in the woods, when walking between vast pillars of beech trees and gigantic pines, through a dappled light that is filtered down from high, high above. It is easy to lose sense of space and scale beneath these giants, especially in the early summer when even the foxgloves tower over me.

It is cool, or at least cooler, under the shade of the Scots pine and Wellingtonia and, protected by the canopy, the sounds of the world around muted and soft, it becomes the sort of day on which I would not mind spending some time lost in the woods, enjoying what the Japanese might call the *komorebi* and *hamorebi* – the sensation of sunlight through the branches of trees, and the light that shines through leaves, respectively. We are drawn to these places in which the trees tower above us – just think of the flocks who travel for hours to view the world's largest tree, General Sherman, the giant sequoia that towers 270 feet above the thousands of acres of Sequoia National Park in California. They put us in perspective.

The same is true of the oldest trees, the ones to which we might make a pilgrimage in order to pass time with these living connections to a history which we cannot even begin to guess. It may be one of the reasons we find it easier, when walking among these tree cathedrals, to put our own lives in perspective, though those who engage in the practice of forest bathing – which the Japanese call *shinrin-yoku* – claim there are countless other benefits, from those of phytonocides, the essential oils given off by trees, to reductions in stress, anxiety and depression and improvements in both sleep quality and the immune system.

The Japanese term *komorebi* has enjoyed its moment in the sun recently, with the uptake of forest bathing. We don't have a similar word in English, though the experience is common enough that poets have coined terms for the same thing. Gerard Manley Hopkins's 'shivelight' from his poem 'That Nature is a Heraclitean Fire and of the Comfort of the Resurrection' described sun lancing through trees. Dylan Thomas's 'windfall light', from 'Fern Hill', offers an alternative, and C.S. Lewis termed the phenomenon 'patches of Godlight', both of which phrases go some way to describing the feeling.

At the opposite end of the year, at the end of autumn, I had walked in the woods at Tomnafinnoge in County Wicklow, Ireland, with Cathelijne de Wit-Peijs, who leads forest bathing walks there.

'We tend to walk at a certain speed, as though we've got an end in mind,' she said to me about ten minutes after we left the car park. She slowed down purposefully to emphasize her point and it took me a moment to adjust my speed to match hers. I had not realized we had been striding rather than walking until then. Why rush, she asked? After all, the walk we were taking through the ancient woods was a circular one. We would end up at exactly the same point at which we started.

Tomnaffinoge Woods, *Coillte Tom na Feannóige* in Gaeilge, the wood of the hooded crow, is one of Ireland's most ancient forests, the last surviving pocket of the great oak woodlands of Tinahely in County Wicklow. And, although the woodland, as it stands today, is just a fraction of the size of the one that existed as part of the Watson–Wentworth–Fitzwilliam Coolattin estate, its towering oaks speak of a continuity of woodland that is rare in Ireland.

The estate passed into the hands of the Fitzwilliam family in 1782 and remained that way until 1977, when it was put up for sale.

At this point most of the forest was cleared, and the remaining 165 acres was only saved after a twenty-year campaign by two locals, Johnny Couchman and Paddy O'Toole, a charity called Artists for Oak and the support of high-profile figures, including the guitarist, The Edge. What saved it in the end, perhaps, was the realization that this was the last woodland of its type here. That when it is gone there will be none left like it.

At our new pace, Cathelijne and I walked in silence for a while. I listened to the flow of the River Derry, along whose banks we were walking, and the sounds of the woodland on the other. As though the rarity of this woodland was not enough to warrant slowing down, Cat talked me through some of the other benefits of engaging with the woods in a way we might not often consider when out walking.

'When I'm leading a group I give people invitations to use all their senses,' she told me as we left the path, walking away from the river, among the giant sessile oaks and the understorey of holly and hazel, the forest floor thick with fallen leaves.

'You get out of your head and into your body. It's good for your mind, your stress. Some people get really emotional when they are forest bathing and they can't really explain why, but it's just your body releasing things you've been holding inside you, which come out when you slow down and listen to your body.'

Often, she said, people find they are a little resentful about having to slow down when they first arrive for a forest bathing walk. 'When we walk, it's often because we want to get somewhere, so when we slow down, our bodies start to protest – "Why are you doing this to us?" It's like a stress reaction.'

I had not realized until then that I was having exactly this reaction myself, and the absurdity only hit me when Cat continued to slow her pace and I felt something inside rail against walking so slowly.

You have to sit with that feeling for ten or fifteen minutes before the reaction passes, she told me, though once you have slowed down and become quiet, you tend to stay that way for a while, and turn inwards.

During a formal forest bathing session, she told me, the group might stop at points on the walk and lie on the forest floor looking up into the canopy or, on a day like this, in the first phase of autumn, sit on the ground and smell the complex aroma of leaves that had just fallen from the trees.

'I often ask people to find a tree and look at it as though it is a piece of art in a gallery. I ask them to look at it as though it is an art installation, for ten or fifteen minutes. People have all sorts of reactions when they do that – they connect to the trees in their own way.

'When you stand right under a tree, or right next to it, for a time, there's a certain energy that's not there when you are looking at it from afar. People get quite emotional when they do that.'

Some people are quite literal, describing the trees in great detail, their colours and textures. Others find themselves hit by powerful emotions, and those of a more spiritual mind talk in terms of a tree's personality and aura. One forest bather, an American woman, Cat told me, described hearing one of the trees here talking to her, in a clear Irish accent. For others, she said, the tree lends itself to metaphor: they describe the ways in which the branches spread out from the trunk as being like the journey they have taken in life, the different branches representing different events. Some people simply enjoy sitting quietly in the shade, their backs against the trunk.

All the while, Cat was slowing down further and further. We had left the huge oaks behind now and were among enormous beeches, and we stood for a while in a woodland that felt completely different to that of the great oaks, where we had crouched down in the leaf litter, observing the fruiting fungus that was beginning to shoot up there. Our hands on the trunks of the elephantine giants, we stopped for a while, observed by a small hybrid sika red deer.

'As soon as you stand next to a tree, you get an impulse to put your hand on it,' Cat said. 'There must be something in our past that makes it natural for us to do this, because everyone does it.'

Back on the search for the Devil's Water, I am striding through humid woods when I pass one particularly large tree that stops me in my tracks. I feel compelled to put first one and then both hands against its trunk. It slows me down and I laugh at the ridiculousness of marching through the woods on a hot day as though the only thing that matters is the destination which, at this point, seems uncertain at best, given my general lack of directional sense.

We touch wood to ward off bad luck, though we do so too for the sense of comfort, for the grounding effect of trees, their solidity and sense of power. But it is more than that. As the Quaker and land reformer Alastair McIntosh said to me, when we spoke the previous month, to touch wood is to re-embed, to remind ourselves of our fundamental connection to our pasts and to the world around us. This is how it feels with my hands against this trunk, and I stay with my hands on the tree for a minute or so, not reaching for that sense of connection so much as wondering how this tree experiences the world. How different that is from my own experience.

The word 'tree' has a shared etymology with that of the word true, derived from *deru*, a proto Indo-European root that links the two, meaning firm, solid and steadfast, three of the qualities for which we love trees.

Leaving the huge beech behind, I walk further into the woods. I have been following the path for some time when I notice a faint buzzing that's getting louder. At first, I wonder if it is a distant chainsaw – after all, this is a working woodland – but become distracted by a column of ants shifting chunks of leaves several times the size of their bodies. The buzzing becomes louder as I watch the ant platoon make their way along a branch and it is only when

I look around I realize I had failed to notice the tens of thousands of ants that cover the woodland floor. I spend the next thirty minutes attempting to brush them from my clothes.

In the end, I stumble upon the gorge by following any path that slopes down into the valley. The dog walker I met earlier was right. The path becomes increasingly precarious as it joins with a small stream and starts to drop steeply on the approach to the gorge, and it *is* worth the scramble. As I emerge from the undergrowth, I come out onto a small beach and a pool in the river beneath sandstone cliffs. There is no one around and as my clothes are still full of unhappy ants, I strip off and dive in, emerging into a small cloud of midges.

The water is a rich, dark loamy colour, and gloriously cool beneath the shade cast by the oaks and pines on the sides of the gorge. I float and breathe in the forest's scented air, look up the steep sides of the gorge to the canopy to marvel at the crown shyness of the pines high above, enjoying what Proust called the 'cool, silent, intimate hours' one can spend beneath the canopy.

I swim with my eyes level with the water, to better watch the gentle eddies and currents of the river in the movement of fallen leaves and small twigs. I am lost in this activity when I notice a couple has appeared on the beach with an aged Labrador, and feel I have to stay in the water to avoid anyone's discomfort. The beach area is small, and they have chosen to sit at a spot just next to where I have left my clothes.

The dog jumps in and swims around me for a while, cooling off too, and the man shouts over to ask if I'm a local. I'm not to worry, he says, it's okay to swim in this section of river, which is a tributary of the Tyne. It's not usually polluted. It's not a given, he continues, and, in any case, it is a little too late to do anything about it if there was a problem with bacteria or pollution. I thank him for the reassurance and wonder how long I will have to wait before getting out.

He has been coming down here for decades, he continues, a regular pilgrimage to check how the woodland is doing.

Sometimes, he says, a patch of woodland he has known most of his life will have been felled in between visits, and the whole place changes. It leaves a hole, a place he thought he knew well changing shape so drastically overnight, though much of the woodland here is a pine plantation and he supposes it is to be expected. The old retriever eventually hauls itself out and the couple stand, waving from the shore as they make their way back up into the undergrowth.

I return to my aimless floating for a while, settling into the space and feeling myself start to cool off before I dry off on a rock in the middle of the river, refreshed.

Retracing my steps, and mindful that I could easily end up hotter than when I entered the woods, I take the return journey at less than half the pace I had on the way down. The path is wide enough for me to close my eyes for a few steps at a time and I listen to the woods.

Woodlands sound different at different times of the year – dependant on whether the canopy is open or closed, what is underfoot, whether fresh fallen leaves or well-rotted mulch, the air pressure, which birds are present.

I only know a few birds by sound, though I am improving with the help of an app called Merlin Bird ID, which listens along with me and comes up with a list of birds.

Emma and I started listening to the birds this way during the Covid lockdowns. Standing outside our house in the wooded valley by the sea, we had the time and space to wonder what the various birds singing in the trees opposite our house were. Like many people, we became more interested in the place we lived, perhaps for the first time, in a concentrated way. Home was no longer somewhere to which we returned, but the place we were in the majority of the time and, like others, we began to notice the rhythms and patterns of this particular place, the ways in which the plants and trees grew, the changing colours of the woods.

For me, it was an act of mindfulness, or of combatting the anxiety that occasionally rears its head, a form, as Cat had described to me, of slowing down and listening to what is going on in the world, rather than what is in my head.

We started in the woodland by our house in the morning and evenings, listening with the app open. The more I listened alongside the app, the better I became at splitting the birdsong into bandwidths, and the less I relied on it. As another writer described it to me, while we were walking in the forest at Abriachan, it was a case of breaking through the green veil. At first, the birdsong is recognizably that but often nothing more; similarly, trees are a uniform mass, one species merging with another. But spend long enough looking and the greens of the woods become rich and deep, astounding in their variety, and beyond the greens, countless other colours of woodland emerge; the trees become individuals, distinct and specific. The same is true of birdsong.

Sometimes, still, I catch myself hearing a bird the app does not recognize and feel a small and pointless sense of one-upmanship on it, though most times the app still recognizes more species than my ears can. It is a meditation of sorts, as good as any other I have tried. Half an hour in the woods, listening to the birds sooths a racing mind. Walking with my camera is similar – I value it for the concentration, the patience it requires more than I do the pictures.

The philosopher Christian Diehm wrote in a paper on our connection to nature that, for most of us, nature is 'a more or less homogenous mass, with only the grossest distinctions apparent: here are flowers, here are shrubs, birds flit about among them'. In other words, we are often unable to see the trees for the wood.

Diehm, in his study, suggested that developing a language of trees, learning their names and features, developing our ability to recognize them, informs our environmental ethics profoundly. Being able to separate the sounds into individual birds, the species of trees within the forest, its lichens and mosses, epiphytes, and scurrying creatures, makes the green veil richer. It increases our sense of wonder.

I have started to attempt the same with trees now, though this is more complicated. For a start, even trees of the same species can look radically different from one another. The bark of a young tree may look entirely dissimilar to that of one that has been growing for several hundred years. And then there is winter.

When I was at Wytham Woods, I had spent some time with two ash dieback researchers, who were taking core samples. The first job, they told me, was to identify all the trees of the species from which they wanted to take core samples. The lead researcher gave me a crash course in identifying sycamores, and, in doing so, realized they may have made a small error and may have been taking samples from beech trees instead. It is reassuring to know that even those who study trees get it wrong sometimes. It struck me, as we moved from tree to tree that theirs is slow, demanding work, which makes it similar to forest bathing in some senses, slowing the pace of a walk to feet per minute rather than miles per hour.

So, I take my time on the walk back to the car, listen to the birds, place my hands on the trunks of trees I pass, crouch to watch a beetle that I might otherwise have missed, or a tiny fungus beneath one of the fallen trees as I retrace my steps.

In Diehm's words, there are 'instances in which one must focus one's attention on a bud smaller than the tip of one's finger, and others in which one must stand back to glimpse a living pattern so immense and humbling it makes some feel they are in the presence of God'.

9

Myth Walker

Walks in the fictional woods at Wenlock Edge, Shropshire

You do not believe in ghosts, nor in poltergeists, fairies or trolls. You are a rational person. So, when you set out with the express intention of scaring yourself by walking through a supposedly haunted woodland, in the full knowledge there is nothing out there to scare you, you wonder if it is worth bothering at all.

You choose your woods carefully, the ones with the highest density of ghost stories associated with them. It is hardly a scientific approach, but Wenlock Edge in Shropshire seems to have a good claim.

The most famous of the stories told about these woods is about the robber knight Ippikin who, in the thirteenth century, terrorized Wenlock Edge with his band of robbers, from a cave in the woods. There are many stories told of Ippikin, including that he struck a deal with the devil for eternal youth, though his luck ran out when he and his men were trapped in their cave by a rockslide and there they died. As the story goes, Ippikin's spirit still roams the Edge, and occasionally he pushes unsuspecting walkers off the cliffs, though he can be kept at bay with the repetition of the phrase, 'Ippikin, Ippikin, keep away with your long chin.' The veracity of this advice is up for grabs, however, as other versions of the story have it that saying this will result in the person speaking these words to be pushed off the Edge, so you take your chances either way.

Another ghost story told of the Edge is that of Major Thomas Smallman, a Royalist officer in the English Civil War, who was surrounded by Cromwell's forces while carrying important dispatches. Instead of surrendering, Smallman leaped off the Edge on his horse, which was killed in the fall. Major Smallman was, apparently, saved by the branches of an apple tree, so why *his* ghost is said to haunt the woods, alongside that of his horse, is one of Wenlock Edge's mysteries.

More sobering, a more convincing claim might be that the woods are haunted by the memories of one particular event, the execution of eleven-year-old Alice Glaston who was hung at Gallows Tree Lease, Edge Top, in 1545. No details of the crime for which Alice was convicted remain, though she is thought to be the youngest recorded girl to have been hanged in the UK.

You find yourself parking in an empty car park on the edge of the village of Much Wenlock at dusk, a few minutes before a man from one of the nearby houses arrives with a heavy key fob to lock up for the evening. You explain to him you are writing a book about woodlands. You don't elaborate too much – it would sound ridiculous to say it out loud that you're attempting to scare yourself silly in the woods – but the man with the keys seems delighted and offers some nuggets of information about the area. He wants you to make sure you call Much Wenlock a town, not a village – it has a mayor, you know, this said with a grin. He asks if you have watched the *Time Team* episode that featured the village. You look like the sort of person who watches *Time Team*, he says. You are unsure what he means by this, but you let it pass. He has decided you can be trusted to have the car park to yourself – perhaps he knows there is little crossover between people who watch *Time Team* and the teenagers who come up here to smoke pot. He agrees to lock you in for the evening. He will come over to unlock gates again at about seven the next day.

You say goodnight, listen to him closing and locking the gate, and walk up through a tree tunnel into the woods in the last of the light. You note the sound of horses stamping in the field to one side as you climb up the limestone path, the stand of trees in which crows are settling down to roost, the scrabble of small rodent feet in the undergrowth. There is a gentle breeze in the treetops. 'Suthering', the poet John Clare called it, a blanketing sound that comforts. You are safe in these woods.

It is only a mile from the car park to Wenlock Edge proper, though it feels much further in the growing darkness, especially when you need to stop to check the path behind you every minute or so. It is now almost entirely black. What moonlight there might be is shrouded in clouds and you purposefully left your torch at home. The tree tunnel ahead, which would seem charming, you're sure, in the daytime, now looks oppressively close. A few flittering shapes emerge from the holloway. You stop in the path and watch the pipistrelles flit in and out of the trees for a while – what you are really doing is avoiding the thought of plunging into the dark tunnel.

You check the heart rate monitor on your watch. It seems ridiculous that this one shift – light to dark – would have this effect, though there it is on a blinking digital display, your elevated heart rate, as though you are jogging and not walking slowly.

You walk on, ignore a rustle in the bushes, the clatter as you disturb some roosting birds. A noise you cannot place. You are just a few hundred feet into the woods.

Another shape, darker than the darkness, appears ahead. It seems to stand in the middle of the path, blocking the way ahead. You stop. You could swear it is moving, though you stay still for long enough to work out it is not. Your eyes have started to play tricks on you. It takes some effort to continue but you push on, and when you get to it, you find the shape is a tree stump about five feet or so tall, on the edge of the path. Your heart is racing now, though all you have seen is a tree stump and some small bats. You have found trace of neither Ippikin's bandits nor ghostly horseback riders, yet your heart is still racing and it takes all your effort not to turn back, to seek the comfort of the van.

The path splits and you hesitate. Deep in the woods, it is easy to get turned around. Even though you know there are a few vast woodlands and forests in the British Isles, it is easy enough to get lost in even small patches of woodland.

You look down both paths. One leads upwards towards the ridge, and the other straight on. Knowing that you might get lost almost never stops you, Red Riding Hood-like, from taking a diversion when the chance occurs, regardless of how many times you have been advised to stay on the path. During the day, you find the desire to leave the well-trodden gravel almost irresistible. The sight of a clearing in the distance. A particularly gnarled tree glimpsed in the far, dark greenery. A fruiting fungus. Or the sight of a deer's flank. Any of these will do it, though sometimes it is simply the depth of the woods that draws you on, as though you really cannot help yourself.

All great woods have this in common, an irresistible depth of field, in which the further we look, the deeper and more multi-layered the image becomes, its pull magnetic. Where an individual tree is a marvel of complexity and beauty – and one can have a life-long relationship with just one tree – a woodland is infinitely rich, and nowhere does that become more apparent than when we are standing in the midst of a forest when the way forward is slightly uncertain, and we have to trust that we will find our way out before the situation becomes too serious. The woods' complex layers, from the undergrowth and deadwood, which make taking straight lines near on impossible, up through the shrubs and trees whose growth was stunted as they were outflanked by those to either side, to the perpendicular trunks and the canopy that draw the attention away and disorient the walker further, it is easy to understand why, even in daylight, we might lose our way. It is easy to see why we might be enchanted by this place, also easy to understand, when we stray too far, that we might feel panicked by it.

During the night, there is a *volte-face* in this dynamic. The tendency towards panic grows the darker it gets, and the more the trees and brush feel like walls, seemingly as impenetrable in the dark as they are intriguing in the light. There are no bears or wolves left in our woods, but who would choose to leave the knowns of a dark path for the unknowns of the darker undergrowth?

These are not the only feelings possible within the woods. Anyone who has spent long enough wandering alone among the trees may be familiar with the feeling of *Waldeinsamkeit*, the German word that translates loosely as 'forest loneliness'. But the feeling that has come across you on your night ramble is more akin to what writer Sara Maitland calls 'forest fear', which goes beyond the fear of getting lost, beyond the fear of coming across other people in the woods and is related simply to the sense of fear one feels when deep in the woods, that sense of being watched – and not just by the deer and the birds.

I often realize, having wandered off the path, that I am no longer quite sure from which direction I came, nor in which direction I am heading. It rarely takes long from that point before I am entirely disoriented, even if I am only a few metres from the path, and the curiosity that led me from the path begins to stray into panic.

It can be no surprise that the word panic originates with the Greek god of the wild, the goat-horned Pan, who is closely connected to woodlands and whose voice was said to cause humans to flee in unreasoned fear when they were in lonely places. The bacchinalian characteristics of Pan – among which are curiosity and joy – both of which we may feel when we enter the woods, can so easily tip over into panic when we realize we are no longer in control of the situation, that we have been turned around and the way back to what is known, and therefore safe, is uncertain.

And we are surely lacking in imagination if we have never, upon being deep in the woods alone, as dusk falls, felt unsure of ourselves, of the danger of the wildwoods and the sensation that we are being watched. We see, in the scars on trunks – a product of our tendency towards seeing the human in the non-human – eyes watching us. And yet we are similarly lacking imagination if we do not, on feeling the sun's rays filtered through the branches (whether or not we refer to this as forest bathing) sense that we are protected by the trees around us, held in a loose, comforting embrace. And these two feelings – of being protected and of being watched – are never quite as far apart as we might hope in the heart of the woods.

It is unsurprising, given the primal emotions that the forest stirs up in us that woodlands and forests have provided our most enduring metaphors for the workings of the imagination. The world of fiction writing, in particular, is full of these metaphors. The journey from the blank page to finished story is so often discussed in terms of walking into imagined woods. It is a process of uncertainty, of diverging and often disappearing paths, a journey of discovery, becoming lost and then found again, of being unable to see the wood for the trees and – at some point – emerging at the other side of the wood, having found a path, and having left a trail of breadcrumbs the reader may be able to follow through the story.

You have reached your capacity for discomfort in the dark woods. You decide to turn around and head back towards the car park. It is all downhill from here though, if anything, as you about face the way back looks darker than the way ahead. You retrace your steps, take care to take the turning at the right point though, even as you were certain of it on the way out, you don't quite recognize the path you take and have to remind yourself that, walking on a hillside, you just need to keep the upward slope to your right and you'll get out eventually.

Your breathing is loud in your ears and you find yourself holding your breath to better hear the sounds of the woods around you. You know there is no one else here, though every noise is now a footstep behind you. As you pass the walls of one of the lime kilns, evidence of one of Wenlock Edge's previous uses, despite the fact you know what these workings are, you begin to fill the darker blackness of the tunnels there with all sort of creatures. There is a pool of water here, from the recent rains, the stillness of which seems unnatural too, and you feel the urge to run, stronger this time, to cover more ground so as to be able to leave the cover of the trees sooner. Now you are in conflict with yourself. Your mind is not your friend in the woods at night.

You hold your breath again when you hear a sound that is neither bird nor badger. Like quiet voices, though you are still well away from the road and the town. It is difficult to tell above the susurration in the canopy. The wind is up now and every now and then, the moon comes into sight, allowing you a slightly better view of the path ahead. In one of these brief moments of illumination, you're sure you see two silhouetted figures some way down the path. You stop in your tracks, rooted to the spot.

The figures ahead are definitely not trees. And like you, they are still, about 60 feet or so from where you stand. You wonder about getting off the path, or turning around and heading back the other way, though that would mean they could follow you.

One of my earliest memories is the illustration on the front cover of a book of Grimm's fairytales I had when I was very young. I grew up in a house full of books, though of all of them, this is the one I remember most clearly. The cover showed a twisting, tangled forest, a dense wall of trunks, roots, branches and brambles. This illustration was a promise to the reader – that the heroes and heroines of these stories would stray from the path that leads through the woods, that they would become entangled in the roots and brambles of the dark forest and have to fight their way out into the open again. For a child with an over-active imagination, it was the stuff of nightmares. The illustration made its way into my dreams, and I recall waking in the night full of forest fear having dreamt I was on the wrong side of that entangled wall, in the dangerous woods with little hope of getting back, so dense and deep was the undergrowth.

The Grimm's fairytales are full of forests, dangerous places into which children are led, in which they are abandoned, into which they are abducted and into which they stray against all advice. The forest as the entrance to another world. The woods as home to goblins, ogres and witches.

These journeys through the forest of fairytale have long been viewed as analogies of coming of age, especially for girls – just think of Red Riding Hood and Rapunzel. Forests are metaphorical spaces of awakenings – a space in which change may occur, echoing the turbulence of the shift from child to adult – and the dark woods of the stories the Grimms collected provide the perfect setting.

To enter the dark forest is to cross a threshold, to enter into an uncertain and dangerous place in which the one who enters the forest will be challenged, face perils, and undergo changes. The one who walks into the dark forest is rarely the same as the one who walks out the other side.

However, these are not the only archetypal forests of story. Walking in the dense spruce and pine forests of Germany is an entirely different experience to walking among the oaks and coppices of the English woodland, the landscape that inspired legends that originated closer to home.

On the face of it, the dark woods of the Grimms and Dante, and the forests of many of the medieval romances of the European mainland, could not be more different from the deciduous woodlands of the stories of Robin Hood in English legend. Along with the Arthurian legends, the quintessentially English stories of Robin Hood are among our islands' most enduring.

Stories of Robin Hood begin to crop up in fourteenth-century England, a figure who robbed from the unjustly rich and redistributed to the deserving poor, perhaps marking a sign of the working classes' discontent with the feudal system. In the earliest stories, Robin Hood is violent, often killing landowners and agents of the government. In one of the earliest written versions of the story, 'A Gest of Robyn Hode', Little John asks Robin to tell them who they shall, 'robbe, reve, bete and bynde', though in many of the later tellings, the outlaws' forest is a place of safety as well as transgression. The Greenwood of Robin Hood morphs into a benign place in which fairness trumps law and in which commons trump ownership. There is less 'reveing' and 'beteing' – the threat is often enough. And the merry men who form Robin Hood's band of outlaws are safe within the wild Greenwood, which seem to stretch out forever beyond the corruptions of the town and city. The wild woods represent lawless freedom or, rather, natural law.

In the majority of tellings of the Robin Hood stories, from the earliest written down, the forest is Edenic, an imaginary landscape in which natural law prevailed though, historically, even in the Middle

Ages forests were ruled by strict laws surrounding the coppicing of trees and the taking of game. In addition, the idea that forests once covered over England is a myth in itself, what Simon Schama terms, in his book *Landscape and Memory*, a kind of mythic memory of the freedom the Greenwood offered.

According to both Oliver Rackham and Simon Schama, by the time William the Conquerer arrived on these shores, no more than 15 per cent of England would have been wooded, an assertion bolstered by the great survey of 1086.

We have clearly wanted to hold on to these woodlands and forests of the mind for centuries – they lodged themselves in our consciousness through the Robin Hood stories, through Shakespeare's wonderfully anarchic Forest of Arden, and the hundreds of retellings of forest stories in poem, novel, film and game in the centuries since. Schama describes the Greenwood as a useful fantasy, flourishing at a time when the economic assets of the country's trees were being increasingly exploited.

Like all legends with any strength, it survived through adaptation. The useful fantasy has shifted over time. In early surviving ballads of Robin Hood, he was a yeoman turned outlaw, and only later a nobleman deprived of his home, a kind of domesticated outlaw, one who may have been more palatable to the ruling classes. Yet, in all of these stories, at their heart, Robin belongs to the Greenwood. If someone is to bring their villainy into the wood, they are fair game to be robbed, beaten, *reved* and bound. As much as he evolves over time, the anarchic figure of Robin Hood has, within him, an echo of an earlier proto-hero, emerging from the woods to dole out justice, the wild man of the woods, a character whose origins may stretch back as far as the history of humankind.

The Green Man at St Ildierna's Church, Lansallos, Cornwall.

My favourite story of the wild man of the woods is one connected to that other great mono-myth of our island archipelago, the Arthurian legend. When I read the medieval epic poem, 'Sir Gawain and The Green Knight' as an undergraduate, the image of the wild man lodged itself in my mind and took root. In the poem, the comfortable Arthurian court, preparing for Christmas, is interrupted by a giant, an alarmingly 'green man', who sets a disturbing challenge to the knights. Like Robin Hood, this figure, who emerges from the woods into the seat of power, is clearly more powerful than the court itself. With his imposing physical stature, green-tinged skin and his party trick of calmly being beheaded and walking out of the party with his head under his arm, he stands as a reminder that the natural world, which is beyond the law of man, trumps all. Gawain, who takes up the challenge, goes out into the world to seek the Green Knight, though wherever he is, whether in the court of Arthur or the castle of Lord Bertilak (a.k.a. The Green Knight himself), the reader is constantly reminded that there is something that stands outside the laws of man, a more elemental nature. The Green Knight, in demanding that Gawain completes the game, asks nothing less than to know who he is in his heart, something the court, even at the height of its power, could not possibly do. And what does Gawain learn from his experience? Perhaps that when he rode out into the wilderness, he found that the wilderness was already within him.

Just as Robin Hood seems to have the Green Knight in his DNA, so the Green Knight echoes the even older figure of the Green Man, the foliate face who appears in rood screens and pew ends, in carvings in the darker recesses of churches across the country, and the *wudawasa*, a mythical forest creature, a hairy, human-like creature that inhabits the woods, who was depicted in a fifteenth-century tapestry about which little is known, and incorporated into several medieval churches across Europe.

The origins of the Green Man and the *wudawasa* are now lost beneath the palimpsest of stories that have grown up around them though we feel we discern within them something original, something true.

Similarly, with fairytales of the dark wood and the peril there, I might be tempted to side with writer A.S. Byatt when she resists the simplistic reading of the forest as a place in which we witness a coming of age of the adolescent. In the stories of *Yggdrasil*, the world tree of Germanic mythology, the ash tree that spanned nine worlds and nine heavens and from which Woden hung himself for nine nights in order to learn wisdom, we see a precursor to the later image of Christ's crucifixion. And the Robin Hood we think we know is a reinvention of a reinvention, any authentic sources almost entirely absent.

In trying to return to the source, we come up against the problem that these stories were predominantly oral, and by the time they were laid down they had already undergone countless alterations and transformations. We see them through a distorted lens overlaid on countless other distorted lenses, though the figures who sit at their centres retain a sort of primal power that resists these distortions.

There is argument among scholars as to when the *wudawasa* and the Green Man first emerged, whether they are symbols of early Christianity or something older. Once seen, he seems to be omnipresent, in story and folk tale as well as in carvings on pews. He is the May King to some, a Dionysian figure to others, a wild man and a Cernunnos of Celtic mythology, or an allegory of Christ, a symbol of birth and rebirth. He is both knowable and unknowable. We have adapted the story of the wild man to our woodlands. We have transplanted him there, though his is a powerful narrative that seems to reach back much further, through other woods and forests, across continents perhaps, from the moment we came down from the trees, when we were foliate faces, and the face that stares up at us, from the pews, reminds us of our wildness. These stories are seeds carried across time and continents.

That is not to say we ought to find the Green Man a comforting figure. A face spewing vines and leaves, which serves to remind us of the wildness within might exhilarate, it might excite, but it ought to provoke unease too, just as the figure of that other ancient mythological figure of the woodland, Pan in the bacchanalian excites and exhilarates, though the fear he could invoke, the panic is never all that far away. The foliate head reminds us that nature will out in the end. The trees and the wild green were there before us; they will be there long after we are gone. And that is a thought that is both thrilling and fear-inducing. It is a reminder that we are not in control, and that change is the only constant, even if it is happening at a pace at which we are unable to grasp it.

The ambiguity of these stories is one of their enduring legacies. And along with these ambiguous stories, we have inherited complex feelings about the wood and forest, and the mysteries that lie at their heart. Maria Tatar suggests that fairytales offer a roadmap out of the woods of confusion, of darkness, back to safety, to home, to the safety afforded to us by the walls we have put up to keep the wilderness out, though I wonder if they also suggest that, once we have been into the woods and experienced the wilderness there, when we return home, we realize there is no real going back. They remind us that, at heart, we all retain the vestiges of the *wudawasa*, and a part of us belongs forever to the wild forest. Regardless of how civilized we have become, like Gawain, we carry the wilderness within us.

You are still rooted to the spot, in the pitch dark on Wenlock Edge, and have been for what feels like an age, full fearful that you have come across two of these woodland spirits or green men. The two indistinct shapes in front of you are not moving either. In the end, you make the first move, pluck up your courage and say a rather awkwardly British, 'Good evening,' gather all your courage and walk forwards. Closer, the dark shapes resolve themselves into a young couple. They are wearing backpacks, a tent strapped to one, and you begin to see the story for what it really is. They climbed the gate and were heading out into the woods to camp in the dark when they saw a shape in the distance, a figure that was definitely not a tree. It was moving towards them, until it stopped in the path. They stopped too, unsure about the movement they saw on the path ahead. If they stayed still, whatever it was might go back the way it came. Perhaps, they may have thought, it was a wild man of the woods. As you pass them, you see they look terrified to have come across someone in the dark woods. At least as terrified as you.

When you emerge from the tree cover, the feeling of enclosure, the rising sense of panic, passes so quickly you would swear it was

never there. If you fancied, you could convince yourself you had not succumbed to imaginary fears. If anything, you feel a bit foolish.

The wind has blown the last of the clouds to one far side of the sky and the thin moon casts a comforting light. You look back towards the block of woodland. It was not that scary, was it? You could head back in just to prove it to yourself. But not tonight. Tonight, you will read a bit before bed, or watch a comforting episode of *Time Team* on your phone before getting your head down in the van.

There is a fine line between exhilaration and panic, and it is within us all. So, when we enter a wood – fictional or real – the danger we find there is, for the most-part, that which we bring ourselves. The trees don't change us so much as we take whatever we are carrying into the woods with us, whether our anxieties and depressions, our joy and hope, our idealism or romanticism, our propensity to create narrative. The wood we enter with the lens of fear is clearly different to the one we encounter with the lens of curiosity, though we may walk beneath the same branches, crunch through the same leaf litter. And somewhere along the path, we change. Some transformation occurs before we emerge at the far edge of the wood, some alchemical process by which we are altered. The wild man of the woods will always stare out of the heart of the woods at us, and we see in him, in the eyes he co-opts on the trunks of trees, something older in ourselves staring back, something frightening and wild.

10

Way Follower

*In the workshops of traditional woodworkers in Takayama,
and a sacred forest in Shibuya City, Tokyo*

I t was somewhere north of 35 degrees Celsius in the forest on
the hillside behind the Soyuji Temple. It had been this way
for months, even high in the hills around Takayama, whose
name means high mountain in Japanese. It was hard to believe,
in the still, humid heat that had sat on much of Japan for most
of summer and which was showing no signs of shifting, that
the *Kogarashi*, the 'tree witherer' wind that comes at the end of
autumn would ever arrive. And just as there was no sign of the
autumn wind, there was no sign either of the maple's shift from
brightest green to intense red – which the Japanese call *momiji* – a
spectacle that draws tourists to the trees as religiously as do the
sakura blossoms of spring.

I had left the crowded streets of the old town and started to
climb out of the bowl in which Takayama lies, hoping to get a
better view of the city; however, when the trees closed in around me,
I found I could not see it at all from the hillside. There was no one
else walking in the graveyard, and the temple yards through which
I passed had been empty too. The only sign I saw that anyone else
had been there recently were footprints running in a line across the

In the heart of the Meiji forest.

garden of tiny stones raked into circles and arcs in the courtyard of the zen monastery through which I had passed earlier.

Sotoba, wooden stakes inscribed with prayers and invocations

Fixed to one of the trees there was a laminated note that warned walkers to keep an eye out for bears. At this time of year, there are regular reports in the papers of elderly mushroom pickers in the woods being killed by bears when the paths of one of these quiet parties crosses the other. The path wandered up the hillside and split amid squat stone pagodas, lanterns and gravestones against which sprang crops of *sotoba*, wooden stakes on which are written the names and dates of the dead, along with prayers and invocations. Several of the larger trees were tied around with ribbons of blue and yellow. Sacred trees in a sacred forest.

I came to the edge of the cemetery where the oldest graves were stacked one against the other in tight rows. Some of them were covered entirely with mosses and ferns, the faces of the meditating Buddhas carved on them just about discernible, at peace in the hot green world. Among these, somewhere, were the graves of the *Kijishi*, the nomadic woodworkers of the forest. I stopped for a while, drank warm water from my canister, and let the biting insects that had followed me up the hill settle on my neck and arms where they were exposed – there seemed no point in fighting a losing battle.

After wandering the winding, intersecting paths of the graveyard for some time, I found the carpenters' graveyard, a cemetery within a cemetery for the *Kijishi*, who worked and lived in the forests. They had been interred in a walled garden of their own, a sign of the high status the woodworkers of Takayama were afforded. The oldest of the graves dated from the seventeenth century, though the *Kijishi* were here long before that. It seemed fitting they would be buried in the forest in which they practised their craft and from which they made their livings, among the cedar trees, in a place that overlooked the temples they and their ancestors constructed with the complex, interlocking wooden joints that they had developed. I sat with the dead carpenters for a while and listened for any sound of bears in the thick forest beyond.

A few days earlier, I drove into the city with Masashi Kutsuwa, a woodworker friend of a friend who lives in nearby Gifu City and had agreed to be my guide and translator when I visited Japan. I asked him what accounted for the concentration of woodworkers here, and for the reputation the city has for being home to some of the most skilled traditional craftspeople in Japan. It was a reputation that had drawn me halfway round the world, from an exhibition titled 'The Carpenter's Line' at Japan House in London, to a city in Japan's mountainous Gifu Prefecture.

'Takayama is the largest city in Japan,' Masashi explained shortly after we entered the city.

He let the unlikely statistic hang as I tried to figure out the puzzle through the fug of jet lag, having flown into the country just hours before. After disembarking, I had travelled through the sprawling urban mass of Tokyo and I had been glad when the bullet train from Shinagawa emerged from the urban sprawl and the landscape gave way to fields and villages, and even more so when the mountains of my destination came into view. Takayama felt objectively tiny in comparison to the capital, surrounded by the densely wooded slopes of the vast area known as the Japanese Alps, even despite the growth the city had seen when Michelin awarded Takayama three stars in its first guide to Japan some sixteen years before, leading to a rush of new hotels and an influx of tourists. Eventually I gave up.

'It's just that 93 per cent of it is forest,' he continued, as if that answered everything.

The 74,000 people who live in Takayama are concentrated in a small area, though the urban centre is surrounded by over 700 square miles of dense forest in which wild boar, antelope and bears roam, all of which form part of the city, which makes Takayama the largest city in Japan by area, and by area of forest too.

Takayama is built on wood, Masashi told me, and a tradition of woodworking that stretches back at least 1,300 years. The heavily wooded, mountainous areas around Takayama were unsuitable for farming, and whereas in most areas in Japan tax was paid in the form of rice, vegetables, fish or meat, in Takayama it was paid in labour. Takayama's young men were sent to other parts of Japan to work as carpenters in cities such as Nara where they built and maintained temples and houses. Over a period of 600 years, some 50,000 carpenters from the area were sent to the city that was then the country's capital.

When they returned home, they brought with them new techniques and skills to build on those that had been developing in Takayama already for centuries, and applied them to their own city, building beautifully intricate temples and wooden buildings, refining their techniques, such as the fiendishly complex multi-angled joints – *shiguchi* – which were used to erect buildings and roofs without the use of nails. I had admired the *shiguchi* in the rafters of the temple roofs beneath which I later stood, as I made my way to the carpenters' graveyard. The master woodworkers took on apprentices – often their own sons – who learnt by watching and copying the techniques of their fathers, and so the woodcrafts of Takayama were established as being particularly fine, particularly refined, a culture created by wood.

Shiguchi *at one of Takayama's temples.*

It was a reputation from which he had benefited, Masashi said. As a woodworker who had learnt his craft in Takayama, when Masashi came to England to work as a furniture maker, he was seen as an expert by virtue of where he came from.

The second value of Takayama was in the forests themselves. It was a sign of their importance that the Edo shogunate, the national government of Japan between 1603 and 1868, established a *Jin'ya*, or government office, in the city, one of sixty built across the country in the seventeenth century. The city was administered from the *Jin'ya's tatami* mat rooms. Trials were heard there, justice doled out, taxes collected, forests managed and trees felled in the surrounding forests were recorded by the *Jin'ya's* scribes, before the logs were floated by river to the country's growing urban centres, a journey that could take up to three years. It was here I might begin to understand the city and its woodworkers, Masashi told me, and to comprehend the precarious position in which the traditional woodcrafts of Takayama find themselves.

Aside from a few multi-storey hotels, Takayama still has a low profile for a modern city. Because they were built of wood, its houses were rarely more than one or two stories high, and for centuries the *Jin'ya* housed the city's tallest tower. It was from here that government officials could look out over the work taking place across the city. Deep inside the complex, the *Jin'ya* director pulled aside a thick rope and ushered us up the narrowest of staircases to the small room at the top of the tower for us to see the city much as it would have been viewed when it was first built, the dense woodlands beyond too on the mountain slopes. Closer in, the tower also looked out over the rooftops of the complex, tiled with over half-a-million hand-cleft cedar shingles and we could see, from the small windows of the tower, carpenters at work in the heat just below its ridges, laying new tiles.

Yoshiharu Matsuyama was sitting on a low stool cleaving and shaping cypress wood roof tiles in the former rice store building, the oldest part of the *Jin'ya*. He was using an ancient technique for splitting wood into shingles, called *hegi*, working with a froe, a blade used for cleaving, and wooden mallet, with a billet of wood held in the groove of a wooden block. Closing my eyes, better to hear the creak of the wood as it split and to take in the scent of cypress that emerged from the block, it was possible to imagine the same scene being played out at any point in the building's history. When I opened my eyes again the billet had become several tiles or shingles, which Yoshiharu then proceeded to shape with another tool, a lighter, angled blade.

There are few people who can still perform this woodcraft, he explained. Although at one time there were several freelance shingle-makers in the city, the last generation had become old and died without taking on apprentices. None of them could afford to take one on. Before Yoshiharu laid his first tiles on the *Jin'ya* roof eighteen years ago, as a young carpenter, he had been a dental technician in Tokyo, though he had abandoned the city for the mountains and turned away from dentistry to focus on a traditional and obscure craft, which he had learnt by looking at the old shingles and replicating what he saw there.

Once Yoshiharu had laid his first new section of roof, Takayama's only remaining living shingle maker, who had long since retired, came to see his work. The older man, after looking at the new roof, told Yoshiharu that he should remove all the tiles he had laid. There was, in his work, the master craftsman said, a small error, barely perceptible. The mistake could not even be seen by looking at the roof from the ground, though the shingle maker had insisted.

"'If you leave false samples on the roof, they will then become the standard", he told me,' Yoshiharu said as he passed me one of the tiles he had just cut. To my eyes, it looked the simplest of things, a thin rectangular board of wood. If it was remarkable to my eyes for any reason, it was for its similarity to the thousands of others that sat in bundles behind the carpenter, waiting to be laid on the roof.

Yoshiharu started again with a new billet and talked through the process step by step. The way the tiles are split, he said, cleaved by a froe rather than sawed, leaves them with a series of grooves, down which water can run freely, and they are subtly shaped so the sides are not quite parallel, ensuring water cannot sit at the point above which the tiles overlap. Each tile must be made to the same length, width and depth, strong enough to prevent it from cracking beneath the summer sun and to withstand the weight of about 5 feet of snow that can sit on the roof in winter. So, the tiles he had laid first came off and Yoshiharu began the job again.

'Those words, "don't leave a false sample", are still in my mind when I teach this to apprentices now.'

The demonstration finished, Yoshiharu stood and we walked beneath the exposed eaves, looking up at the patchwork of tiles from below. Each tile lasts about twenty years, he explained, and they are turned and flipped over every five years to extend their life, though thousands have to be replaced each year. It is an ongoing job, expensive and time-intensive, and one which few carpenters now have the skill to do.

Roof shingles at the Jin'ya *from below.*

Beyond the shade of the eaves, a ladder led up into the scaffolding that had been erected against one of the walls and we climbed up to find one of Yoshiharu's apprentices, Shusei Kawakami, laying the new roof. The younger carpenter nodded a welcome as we emerged, though said nothing. He worked quickly, choosing tiles from a stack and pinning them down with a small hammer. As Yoshiharu talked, Shusei worked quietly. One row completed, he laid down a mark for a new with the *sumitsubo*, the carpenter's line, a tool for measuring and marking that has remained almost unchanged for centuries. I wondered at first if Shusei's silence was out of some diffidence to his boss being present, or if he was simply deep in concentration. Yoshiharu explained it was because he had a mouth full of nails.

'He holds about thirty in his mouth at any one time. As he hammers one in, he shifts the next to the front of his mouth, tip first.'

Under the hot sun, the freshly laid roof became a glowing, fragrant sea. I half-listened to the talk about hammers and alignments, the costs and difficulties of keeping the craft going, and half-watched the silent carpenter at work on the oceanic tiles, navigating a craft that stretched back over a thousand years, preserving a building to ensure it would live on for hundreds more.

The rooftops of Takayama Jin'ya.

Later, as we walked through the streets, the old town abutting the new, the modern and touristic alongside the carefully crafted, Masashi pointed out fine wood-turned cups, finished with deep red urushi wood lacquer; steam-bent boxes of cypress, crafts shaped by the landscape.

We stopped at one, a small shop, cramped even, its shelves crammed with traditional woodcarvings, intricately carved buddhas and animals. In a workshop at at the back, two men sat at low tables, their tools – chisels, gouges and knives – laid out alongside the pieces on which they were working. They were brothers, Suketomo and Sukeyoshi Tsuta. The younger of the two, who must have been in his late sixties, was carving a dragon rearing up on its hind legs, some 2 feet tall, copying the intricate design exactly from a carving, the yew wood darkened by aged by time. The skill, he explained, was in producing an exact copy, using the same skills, techniques and tools as the woodworker who had made the much older piece. The dragon, he said, was a complex carving, completed in parts, with most of the woodblock and the original swathed in cloth, while he worked on one aspect, a claw or tail.

Suketomo's carving of a dragon, based on
copying an existing carving.

Apprentices begin with simpler carvings and the apprenticeship is a long one. Woodcarvers can spend up to twelve years perfecting each of the twelve animals of the Chinese zodiac, carving the same animals over and again to develop the skills and techniques necessary to tackle more intricate, complex designs.

These woodcarvers were practising a traditional form of carving, a craft known as *ichii ittōbori*, yew woodcarving. It is a tradition that stretches back to the early nineteenth century, during the Edo period, to a carver called Matsuda Sukenaga, whose family ran a chopstick making business in Takayama. Having learnt woodcarving from the master carver, Hirata Suketomo, Matsuda started to carve with Japanese yew wood after seeing heavily painted dolls in the country's capital, Nara, establishing the tradition of *ichii ittōbori* woodcarving. He could not understand why anyone would want to paint over something made from an inherently beautiful material, and dedicated his life to creating *netsuke* – the beautiful, intricately carved toggles that were used in Tokugawa-era Japan to secure small bags to pocketless robes.

When he returned home, Matsuda began to work with the yew from the forests around Takayama which, like European yew, has dark reddish heartwood and a much lighter, contrasting sapwood. He used the contrast in the two tones of wood to create beautiful objects that made not just the most of its natural colours, but also the direction of the tight grain of wood of a tree that might be three or four hundred years old. This was wood that would develop a deep lustre over time, the objects becoming more beautiful as they aged, the carvings drawing out the yew's natural beauty.

The brothers, Suketomo and Sukeyoshi, carving in the small shop, were of the sixth generation of Matsuda Sukenaga's line and, while they were not direct descendents of the master carver, they inherited the '*suke*' of their names from Matsuda's given name, marking them out among the most traditional of Takayama's woodcarvers.

Takayama is still known across Japan for the quality of its traditional woodwork and the skill of its woodworkers, enshrined in

A netsuke *of a daruma by*
Matsuda Sukenaga (1800-1871).

the honorific title that was given to the master craftsmen of Hida, *Hida no Takumi.* Though like the roof of the *Jin'ya*, Masashi told me, as we left the small shop, the majority of this craft was under threat.

'There are three shortages: apprenticeships, tools and materials. It's a perfect storm.'

Like the tile-makers, fewer of the older generation of wood-workers in Takayama's other traditional practices are taking on apprentices. Fewer people are making the specialist tools – the planes and gouges – necessary for traditional craft and there is a national shortage of materials such as the urushi lacquer, as fewer people are cultivating urushi trees. Although there are still carpenters and woodturners working in the traditional way, in pockets across the city, all these crafts are at risk of dying out. For the moment there was a stay of execution on tile-making as a new generation of tile-makers had emerged, though in other areas of traditional carpentry many of the current generation of traditional woodworkers were approaching retirement and had no one to continue their practice.

The conversation about the future of Takayama's traditional woodworkers spans the whole city, Masashi said, as we left for a workshop on the city's outskirts. There were those few remaining, ageing woodworkers still clinging on to the traditional ways as they had been practised for centuries, and those who were looking for ways to reignite the traditional crafts, to bring them up to date for Japan as it is now.

Ayayuki Kosaka, one of the city's most celebrated woodworkers, still carves *netsuke* and highly traditional works of *ichii ittobori* for shops like the one we had visited. He comes from a long line of woodcarvers, Masashi informed me as we entered Ayayuki's workshop. He had recently split with the association of yew carvers in the city, the majority of whom were taught by Ayayuki's father, to set up a new association, one which looked to the craft's future as much as its past.

'The members of the yew wood association keep the tradition the same,' Ayayuki commented. 'They continue to make the same things using the same woods, in the same tradition and if you're a member of the association you are only allowed to use yew. When I started out, I only knew about carving with yew too, though gradually I've become interested in the characteristics of other woods.'

He passed around carvings made from katsura and cypress, two of the woods that grow in the forests around Takayama. Each wood has a different character, a different sort of beauty. There was a reverential quality to the way in which he talked about the woods he carved, a respect for the material that reminded me of one of the other woodworkers I had met, a maker of steam-bent boxes, who said of the cypress wood he used, 'If this wood is three

In this netsuke, *created from one piece of yew,
the heartwood and sapwood provide a contrast
between the frog and the coin.*

hundred years old and I plane the surface, when the new surface is revealed, it's like I'm breathing the air from almost three hundred years ago. That realization makes it truly precious each time I work with this material.'

Kiyosi Seike, author of *The Art of Japanese Joinery*, wrote that he could not help but see the divine nature of the tree when he looked at a beautifully constructed wooden building. It seemed to speak of an expression of the soul of the wood itself. The way the traditional carpenters of Takayama spoke to me of the material with which they have such a close relationship seemed to echo this sentiment, a true reverence.

A corner of Ayayuki's workshop was dedicated to his father's carvings: buddhas, animals, traditional *noh* masks, and *netsuke*. They were dark with age, having developed the lustre that aged yew takes on. This was how he learnt, he explained, by copying his father's carvings exactly.

'*Ichii ittōbori* carving will die out in the next ten years, I think,'
Ayayuki told us as we examined these pieces.' Of the twenty members of the yew carving association, none of them has taken on an
apprentice for the last ten years. The only way for it to continue is
for it to change. You have to respond to the way life is now, otherwise the tradition will die out, if you simply continue to create the
same forms over and again.'

In contrast to his father's, the carvings on Ayayuki's own shelves
looked entirely different. Here, carved frogs rode surfboards down
the faces of wooden waves and a *yokai* – a ghost from Japanese
folklore – in the form of an upturned umbrella with its arms outstretched – loomed over a more traditional carving of a frog sitting
on the end of a branch. In one of his carvings, a photorealistic
carving of a crushed drinks can, the wood took on the exact look
of thin metal.

Ayayuki took down a piece from the shelf, studying it – a plank
of wood which bulged improbably in the centre into a latticework
that looked almost impossibly delicate.

'For this craft to survive, it has to continue to develop, otherwise the people who buy it will become bored and it will die out
entirely. What matters is that we keep learning the same skills and
techniques, the same sharpness of the blades of our chisels, and we
use traditional skills to create new forms.'

To my eyes, the carving bore no resemblance to his father's
work, though when he took one of his father's carvings down, a *noh*
mask of a child's face, laying it alongside the Matrixesque piece,
and turned both pieces upside down, the relationship between the
two became clear. The technique for creating each was the same,
the way in which the front face looked as though it was thin and
delicate, an illusion created by the technique practiced on the back.
Ancient techniques used for innovative forms.

In the new association, Ayayuki had gathered together a
group of likeminded woodcarvers, all forward-thinking and
committed to retaining the skills of traditional woodworking

A latticework carving by Ayayuki Kosaka.

and developing the possibilities of the craft. It was why, after resisting for some time, he had decided to take on an apprentice and had just advertised.

It was no small thing to take on an apprentice. 'You become responsible to them, to their success, their ability to make a living from the craft you have shared with them.' He weighed the words carefully. 'You are not just ensuring they learn, but that they develop the right attitude and temperament for the job. You are responsible for ensuring the craft continues through them, and you are responsible to the woodcarvers who went before you too.'

He had received more than thirty applications for the apprenticeship. In some ways it seemed surprising. There is still a flow of young people out of the towns and villages of rural Japan towards the larger urban centres, drawn away by highly paid roles in new sectors like AI. Yet, at the same time, Masashi had told me that people working for big companies had been thinking about making changes in their lives since the economic crisis in the 1990s, and more recently the earthquake and the meltdown of the Fukushima power plant. The Covid pandemic, for many, he added, had further accelerated change of life decisions.

So, there is now a two-way migration. People unable to make a living in the world of traditional crafts are heading for the city for the higher paid jobs in technology. And those in those higher paid jobs in the cities, burnt-out or looking for work with more meaning, are leaving in search of a life that is gentler on the environment, working with traditional skills and are making for places like

Takayama to look for apprenticeships in traditional crafts, or to one of the area's woodworking schools.

There is also a corresponding growing resurgence of interest in traditional Japanese culture. Whereas many of the previous generation looked to American culture for its idea of cool and considered Japanese culture as old fashioned, the pendulum is swinging back towards that which is traditional and connected to the earth for a generation who have only ever known a precarious, rapidly heating world. The growing interest in Japanese traditions such as the tea ceremony, traditional crafts, music and clothing seems to correspond with the growing interest in the UK and Ireland for green woodworking and traditions that the previous generation have seen as deeply uncool in their youth – traditional dancing and rituals from an earlier age.

Ken'ichi Kawakami turning a bowl on a Japanese lathe.

Sitting at a low table in a restaurant later that evening, with a group of the younger generation of carpenters including the tile-maker Shusei, who was more talkative now he no longer had a mouth full of nails, Shinji Kawakami, the son of one of Takayama's few remaining master woodturners, recalled overhearing his father saying he would never take on one of his sons as an apprentice. It did not bother Shinji too much at the time, though he had always been interested in the work his father did. At the time, his ambition was to become a professional baseball player or a musician. When he left school, he and the friends with whom he was in a band packed their guitars and left Takayama for Tokyo. They knew three songs, he grinned, and they were convinced that fame awaited in the capital.

Shinji's band never made it to the heights of fame, and he returned to Takayama a few years later when his father developed stomach cancer to support him in his recovery. He took a role at one of the city's largest furniture companies. When he was made manager, though, he quit the job. It was not the life he wanted, to be sitting at a desk. The idea of following in his father and grandfather's footsteps came back to him, but when he took the apprenticeship form to his father, he refused Shinji. They had not spoken about it again since.

I had met Shinji's father, Ken'ichi Kawakami, earlier at his workshop on the city's outskirts. Ken'ichi was an energetic man, with a broad and generous smile as he showed me the woods he used, the gouges, callipers and files he had made himself and the Japanese lathe on which he performed his craft.

A woodworker's tools, he explained, become an extension of their body, so it made sense that he would learn to forge them himself. The pleasure with which he talked about his craft was magnified when he sat at his lathe. As soon as he was seated and loaded a walnut blank onto the lathe, he became entirely absorbed. He worked with a speed and lightness of touch that spoke of an intimate relationship with machine, materials and tools. When he finished, just minutes later, he pressed the bowl into my hands, along with two fine-walled cedar sake cups, insistent that I should take them, examples of the fine craft to which he had dedicated his life.

I could not help but bring up that I had heard he had refused to take his son on as apprentice, that I was surprised he would not want to pass on the skills of which he was clearly so proud.

'I was happy when he asked me,' he replied. 'Though at the same time, I wanted him to see the reality of the situation. Look at the lacquerware shops – none of the families who run those shops wants their children to become the successor to their businesses. And the same is true of the urushi workers. None of them want their children to follow in their footsteps. Anyway, I'm too old to become master to an apprentice now.'

Of the three remaining members of the association of wood-turners in Takayama still alive, Ken'ichi, at seventy-three, is the youngest. The others are in their eighties now and all of them have concluded that, while it was once sought after, the demand for this craft has been in decline for years. It is dying out.

The woodturner picked up from his desk the cup from which he drank his daily coffee, made from cypress he had turned some forty years earlier and coated with deep red urushi lacquer. 'You can use a cup like this for life.'

It is an object that represents a tradition and the development of rare skill, though one for which there is a diminishing demand. Some years ago, he said, he was employed to create presents for the computer company IBM, given to staff in recognition of long service, retirement or special achievements. At its peak, the computer firm commissioned 600 bowls and cups from him a year but they have, more recently, turned to catalogues for more generic, more modern presents. It was indicative of a broader trend. In a few years, it seems there will be no demand for it at all, this tradition that stretchs back thousands of years, beyond woodturners like Ken'ichi and his father, with their electric lathes, back past the turners, who carved bowls by foot-powered lathes, to the earliest woodturners, who powered their lathes by hand, one person pulling a rope to turn the cylinder and the other carving, to the ancient *Kijishi* who are buried in the forest above the city.

As he was telling us about the decline in traditional crafts, he took down from a shelf a stack of bowls Shinji had turned and passed them around with paternal pride. He showed us the workstation he had set up for his son, at which he had taught him to turn bowls. When he retired, all this would become Shinji's, he said, and his son could make his own decisions then, though nothing would change his mind about the apprenticeship.

'He could do it as a hobby or at the weekend,' Ken'ichi said. 'But not as a career. He should get a proper job.'

It is a dilemma for our times, the balance between a job with meaning, with which it is difficult to make a living, and one that provides money but little satisfaction. Traditional crafts, though they may be precarious in terms of making a living, often have encoded within them values that make them worth pursuing in terms of a life well lived, values of quality, patience and persistence. They are typified by skill and purpose, the creation of physical objects by hand, objects with meaning and use, based on skills developed over centuries. In short, it is work with soul.

Back at the restaurant, Shusei took from his bag one of the wooden tiles he had made which, no good for the roof for some almost imperceptible reason, he had coated with urushi lacquer and made into a serving dish. It was no longer okay to waste material, he said, and this was a way of using the same techniques for a different purpose, another way of making his craft pay. He transferred the next dish that arrived at our table onto the lacquered tile and photographed it for his social media accounts.

Shinji was telling us about his plans to turn bowls and cups and to coat them in bright colours to suit today's tastes – yellows and blue neons to match neon times. As he talked to us about the possibilities of using fast-growing woods like bamboo as well as older timbers like the cypress and walnut his father used, wrapped up in his dreams for the bowls he would turn, it became possible to see father in son, a new generation trying to keep old techniques alive, undimmed by the challenges ahead.

The torii *gates at the Meiji Temple, Tokyo.*

After I left Takayama, I spent two days wandering the streets of Tokyo, attempting to keep in the shade of the high rises. After the mountains and forests of Takayama, the city was a shock. I was carried along by the crowds in Akihabara, Tokyo's electric city, with its walls of screens, its neon and flashing lights, and walked, dazed, through the intensity of the fashionable district of Harajuku. I stumbled onto the Shibuya Scramble Crossing, the busiest junction in the world, at which two-and-a-half million people cross each day, swept by tides of commuters and shoppers, tour guides and tourists. There were protesters there too, a long line of young people carrying placards demanding action on climate crisis, though they too were swept up in the currents of the city, their chants absorbed into the louder rumblings of traffic.

I was flagging when I came across the enormous *torii*, the wooden temple gates, of Tokyo's Meiji Jingu, or Meiji Shrine. Here, more than anywhere I had seen, the temple gates – a symbolic transition point marking a shift from the secular space to the sacred – felt charged, with the traffic roaring behind me and the trees thick ahead. As I had in Takayama, I left the city for the trees, though here I felt an acute sense of inversion as I entered the small forest in the centre of a vast city.

Beyond the gates, the clamour of Tokyo fell away almost immediately, absorbed by the canopy. The sound of cars and crowds were replaced by those of birds and insects, the trees acting as a sound curtain so effective that it was difficult to accept the contrast for the first few minutes, and to believe that the busiest intersection in the world was less than mile away. There were few other people on the wide avenue through the forest towards the central complex of one of the capital's most well-known Shintō shrines, and those who

The sacred forest surrounding the Meiji Temple, in the heart of Tokyo.

were walking there were mostly silent or talked *sotto voce* in order not to disturb the peace, tourists and business people, presumably on lunch breaks, young students carrying the longbows that marked them out as practitioners of traditional archery, elaborately dressed men and women on their way to weddings at the shrine.

Although it is by no means an old shrine – it was built in the early twentieth century – Meiji Jingu was designed as an eternal forest, a statement of Shintōism's relationship to *kami*, to the spirit of nature, the trees chosen for the way they would look in a hundred or two hundred years. As is the case with most Shintō shrines, most of it is off-limits to walkers, its visitors keeping to the paths.

The 175-acre forest contains 234 species of trees, 100,000 of which were donated by people across Japan. Planting began in 1915, ending five years later in 1920. Although the shrine buildings were destroyed in the Second World War, in the firebombing that razed much of Tokyo, a good deal of forest survived, and it is now being left to regenerate naturally.

Shintōism imbues ancient trees with meaning, as the home of spirits, to be revered and protected. When I asked Masashi about it, he said that many Japanese people no longer consider themselves to be particularly religious, though they continue to visit Shintō shrines and Buddhist temples on special occasions and holidays, and the residual practice of worshipping, or at least respecting, ancient trees continues. Truth told, the walkers in the woods around the Meiji temple complex were as likely to be engaging in *shinrin-yoku*, forest bathing, as they were praying at the temple, in the knowledge that spending time around trees influences us, our mental states and behaviours. *Shinrin-yoku* is a legacy of Shintōism, one that has travelled far beyond the borders of the Japanese archipelago.

It is a sign of the importance Japanese culture places on its woodlands that there are forests within the country's capital city where space is at a premium, natural places that are allowed to develop in ways that are not to do with increasing profit.

The UK shares much with Japan. We are both island archipelagos of roughly the same size, with similar climates and bio-systems. Historically, too, there are similarities, with our monarchies and our sometimes problematic relationship to a larger continent on our doorstep; however, in our relationships with trees we diverge. The UK has a paltry 13 per cent woodland cover, yet almost 70 per cent of Japan is forested.

At the centre of the complex, the shrine was busy with weddings and tourists. From the shade of one of the complex's sacred trees, I watched the intermingling of tourists and the workers from Tokyo in the courtyard, and the slow wedding processions, the ornately dressed brides, grooms and their wedding parties, sweating in the full sun before they reached the shade of the central shrine.

To either side of the main shrine there were *shinboku*, sacred trees where groups filming and photographing the wedding parties stood. Two of these, named *meoto-kusu* – the marriage trees – stand close to one another, connected by and wrapped around with *shimenawa* rope, a sign of their spiritual importance. They are considered shrines in their own rights. These camphor trees were burnt in the firebombing of 1945, but survived and regrew and it is easy to see why they are considered sacred. They stand together but not too close, their trunks separate and their branches touching so that from some angles they might resemble a single tree. As such, they bear a resemblance to the way Kahlil Gibran writes of love in *The Prophet*. 'And stand together yet not too near together,' he writes, 'For the pillars of the temple stand apart, And the oak tree and the cypress grow not in each other's shadow'. The *meoto-kusu* have become the focus of a popular pilgrimage for those who wish to pray for their own relationships and the relationships of those close to them.

The sun was intense in the temple courtyard and I kept to the shade of the sacred trees, thinking again of the *Kogarashi* wind, which would have been welcome at that moment and which signals the end of autumn, marking a moment of change. At the other end of the year, *Zan'ou* is the Japanese word used in haiku or tanka poetry to describe cherry blossom left on the branches of the tree, marking the end of the spring. Both are defined by a word for which we have no direct English translation, *Mikkaminumanosakura*, roughly 'the cherry blossoms have all fallen since I took my eyes off them three days ago', used to describe change that occurs suddenly and intensely.

Standing in the shade of the *meoto-kusu*, I found myself thinking about the sudden and intense changes that are occurring to our trees and woodlands. I thought of the traditional woodworkers of Takayama who find themselves at a crossroads, a moment of change, at a point at which they must adapt their traditional crafts for the world as it is now, and choose the elements of the past to retain, those they will discard, and those they will develop. I saw in them a microcosm of all of our relationships with wood and with trees. Like the *Hida no Takumi*, we shaped and were shaped by trees and woodlands and, in shaping the woodlands around us, we shaped our cultures.

Now, finding our forests and woodlands in crisis, we find ourselves at a crossroads at which we must work out a new relationship with them, in need of a new way, perhaps one in which we revere the spirits of trees far more than we currently do, in which we develop our practices of planting and protecting, developing and nourishing, in which we plant more eternal forests, and respect the wood we do use, making of it things to cherish, beautiful things that will endure for a time. If I prayed for anything at the shrine of the marriage trees, it was that we might find the means to follow that way.

The Meiji Temple marriage trees.

11

Seed Collector

Ireland's ancient trees and a hidden fragment of
oceanic rainforest in County Clare, Ireland

'The Irish are a forest people without a forest,' Jeremy said as we climbed into his beat-up van. 'You can still find that forest culture kicking around in the music, the dancing and crafts. You can find it there in the language and the stories. All of it points to an indigenous forest culture, though the forest itself has been deeply forgotten. You can only find the old growth forest in these small fragments and pockets now.'

It was one of these few remaining fragments of ancient woodland that are found on the far fringes of the country's west coast to which we were heading, in search of the roots of one particular tree.

I had experienced something of how deeply forgotten Ireland's woodlands are just a few hours earlier when, lost on the drive west from Dublin, I had flagged down a walker in the village of Ennistymon and asked for directions for my destination, the charity Hometree. The man drew a blank and asked what Hometree was. When I replied it is a charity dedicated to restoring Ireland's great Atlantic rainforest, he laughed: 'A rainforest, in County Clare? There are few enough trees in Ireland, and nearly none in Clare.'

When I recounted this in the van, Jeremy nodded. It is a popular perception that Clare has few trees, though it is actually one of the most wooded of Ireland's counties. It's just that many of the remaining woodlands are hidden, overlooked or ignored.

There are few people in Ireland who know these rare fragments and pockets as well as Jeremy Turkington, Hometree's seed collector. He is one of a small group of conservationists operating out of the charity's base on the fringe of County Clare, attempting to tip the balance through growing trees from seeds found in these ancient fragments, in an attempt to let the ancient Atlantic rainforest get a foothold again in a country where it is currently on the brink of total collapse.

In general, though, the man I had flagged down was right, Jeremy agreed. Ireland is one of the least forested countries in Europe. Ireland rivals only Iceland for lack of trees, with woodland

covering just 11 per cent of the land, compared with 70 per cent forest cover in countries like Finland and Sweden. And it is easy to see why County Clare, in particular, might be considered tree-less. The limestone pavement of the Burren, one of the largest expanses of karst in Europe, dominates much of north-west Clare and is famously barren, in terms of woodland at least, much of the vegetation being confined to grimes and clints, thin fissures in the rock between which Arctic alpine plants grow.

Walking across the stark, stunning landscape of the Burren now, it is difficult to imagine it as it once was, covered with pine, hazel and yew, huge forests inhabited by bears, the skeletons of which have been found in caves on the Burren, such as those discovered at nearby Aillwee. These bears once roamed the great forests of Ireland and the Irish were hunter-gatherers on the forest's edge, before they became farmers some 2,500 years ago and began to clear the land for grazing and growing.

The legacy of this shift is still felt on the Burren, where sheep and goats graze year round, keeping check on any saplings that might spring up, and the memory of the forests that covered the karst is kept confined to the pollen record.

On the way through the village, we stopped for coffee at a bakery and while we were waiting, a woman, sitting by the door, asked us what we were doing with our day. She laughed when she heard we were on our way out to explore a patch of ancient woodland.

'What woods?' she responded. 'The English cut down all our woods.'

The history of trees in Ireland is complex and controversial, Jeremy told me as we left the bakery. The memory of the damage done when the English Crown confiscated huge swathes of land owned by Irish Catholics during the Plantations of the sixteenth and seventeenth centuries is still very much still alive. In County Clare, where the Cromwellian invasion was particularly brutal, one soldier is reputed to have said of the Burren, it was: 'a country where there is not water enough to drown a man, wood enough to hang one, nor earth enough to bury one . . . yet their cattle are very fat'. And there's a grim sort of irony, Jeremy commented, in the fact it was not the English who cut down the trees – some of the most established of Ireland's remaining woodlands are on the former or remaining large estates that were not enclosed when the Irish gained the right to buy their own land back – it was more the effects the Plantations had on Ireland that led to the deforestation of a forest people.

A mile or so outside Ennistymon, he pulled the car over at the roadside and we looked out over a patchwork of small fields that stretched out to the sea at Lahinch, on the north-west coast of County Clare. In just this small area, he told me, there will be tens of different landowners. Each of the compact fields here may be owned by a different family.

The tight patchwork field system across much of Ireland is a result of a series of Land Acts of the late nineteenth century, which gave tenants the right to buy back the land on which they worked. By the beginning of the twentieth century, tenant farmers had bought back over two-and-a-half million acres of land from often absentee English landlords. In addition, in 1917, tenant farmers were given the right to buy small areas of land to grow their own food, with many buying a single field, all they could afford. It was the pressure to make each of these fields productive that led to the majority of the remaining trees being felled, leading to a situation in the late 1920s in which just over 1 per cent of Ireland was covered with arboreals.

'Land ownership's a sensitive topic around here,' he continued. 'As soon as you mention trees, that equals land, which equals oppression. And land in Ireland is owned by so many different people. In mainland Europe, land changes hands about every fifteen years – in Ireland, it's every 300 years. There's a genetic cell memory in Irish people about what it took to clear the land, the blood, sweat and tears that went into making these fields.'

This complex history makes getting ecological messages out more difficult. Histories driven by memories of oppression and the fight for the right to determine one's own future are powerful narratives with long lives.

'Those narratives need to be challenged, though,' he said. 'There are no fish in the rivers, hedges are still being ripped out, bogs are being drained and we're there singing rebel songs at twelve o'clock in the pub and thinking this is Ireland. But it's being destroyed every day. It's being eroded. There's so much land in Ireland that could be rewooded, we've just got to get on with it. So much of it is about us getting over our histories.'

Jeremy comes from people who got on with things in places where the narrative was complex and convoluted, where controversy was never far off. He talked about growing up in Northern Ireland, where his parents were the first people to set up an integrated school for children from Protestant and Catholic backgrounds, and the battle they had in the nineties just to get people from the same religion into the same school.

'This could all be different though.' He gestured towards one of the fields ahead. 'There's a seed bank already in that soil that would come back if you just took the sheep off the field.'

We turned away from the patchwork of fields to look up at the hillside behind us. This bank was an example of the way modern Ireland treated its remaining forests. This thin band of oaks, showing light grey in their winter guise, clinging to the hillside, was one of the rare pockets he had talked about.

'My job is to find these tiny fragments of ancient Irish forest, the 5 per cent of 1 per cent remaining that Oliver Rackham talked about, and collect from those trees and from that stock, to ensure continuity,' he explained.

What we were looking at was an example of a hyper-oceanic rainforest on a shale bed, hiding in plain sight by the side of the road. In view of the Atlantic Ocean, it is permanently wet here, never getting too warm nor too cold, the perfect environment for rainforest, the trees so wind-pruned that the canopy stands at just 4 or 5 feet tall.

We scrambled up the hillside and looked down, momentarily giant-like, on the dull silver of the canopy of dwarfed sessile oak with their tentacle branches and sprawling trunks, a picture punctuated by the occasional rowan or willow, the forest floor a rich bed of woodrush, one of the indicators that this is a truly ancient woodland. It was a shock to see, from this vantage point, that beyond the small strip of woodland, the landscape of the hillside was dominated by a huge shale quarry.

'This is typical Ireland and how much we appreciate our ancient woodlands,' Jeremy waved at the landscape of blasted rock onto which we were now looking. 'They've quarried the entire centre out of the woodland. All of that oak that would have been growing there for centuries and now it's a quarry for shale, with just a tiny fragment of oak hanging on to the side.'

Many people passing would most likely see that whole rainforest as scrub, useful for nothing other than digging up as the need for more shale grew, though within the seeds of these trees was contained all the information they needed to thrive in this place, a result of the centuries they have endured here.

According to Jeremy, the ideal situation, looking back again at the fields between the forest and the sea, would be to buy the land, take all the herbivores off it, fence it off, right to the coast and let it regenerate, though getting the tens of land owners – many of whom may have their own long-standing arguments ongoing – to agree to plant trees or to sell the land for reforestation, might be a tall order. If they could buy the quarry too, it would eventually return to rainforest, the pits, once they had been cleared of the rubbish dumped in them, filling with water and becoming rich habitats.

The landowners were reachable. They just had to be convinced and buy into stories they understood. Often, Jeremy told me, it took a memory to hook them in. In one project, Hare's Corner, run by the Burrenbeo Trust, Jeremy works with farmers to fence off a corner of their fields to allow for a more natural landscape to sit alongside their productive land, planted with native broadleaf

Hyper-oceanic oaks.

trees. 'Hares' Corner' is an old farming expression he could remember his grandfather using for the area in which they couldn't get machines, so they would just leave it wild. It was a term other farmers could connect to, a cultural memory that could be tapped.

One of the answers to the intractable problem of the treeless landscape lies with the children of the landowners. As land in Ireland does not change hands often, the likelihood is that the children currently in school will inherit these parcels of land and, being younger, they may be more open to ideas of change. It is important, in Jeremy's words, to get them 'when they are still open to wild things'.

By the van, he told me about a school project in which he went out seed collecting with children, who were aged ten. Subsequently, they grew saplings in the classroom from those seeds for two years, at which point the same children took them back out to plant, giving them a sort of ownership, a knowledge of the land and a different sort of connection to it than the one their parents had, one in which trees featured more prominently.

'I'm at the stage now where I'm seeing these children bringing their parents round to the idea,' he commented, 'these hardened, almost anti-environmentalists. Their kids have seen this works and that the trees are still there. Those children are the ones who are going to be taking over that land, though now I have parents coming to me asking how they can get involved too.'

Rowan seed.

As we drove on, I noticed Jeremy was making small notes, marking trees as we passed them, the ones he knew, the places from which he had collected seeds before. At this time of year, mid-November, most broadleaf trees had gone into dormancy, though the rowan trees were heavy with seed, and he scouted two that we would stop by and collect from the next day, and some hawthorns too, their brightest red seeds ready to harvest.

Parking the van again, we climbed a fence and it became clear why Jeremy had insisted we stop to pick up some full length welling- tons on the way. As I jumped down from the fence into the field, I sank up to my calves. The bog through which we would pass was bordered on two sides by conifer plantations, the road behind us and – though it was still out of sight from here – ahead of us was another small area of temperate rainforest. I should watch my step, Jeremy said. Step on the wrong piece of ground here and I would find myself eyeball deep in the bog. It was a lesson he had learnt by experience and one I was to learn too just a minute later when I missed my step and ended up face down in the water.

There is no map of these pockets of ancient forest, no definitive list. It lives in the heads of those who seek them out and care for them, those who stop the car to take a look at what might appear at first to be a patch of scrub land, or an inaccessible stand of trees in a valley in the far corner of a field. Like all maps, it is one that includes the details relevant for the one who uses it: the safe path through the blanket bog, where in the thick tangle of hawthorn there might be an entry point, landowners who were amenable to visits like ours.

Constructing the map is an art, as Jeremy explained it to me, one with many starting points. One of these might be the names of places, many of which are associated with the native trees of Ireland, names that give hints about the geography, geology and topology of a place. So, places with derry (and its relatives, *dare*, *duire* and *doire*) in the name are associated with oak woods. Kildare is the church of the oak, Derry and Derrylanan both oak groves. Col means hazel, so you'll know there's a good chance of finding hazel there, Mayo means the plane of yew, Cuileannach is the place of hollies, Draigneach, the place of blackthorns. Some of these are ghost names, a memory of what was once there, though others are markers that these trees may still be there somewhere, maybe well-hidden, but holding on.

Ireland was well mapped in the 1800s, and it is now possible to overlay those maps with satellite imagery to see better if the areas named after trees still have their woodlands. This gives you a good idea where you might look, though the last piece of the puzzle, Jeremy told me, is usually found by delving back into Ireland's forest culture.

In this game, local knowledge is everything. As in England, there is no right to roam in Ireland, and much of Jeremy's work involves talking to landowners and gaining the necessary permissions to collect seed in these out-of-the way woodlands. If he does not know the area or the people there, the first place he heads is to the pub – to the musicians' table rather than the bar.

'If you can play an instrument, you can go anywhere.'

Jeremy plays the traditional Irish frame drum, the *bodhràn* and looks out for traditional Irish music sessions to join when he is travelling. An instrument is a ticket into a community that revolves around the forest culture that led to the instruments of Irish trad music, the *bodhràn* made of ash, fiddle of spruce, Irish harp of willow.

'If you want to know where the old woodlands are, get involved in a session. In most of the places I collect seeds, there are people locally who care for those woodlands. You usually meet them in sessions,' he explained. 'The temperate seed zone for one tree nursery I worked for in Northern Ireland is the whole of Ulster, all the west coast of Scotland and all the islands in between, so if we needed acorns and I didn't know an area, I would go into a session, say on the Isle of Skye, and play a bit of music. People always want to know what you're doing there and when you tell them, that's it, you'll find within an hour you'll have found someone who knows where those trees are, happy to take you there, happy to keep you informed. Or they'll know someone [else] who can help you.'

We moved carefully through the bog to the rhythm of the water sucking around our boots, between the waterways and the beds of sphagnum moss, around the small herd of short horn cattle that somehow managed to survive in the constant wet.

Jeremy has been seed collecting for twenty years now. He has collected from all over Ireland, and grown hundreds of thousands of trees, many of which he has returned to grow alongside the mother tree from which he took the seed. Over that time, he said, you get a sense of how trees will behave.

'You get a feel for when a tree is going to drop seed and when it does you just get completely obsessed with getting that particular thing,' he told me, as we made our way across the bog. 'Earlier this year I was travelling around Atlantic hazel woods, and I just had a pure obsession for hazel for a good couple of months. Then you move on to the next thing.'

When we had met at Hometree's base, he had shown me the results of his recent seed collecting in the charity's polytunnels and tree nurseries, in the crates of alder and spindle seeds drying out by the woodburner, in sealed boxes in fridges and in seed beds, where dormant seeds are protected until it is time to propagate them. Each type of seed is treated in a different way, some requiring intricate methods for encouraging them to propagate, like those that needed to be dried out before they can be brought on.

Walking to the van, I had seen saplings grown from the acorns he had collected from the Belvoir Oak in Belfast, thought to be the oldest tree in Northern Ireland and now little more than a huge hollowed out bowl, with a tiny branch that, each year, produces a few acorns. It had seventeen acorns on it one year and, having collected them all, Jeremy had managed to grow sixteen trees from them.

Another oak sapling, growing slowly in the lee of a boundary wall was one grown from acorns of the iconic Brian Boru oak at Tuamgraney. Named after the first king who could properly lay claim to rule over the whole island of Ireland, the thousand-year-old tree, some 26 feet around at the base, is the last remnant of the

ancient wildwood of Suídain in the Sliabh Aughty Mountains of
East Clare and south-east Galway. The forest is now long gone,
replaced with commercial plantations of sitka spruce and Douglas
fir, the forest decimated for charcoal to fuel the ironworks. Where
the English had developed a culture of coppicing for charcoal, the
same was not true of the Irish, and old growth woodlands here fell
victim to the furnaces of the Industrial Revolution.

In other parts of the field there were Burren pines, a species
thought to be extinct until recently, when a pocket of the only
Irish indigenous pine was found growing on the Burren, and
Irish whitebeams, which are endemic to Ireland. They were on his
mind as the previous week, Jeremy had been working in Killarney
National Park.

'There's a whitebeam called *Sorbus scannelliana*. It's endemic to
Killarney and there are only two of them, both of which grow on
islands in the middle of the national park.'

These trees are some of the rarest in the world with only five
individual plants known to be alive. The park manager had been
trying to propagate them from seed for six years, with no success,
so they had hatched a plan that Jeremy was going to take grafts
from the existing trees to help ensure their survival. The plan was
to row out to the islands on the remote lake in January to collect
the grafts, while the trees were dormant, and preserve them until
the sap started to rise in the spring.

The way Jeremy talked about collecting seeds, grafts and
cuttings, reminded me of the collectors of shells, driftwood and
wreck I had met while researching my last book, *The Draw of the
Sea*, about the relationship between the people of Cornwall and
Scilly and their coastlines.

Jeremy nodded when I put this to him. There is a small, dispersed
community of seed collectors and conservationists across Ireland
who share his passion and obsess over the seeds they have and
the ones they would like to have. There is no national network for
this in Ireland, but these individuals comprise an informal group,

people who are passionate about preserving species that have all the information about how to live in that particular place encoded in their genes. They meet up occasionally and swap stories of new finds, and rare seeds.

'It's like swapping Pokémon cards,' he laughed. 'We're all collectors.'

The cuttings from the rare whitebeam would be like getting one of those 'special cards', only instead of cards, what they are collecting and exchanging is variety, preserving the genetic diversity of Ireland's woodlands.

Coming to the edge of the bog, we stopped by some small hummocks, the lichen and moss-covered stumps of vast Scots pines that once stood here. From here, with the monocultural commercial forestry plantations to either side, the bog behind and a recently clear-felled hillside ahead, its pine logs piled high on the bare slopes, we looked across the canopy of another small corridor of temperate rainforest.

This is typical. The short horn cattle in the bog are low in terms of numbers, but they're a limiting factor for the ancient forest, keeping it from making progress any further up the hillside and, on the other side, the commercial forestry has little interest in allowing the oak forest to regenerate in the clear-felled land.

'That's the seed source we have to work with. It's been backed into a tiny pocket here. The only reason this patch is here is this field is privately owned, and it's too steep down there for the cattle to graze.'

The ideal situation, Jeremy continued, would be if the forestry company who had clear-felled the land on the other side of the forest allowed the rainforest room to spread itself out, though these trees would be no good for a 'productive' forest. It's a case of not all woodlands being equally beneficial.

The dangers these small fragments of rainforest face are numerous. Hemmed in on all sides by agriculture, commercial forestry and roads, they are under attack by agricultural runoff and glyphosate, pushed out by encroaching rhododendron and sika deer, introduced by wealthy landowners to hunt, and nibbled by goats and sheep.

One of the hidden dangers, though, is that, cut off from other similar forests, the trees inbreed by necessity. The quality of this seed, the product of a lack of genetic diversity, is poor, and because of that fewer grow into new trees, there is less food for the animals that live in these woodlands and the whole ecosystem is beginning to collapse. From our vantage point above the canopy, the fragment of rainforest looked perilously fragile.

'Nature wants complexity and diversity. These trees are in desperate need of fresh pollen. That's one of the reasons for making seed orchards, planting it all together and getting really good diversity and a good quality of seed. It's the reason I'm always looking out for new woodlands,' Jeremy ended.

It was late autumn and the leaves in the canopy had already fallen, so we were looking down on grey branches. We circled the walls of an Iron Age hill fort on the edge of the bog before scrambling down the steep ravine into the forest itself, where we found ourselves surrounded by brightest green, branches thick with moss, in total contrast to the view from above. Climbing down into the forest, was something alike to what I imagine entering Narnia or Mirkwood might be – the vividness of the greens, the lushness of the understory, all lichen and fern, fungi and epiphyte, bromeliad and bryophyte. The first patch of forest into which we dropped was mostly hazel, which gave way to gnarled sessile oaks, their branches outstretched in twisting spirals. The forest floor a labyrinth of roots, living matter and decay, the tangle of the understorey. I am always struck, in these woodlands, at the intensity of colour, the complexity of life concentrated in a small area, though it should not be a surprise: they are the most biodiverse landscapes on these islands. Walking in this hyperreal, fantastical environment, it became easy to see how these forests inspire fantasy landscapes – trees on which other trees grow, each an epic landscape in itself.

It is easy to see how they inspired our ancestors too.

These trees are deeply embedded in the culture, so much so that Irish folklore has it that women were created from rowan trees and men from alder. In the *Dindshenchas*, the 'Lore of Places', a collection of early Irish poems, prose, legends and myths that describe the history and the etymology of place names across Ireland, there were five sacred trees: three of ash, one of oak and one yew and the ancient poem cycles are rich with talk of trees.

As we scrambled over roots and under branches, we talked too about the ways in which trees are embedded in the Irish language itself, or at least in its precursor, Ogham, the old Celtic alphabet.

A good friend of Jeremy's had died recently, he told me, the wood sculptor and activist Andrew St Ledger. A group of Andrew's friends, led by a professional local basketmaker, had woven him an elaborate wicker casket in which he would take his final journey and, on the top of the coffin, there was a slab of wood with his name inscribed in Ogham, a nod towards the tree culture in which he was embedded.

A good thousand years older than English, Ogham is one of the oldest alphabets in Europe. It spread from Ireland to become the basis of the language of the Bardic cultures of the Scottish Highland clans. With the associations between each of the letters of the alphabet and a tree, it is language learnt by looking at the world. It is a language that speaks to ancient cultural connections and relationships between people and trees, between people and the landscape in which they were embedded.

The poet Robert Graves believed the Ogham alphabet encoded beliefs that originated from sometime in the Stone Age, possibly in the Middle East, which made its way across continents, across the centuries, and was taken up by the druidic and Celtic peoples of Britain and Ireland. It was Graves who proposed that the order of the letters made up a kind of seasonal calendar of tree magic, and though some of Graves' scholarship has been disputed, many of the letters clearly correspond to trees. One of my favourite aspects of Ogham are the *bríathograms*, two-word kennings from early Irish literature that explain the meanings of the names of the letters of the Ogham alphabet. So, the Ogham letter for C, *Coll*, represents hazel, and corresponds, in the *Briatharogam Maic ind Óc* in terms of the kenning *carae blóesc*, friend of nutshells.

Even the written form of Ogham relates to trees, the symbols based on a trunk with different numbers of branches on each side.

This patch of woodland is particularly interesting, Jeremy told me, in part because this forest of oak, holly and hazel also contains one of the only aspen trees in West Clare, a species found in Ireland for over 10,000 years.

Aspens are particularly rare as they are not considered productive for either timber or firewood, though more than that, as a result of the fact they are dioecious, with male and female catkins growing on separate trees. Dispersed by the wind and elusive, it is difficult seed to collect and it has just a few days from when it leaves the parent tree to find suitable ground in which to germinate.

Aspens need perfect conditions to produce and pollinate seeds and as they rely on wind pollination, if there is no tree of the opposite sex nearby, reproduction is all but impossible, and it becomes clear why they are under pressure. After half-an-hour scrambling around happily on the steep-sided valley, Jeremy brought us back out to the bog: we had been so deep in conversation, we had missed the tree we were looking for entirely, so we walked along the fringe of the forest until he spotted three tall stems that stood above the oaks and hazels.

We dropped back down into the woods and found the aspen sitting in the boggiest ground at the foot of the valley. There is no evidence of native aspens growing through reproduction for hundreds of years, he said, as he showed me the trunks and the mother tree. Aspens, like cherries and elm, have the ability to put up suckers from their roots, some at a fair distance from the original tree, so all the aspens in this patch of woodland were really all simply clones of the same tree. Just a few remaining native aspens have managed to hold on through putting out and growing suckers of themselves.

Jeremy knelt, dug around in the wet earth for a while and followed the root paths along to where small stems were shooting up from the ground.

'They can live for thousands of years, just doing this.'

As they could clone themselves rather than reproduce, the plan was to take root cuttings from aspens in other parts of Ireland and plant them close to one another, mixing them up so there was at least a chance of getting a male and female in the same place. As Jeremy was talking, he was breaking off small sections of roots, which we were to take back to the nursery where they would be planted and tended until they were ready to be returned to the woods, along with the others.

Hands black with the rich earth, I emerged again with Jeremy from the forest. We made our way back across the sodden field, picking our way out of it as though we were navigating a wall-less labyrinth, clutching the prize found at its heart.

Later, I drove across to Ennis to listen to a traditional Irish session I had heard was on that evening. I have been to scores of trad sessions, listening to the musicians play instruments of wood – squeeze box, fiddle, flute and Irish *bouzouki*, an instrument that, while of Greek origin, has been a staple of the Irish music scene since the 1960s. That night, I listened for traces of the forest culture Jeremy had talked about as the musicians spun their tunes.

When I arrived, it was still early. Take a seat, the barman said. Anywhere you like, though not that one, he pointed, that table there is for the musicians.

The pub began to fill. Others had had the same idea in the early dark of a November evening. At some point, after a few drinks had been drunk, a few conversations had, one of the musicians, a squeeze box player sitting at the musician's table, started up a tune. There was no announcement. It began by tacit agreement, a sense that now was the right time to start playing. More instruments appeared from beneath tables – violins and a *bouzouki*, and the tune gathered pace and volume, the different instruments slotting into the mix. No one called for quiet, but quiet fell, for a while at least, until the music was loud enough to accept conversation and the noise in the room rose again until the music had become something else, part of the room's tapestry. More musicians arrived and the pile of instrument cases on the floor grew. The newly arrived flautists and fiddlers dipped in and out of the tunes, sitting back and listening to some, diving into others.

There was no dancing, though there was swaying at tables, and a kind of transfixed look on the eyes of the listeners, drawn in by the reels and jigs, the hornpipes, polkas and dances. At some point, after a few more pints had been taken, some, caught up, found their eyes glassy and mirror-like, moved in a way you know they would not be able to explain if you were to ask them. It can happen in other places, and with other genres of music, but there is something about the intimacy of traditional music, the proximity of the player to audience, the fluidity between them, the directness of it all – there were no microphones nor amplifiers here, just instruments and ears – that has a unique power to move.

No one was recording this, nor filming it. You had to be there.

A red-faced man from Tipperary sidled over to the musicians and after a short discussion began to sing, straight-backed, in the old way, accompanied by the button accordionist. His voice filled the pub and silence fell until the last notes faded. A woman sitting at the bar cried and apologized for crying. That song was her husband's favourite, she said. A man sitting along from her stared, glassy eyed into his pint. The lament finished, the squeezebox player picked up the pace and I watched the musicians as they watched each other, anticipating the next shifts and the repeats, for the swells and dips, for tempo and pace, though mostly I watched the watchers. It is a kind of magic, watching the effect music has on an audience, watching waves of emotion run through a crowd through nothing more than vibrations caused by plucked strings over a wooden sound box and air blown through wooden tubes, thumps on the skin of a wooden-framed drum.

Driving back across the Burren, the night sky was completely clear, the first time it had been that way since I had arrived. In the small wood cabin in the heart of Hometree, I set the woodburner on and hung my clothes by it to dry. I sat in the spindle-backed chair and listened to the rain battering against the windows, a squall that blew in without warning from the Atlantic. Mice scrabbled in the roof, and I studied the flames of

the fire. Late in the evening, after the rain had passed, I emerged
to see a comet flare across the sky, its tail streaming behind it. It
seemed consistent with a day spent in a folkloric woodland. A
fitting conclusion.

One of the ancient bardic names for Ireland was *Inis na bhfiodh-
bhadh*, the island of the sacred trees. They are still there, the island's
sacred trees, though in small pockets, and in seeds lying dormant
in fields, and in music and songs, dance and stories. Perhaps they
can grow from those seeds again, if enough are given the space
and some help from those who care enough to seek them out in
the hidden places and forgotten forests, give them a hand before
returning them to the soil, encouraging them to recall what they
know in their hearts.

I2

Fire Lighter

*The stories we find among the flames
and embers, Penzance, Cornwall*

Among my favourite stories of the woods and trees are the
ones that concern how we came to harness fire. In many
of these myths, fire is so powerful a force for creation
and destruction it is not given freely but has to be tricked from
the deities. These stories of the theft of fire span the whole globe,
from Prometheus of Greek mythology to IKaggen in the stories
of the San of Southern Africa, to Nanabozho of the Ojibwe, the
indigenous people of the sub-Arctic and north-eastern woodlands
of Canada and the United States, to Coyote of the Shoshone
indigenous people. Theft, trickery and mischief are inextricably
linked to our acquisition of fire, a secret so valuable that the deities
wanted to keep it for themselves, or rather, they did not trust us to
use its power wisely.

It is hardly surprising that this is the case. The taming of fire
from wood allowed us to cook and therefore draw more nutrition
from our food. It allowed us to survive the cold, to farm and create
industry. The harnessing of fire allowed nothing less than the
transformation of human life. It brought us together and around
the flames of the fire we have told some of our greatest stories.

The Polynesian legends of the shape-shifting trickster demigod Māui, who could take on various forms including a pigeon and a lizard, appear on islands as far flung as Hawai'i, New Zealand, Tahiti and Tonga. In some Māori retellings, as well as raising islands from the sea and lengthening the days by ensnaring the sun, Māui was responsible for tricking the fire goddess Mahuika into revealing the secrets of fire. In this story, Mahuika, who lived in the heart of a volcano, had gifted a single flame to the villagers who lived at the foot of her lava field. The villagers, for fear of facing her anger – after all, Mahuika was the sister of Hine-niu-to-te-pō, the goddess of death – kept their one fire burning day and night, though one night, in a fit of curiosity, Māui put out the fire and the villagers were bereft at their loss.

The young demigod, who was Mahuika's grandson, volunteered to climb into the volcano and ask her to give him another of the flames that burnt at the end of her fingers. Māui travelled across the lava fields until he came up against the sheer face of the scorched mountain, where he spoke a *karakia*: 'Rock, I am Māui – open to me.' Travelling deep in the mountain, Māui woke Mahuika from her sleep, whereupon he told her the fires of the village had gone out. Mahuika pulled off the smallest of her burning fingernails and Māui carried it away. When he reached a stream, he dropped the flaming nail into it and returned to the mountain. There, he asked Mahuika for another of her fingernails, which she gave him and when he reached the stream, he dropped that burning nail into it, too. He did the same with each of Mahuika's remaining fingernails, and each time the goddess became angrier and angrier until, as she threw her last fingernail to the ground, she caused the volcano to erupt. Flying high into the air as an eagle, Māui called to his ancestors, Tāwhirimātea, the god of the weather, and Whaitiri, the goddess of thunder to send rain, which doused the flames and Māui watched as, with the last of her breath, Mahuika blew her final dying spark, the last of her fire, into the heart of the forest, where the water could not reach it.

When the waters subsided, Māui wandered among the trees and eventually he found fire, hidden in the dry sticks that lay beneath the banyan tree. He found traces of fire, too, hidden within the dried branches of the au, the fig and the lemon hibiscus, and he gathered an armful of the dry wood, and carried it back to the village. He showed the villagers how to release the fire within the wood to cook their food and keep themselves warm, and around which to tell the story of how he, Māui, had brought fire back to the village.

On an overcast afternoon in mid-December, as what little light has shone on this shortest day of the year fades into its longest night, a crowd gathers at the top of Causewayhead, in Penzance, at the furthest tip of England. As the crowd grows, carols are sung, masks donned, and a banner raised with the words *Goel Montal* emblazoned on it, gold on black.

In the crowd, there are groups wearing Venetian carnival masks, masks depicting horned beasts, winged creatures, birds and plague doctors, top-hatted faux gentry, people bedecked in ribbon and lace, foliage and glitter. One man, with a huge white beard, is wearing a hat made from cabbage, a long necklace of sprouts and another cabbage atop his staff. And towering above them are the skeletal faces of two Penglaz or grey-headed 'Obby 'Osses and a huge paper sun. And somewhere among them is the figure who has been chosen to be Lord of Misrule, whose role it is to disrupt and confuse the natural order.

Once the crowd has reached a certain mass, those carrying tin whistles and drums, accordions and fiddles begin to play and the crowd becomes a procession, which begins to make its way slowly through the town, gathering more masked revellers along the way.

Like many midwinter festivals, the winter solstice Montol Festival, in Penzance, is one celebrated with fire and as darkness takes hold, smoke pours from censers and fire dancers whirl flaming chains around their heads. In an event that lasts all day, the first of its rituals is the Progress of the Sun in which this motley crew of guisers will accompany the huge paper sun to a midwinter bonfire on which it will be ceremonially burnt.

The name *Montol* comes from an early eighteenth-century manuscript of Cornish language in which Edward Lhuyd translates the word as meaning, variously, the 'winter solstice' or 'balance', though this festival is a new one. Although it borrows from older traditions – the 'Obby 'Oss, an invention of the early nineteenth century, the Guise dancers of Penzance who were wearing mock finery and dancing in masks in the 1700s, Morris dancing and mummers' plays, from traditions dating back to the Middle Ages and the gathering of people around a fire, which goes back far, far further into our histories – Montol itself began in 2007. It is easy to forget this when the dark comes and the streets are crowded, full of smoke and fire. It has the feel of something much older, something similar to those origin stories of the harnessing of fire.

The procession has now reached the recreation ground at the top of town where, with the wind threatening to blow the banners away and the fires out, the bonfire is lit and the paper sun laid on top of it. A cheer rises from the assembled crowd, though following this, there is a moment of quiet as we watch the sun burn at the beginning of the longest night.

In *The Old Road*, Hilaire Belloc wrote of the 'primal things that move us'. Among his list of such things were fire and voices in the night after silence.

As the fire blazes, I hear one of the masked figures say, 'It could only happen in Penzance,' and at that moment it feels it could be true. At the far end of the train line, the terminus, it has attracted the weird and alternative for decades, and, at Montol, all that weirdness concentrated into the hours of darkness at the point at which the balance shifts back towards the light.

Another says, 'We need this. When else do you get everyone in town together, those of us who don't go to church anyway?'

The sun now burnt, an entreaty for its return in a ritual of sacrifice, the procession begins its return journey into town and what feels like most of Penzance walks together in the darkness to the town centre where groups of guisers gather in squares and on street corners to tell stories and put on plays.

I might add to Belloc's list of primal things the telling of stories around the fire. The anthropologist, Polly Wiessner has a suggestion as to why we might continue to celebrate and venerate fire, well into the age of the electric light. Fire, she suggests, made us who we are, storytelling creatures. In her 2019 research paper, 'Embers of society: Firelight talk among the Ju/"hoansi Bushmen"', Wiessner suggested that firelight extended our storytelling abilities by allowing us to extend the day into the evening. Studying the differences between what she called day talk and night talk in her observations of the hunter-gatherers of Southern Africa, she noted that day talk tended to focus on practicalities and gossip, whereas night talk, conducted around the fire, tended to centre on imaginative storytelling as well as singing, dancing and religious ceremonies.

Firelight time, regarded as 'unproductive', she posited, gave rise to 'higher orders of theory of mind via the imagination'. Firelight encouraged intimate conversation and the telling of stories at night, once the mundane tasks of the day were done. She suggested that the harnessing of fire, presumably for its practical benefits of allowing us to cook the food we gathered and hunted, led to the development of story in the mellow, otherwise unproductive extension of the day it allowed.

'Stories told by firelight,' Wiessner wrote, 'put listeners on the same emotional wavelength, elicited understanding, trust, and sympathy, and built positive reputations for qualities like humour, congeniality, and innovation.' In short, the telling of stories around a fire may have been responsible for nothing less than the expansion of our imaginations, our flair for drama and our love of creative narratives.

In setting the fire and extending our days, we are all made tricksters, like Māui, Prometheus, Coyote, IKaggen or Nanabozho, or the Lord of Misrule on Montol eve. We are made imaginative and subversive by firelight, a gift from the woods.

In Penzance, the last of the evening's processions is taking place, a sea of people making their way down to the very edge of the land, carrying flaming torches aloft in a ritual called the Chalking of the Mock. A Cornish take on the Yule log, the mock is a yew log, swaddled and placed in a pram, an echo of the birth of Jesus. The mock is carried at the head of the procession at the conclusion of which the 'Oss choses one of the guisers to chalk a figure onto it and place it on the bonfire before it is set alight. Montol is a night for tricksters, parading fire through the streets in defiance of the long night and so the new traditions echo the old. The tricksters carry fire gleefully from the gods, in a story we have told for centuries now, for millennia.

And yet it is not the gods we have to thank for fire, for story and imagination, but the trees.

13

Apple Wailer

*An orchard in St Day, Cornwall, and
the Globe Theatre, London*

The hand-drawn poster read: 'meet by the village clock at seven p.m.'.

I was only a few minutes late, though I was unsurprised to find no one waiting beneath the clock tower. There was a storm in full flow. Rain was gusting in sheets through the darkness. It was difficult to imagine anyone would want to sing to the trees in this weather. It was more reasonable to assume the whole thing had been rained off, though as this was strictly an analogue affair, there was no way of knowing. There were no Facebook messages or WhatsApps, just word of mouth and a poster taped to a wall.

A young couple, shivering outside the Spar on the high street, with a 2-litre bottle of cheap cider in a plastic bag had heard nothing about the wassail nor whether it was going ahead. They turned their heads to the side in unison at the word, as though I might have made it up and was having a laugh at their expense. As I was attempting a garbled explanation, another couple walked past, wrapped in raincoats and holding their hoods up against the wind; they looked more promising. When I caught up with them, it turned out they were looking for the wassail too. They were, in

A single apple remains, marcescent on the tree in mid-winter.

turn, following a group further down the street in the hope they would end up in the right place.

As we walked, more joined the wind-buffeted column, though no one seemed sure if we were heading in the right direction until, outside a pub on the edge of the village, a boy of about twelve ushered us round the back of the building, where a band was playing in a marquee. At first, I wondered if I was in the wrong place and had accidentally joined a wedding party, though the Morris dancers made that seem less likely.

I was in St Day on Cornwall's north coast, to take part in a tradition of the apple-growing regions in the south of England that usually takes place around Twelfth Night, although this was the week before Christmas and there would be other wassails taking place across the southern counties until the end of January.

Depending on where in England you are, a wassail looks quite different. There are regional variations and many villages and towns across the south and the south-west have their own wassails, their own spin on the tradition and the order of events changes depending on where it is celebrated. Some involve processions through a village or town, while others are gatherings in clearings in an orchard. In some parts of Wales, wassails are accompanied by the *Mari Lwyd*, or Grey Mare, an 'Obby 'Oss figure similar to that seen at Montol in Penzance. However, many elements are common: the passing around of the wassail bowl or cup filled with cider, the drinking to the trees' health, the circling of a tree and singing or shouting to it, the rapping of the tree with sticks and the firing of imaginary guns into the canopy to bring down imaginary birds.

There is a reasonable argument to be had that wassailing has always been an excuse to drink in the dark times of the year, one strengthened by the etymology of the term, which comes from the Old Germanic toast *ves heill*, or 'be in good health'. Depending on who you talk to, the tradition arrived with the Danish Vikings who passed it on to the Celts. Otherwise, it was originally a Saxon or Celtic tradition or, as with so many of these festivals, a kind of amalgam of similar ideas. A celebration with heavy drinking at its centre hardly seems like the hardest sell.

In Cornwall, wassailing appears first in the medieval mystery plays of the 1400s, though it seems likely that the apple tree would have been blessed or importuned for a good harvest for as long as it has been cultivated, stretching back beyond the point at which the Romans introduced the fruit to these islands, back through to when the first cultivated apple trees appeared in Kazakhstan some 4,000 to 10,000 years ago.

The orchard we were to toast that evening was one of the youngest in Cornwall, having been planted the previous spring from a small selection of the 7,500 or so heritage varieties, with names like Venus Pippin, Cornish Honeypin, Polly Whitehair, King Byerd, Manaccan Primrose and Onion Redstreak.

The marquee was already full when I arrived, humid with bodies soaked in the rainstorm. Among the crowd, I found Sally Pyner, who works for the Kehelland Trust, the charity that supplied the community orchard at St Day with its apple trees. Community orchards, like this, she said, are particularly important in a country that has lost 90 per cent of its orchards since the 1950s, as farmers grubbed out the ancient apple trees on their land in favour of other crops, coinciding with the time at which we came to expect uniformly sized, shaped and coloured supermarket apples.

'It's tragic,' she said. 'A lot of orchards are just gone now, and like with any ancient forest, you can't just get them back. It's madness that we've lost those traditional orchards just because money was paid for that land to free it up for something else. It's a massive crime. However, what we have now is a resurgence in interest in apples. Apple days have become really important to a lot of people now, and there are lots of stewardship schemes that have come about recently.'

Sally has been running apple days and wassails since 1997. While wassailing is ancient tradition, Apple Day was an invention of the charity, Common Ground, which ran their first in 1991, a deliberate attempt to change the way the apple tree was regarded at a time it was in huge decline. Where wassails are held in winter, the tree blessings of Apple Day take place towards the end of October, around the time of the apple harvest. During this festival, there is a procession of apple juice from the previous year's harvest, at the end of which children wrap the trees in crepe paper, make clay pixie faces and press them into the bark of the trees.

'It's there so the children get a connection to these trees,' Sally said, 'and the idea of protecting the harvest, protecting and honouring the trees.'

The invention of the new festival came along at a time when orchards were being destroyed at an alarming rate, as a marker of the importance of the diversity of the apples themselves and of the cultures that surround them.

'In my opinion they're as important as oaks,' she stated. 'We have a spiritual connection to apples and the beauty of them is – because they don't grow true from seed – there are so many stories and connections with them. You could eat a different apple every day for six years and you still wouldn't have tried all the varieties that are growing in England.'

That apples are important is apparent in the extent to which we have carried them around the world – apples now grow in most places on Earth – and the extent to which they are embedded in our oldest stories. Even though the tree of knowledge of good and evil of the Bible is unnamed, it makes sense that it might be depicted as an apple tree in Christianity in the West, for its sweet fruit and its sheer cultural importance. The theory that it may have stayed that way as a result of the fruit being so culturally important is backed up by the way in which it is viewed in Jewish and Islamic traditions, in which the same tree is often considered to be a fig, a tree that, like the apple, is culturally important across much of the world, and a decent contender for the title of the tree of immortality.

Later in the evening, I found a friend, Jack, sitting at one of the trestle tables, where he had been set to work felting apples, though the purpose of this felting was unclear. One of his sons, dressed in a black top hat and carrying a whistle, was part of the Morris troupe performing as part of this blessing of the new apple trees. Jack's son had found his own way to Morris dancing. There was no parental encouragement necessary, he said, rather an example of the younger generation unselfconsciously embracing folk traditions at which the previous two or three generations might have winced, desperate as they were for the new.

As with many rituals, there is something deeply performative and theatrical about wassails. Both are shared experiences that transport us into the realm of the imagination, community events in which the normal rules of society do not apply, for a few hours at least.

Jack has, perhaps, more knowledge than most in this area. He was the first stage manager for the newly reopened Globe Theatre in London, in 1997, that impressively analogue, wooden 'O' set amid the city's towers of steel and glass. I always felt torn, when watching Shakespeare at the Globe, as to whether to watch the action on stage or to watch the building itself. Being there evokes the feeling of being in a forest clearing, as though both audience and actors have converged in a wooded glade, improbable as that might be in the heart of the city.

The famous line 'this wooden O' appears in the prologue to Shakespeare's *Henry V*. It was the first production to be staged in the new Globe Theatre and later Jack sought me out and gave me a wooden spoon that had been used as a prop in that first production, and which had been stuck in the hat of the actor John McEnery who played Pistol, the sidekick of the charismatic, bacchanalian Falstaff. Jack later found the spoon was being used in the theatre's canteen. It had acquired a small crack and was about to be thrown out when he liberated it. Knowing I spend my spare time carving spoons, Jack gave it to me to use as a template.

On a crisp, cold morning a year on from the wassail at St Day, I walked through London with Pistol's spoon in my pocket. When I reached Bankside, I passed through a market where actors in

Georgian dress were promenading among the stalls, and a folk duo were playing ballads of old London. One of the actors handed me a flier that told me this was the Frost Fair, a resurrection of a festival held on the Thames tideway from the seventh to the nineteenth centuries. The Frost Fair's heyday, though, was in the early seventeenth century, which coincided with the early years of the original Globe. I was heading towards its newer incarnation to meet with the actor Mark Rylance and the Globe Theatre's architect Jon Greenfield.

The original Globe was built in 1599, by the Lord Chamberlain's Men. It was rebuilt using the timber bones of another playhouse that had sat on the opposite bank of the Thames – the first of London's purpose-built theatres, simply known as The Theatre. When the Globe opened, a flag of Hercules carrying the world on his back was reported to have been hoisted above the theatre, displaying the Latin motto '*totes mundus agit histrionem*' – put simply, all the world's a playhouse. That incarnation burnt to the ground just fourteen years later and the Globe that was rebuilt in its place was closed after just twenty-eight years, in 1642, by Puritan decree, an order which led to all London's theatres being shut as 'chapels of Satan'. Just two years after that, it was demolished. As well as shutting the theatres, the Puritans came for the wassails too, as rowdy, drunken events. They were similarly banned in the 1640s.

The Globe Theatre now sits not far from where it would once have been, almost five centuries ago, still on the banks of the Thames, facing St Paul's Cathedral, itself a recreation, the first having burnt down in the great fire of 1666. So we have a sacred stone O, in which stories of God are told, facing a wooden O, in which stories of flawed human beings are told, heaven and earth watching each other across the river.

Everything in the rebuilt Globe was designed to be meaningful and symbolic, Jack had told me, not least the 28-foot Herculean columns, created from single trunks of oak, which hold the 16-ton pentice roof in place. The rebuild, to Jon's design, which made use of sixteenth-century techniques for squaring the green oak used to build the theatre, was an act of cultural afforestation. It made use of a thousand oak trees in its construction, many of which came from the Forest of Dean.

'It's a profound building,' Mark commented, as we sat face to face across a table in the Globe's café. 'A round theatre is so unusual. It's such a beautiful, classical, geometrical shape and I do think that's powerful. When people come here, I think they feel "1,000 trees have turned up and here I am sitting among them too".'

There is certainly something of a sanctuary about the Globe. It's an intimate space and I have sat, uncomfortably, on its wooden benches, shoulder to shoulder with people I have never met before, eye to eye with those sitting opposite, the sounds of the city beyond the playhouse washing in every now and then, as the drama played out on stage.

Mark referred to the circular theatre, its centre open to the sky, as being like a nest. 'In their day, these theatres would have been the only way people could gather apart from churches,' he continued. 'It was equivalent, in my mind, to the arrival of the internet in our time. It was a place people could go where they weren't dominated by priests. And within this place, they could dress in a way that they'd be executed for outside . . . It was a place of enormous freedom, held by this forest of trees.'

Actors often call the Globe a 'wooden instrument', to be played gently or roughly, an instrument out of which to coax music. The theatre critic Richard Horby echoed this, on watching that first 1997 performance of *Henry V*, described the Globe: 'as if someone unearthed an ancient musical instrument . . . and discovered it can emit a sumptuous, resonant music no living person has ever heard before.'

It was a fair analogy, Jon agreed. As a faithful reconstruction of an Elizabethan playhouse, there is no amplification on stage at the Globe – the actor has only their voice and personality to work with, and the wooden building itself.

'There are parallels in everything that's going on here.' Jon gestured at the building around us. 'It's a case of getting the right kind of wood and using it in the right way, and in the right shape. It's like when you're playing an instrument and you've only got your finger strength or mouth to play it, so you need the instrument to reinforce the sound and to give it colour. So, when you're making a violin, if you change the shape slightly, you change the sound, and the same if you change the kind of wood it's made from, or if you change the varnish that goes on the wood.'

Modern theatres rely on acousticians with computer simulations to work out how sound will act within a space. With the Globe, the team chose to trust the history of the building to lead the way, and to give it over to the artists to work out the problems with the space and how to work around the challenges of making themselves heard in a building full of complex shapes, thousands of pieces of wood which sound would reflect off and into which it would be absorbed.

'We imagine the people who built these theatres knew a lot about acoustics,' Mark said. 'There were so many built, and each one is different, so they were clearly learning from each other's mistakes and improving. And the actors were shareholders; they wanted the audience to be able to hear. We assumed if we followed the archaeological and documentary evidence that we would get to a good sounding building.'

It was not a good sounding building to begin with. Contrary to Horby's report, Mark argued that to him the sound in the theatre did not begin to improve until the Globe's third season.

'The problem was the oak was so wet, it was like playing a wet piano or a wet violin.' He made a wringing motion with his hands. 'It's made out of a thousand, massive living beings, so I always had this feeling that one was in a forest, particularly because when it was built, the timbers were so wet ... It was so moist. And you felt their spirits were probably still in them. Or I certainly did.'

It was not until the oak began to dry out, a process that continues to this day, that the sound began to improve. Roughly speaking, wood dries at a rate of a few centimetres a year, and as the largest timbers at the Globe are some 100 centimetres across, some of them may not be fully dry for another fifteen years. So, it stands to reason, the sound in the auditorium will continue to be shaped by the trees from which it was constructed.

It was not a problem that would have affected the actors of the Chamberlain's Men in 1599, that said. The timbers of the original Globe, repurposed as they were from those of The Theatre, would have been well dried out by the time *Julius Caesar*, most likely the first of Shakespeare's plays to have been performed there, found its audience.

Several times during our conversation, both Mark and Jon referred to the Globe as a 'teacher'. They have known it for more than twenty-five years now and have watched it shift and settle. They have observed the ways in which the audience have left their mark in the transference of oils from hand to timber, patches of which have grown smooth, as the squared beams of oak have started to show rot at the outermost points, where the wood was closest to the bark, the legacy of being left open to the elements.

When Mark came on board in 1995, when the theatre was still in construction, he drew a comparison between what Jon and theatre carpenter Peter McCurdy were doing with timber, and the way he viewed the role of the actor, in particular in Shakespeare's plays.

'I had made an amateur study of Renaissance and hermetic philosophy – the classic image of the Renaissance man standing in a square and a circle.' As he talked, Mark sketched out an image of Leonardo da Vinci's 'Vitruvean Man', a figure within a square within a circle, on a paper napkin.

'It squares the heart so that his senses, his consciousness, are in touch both with the physical world – four directions, four elements, all the things that the square suggested of our physical existence – and also the united spiritual world of imagination, of dreams – the circle – at the same time.

'Squaring the heart connected perfectly for me with the issues in Shakespeare's plays of making manifest your heart's desire. You have a desire and you make it manifest. You act. And this is what acting is about all the time. A formless motivation comes up – it might be a desire for power, for security, for sex, for food – and then you put it into the physical world with your will centre. So, the trinity of the heart, the mind and the body of enacting things is what I work with all the time.'

He saw the carpenters at the Globe doing just this as they shaped the posts with which to construct the theatre and took cylindrical oak trunks and squared them. It was, he said, 'the very timber of the imagination being made manifest'.

The building itself became Mark's teacher too. Acting in this analogue space in which the lights did not go down before the drama began changed the way in which he related to the audience. He described the need to befriend the building, to work with it, and with the audience too, in a way he had not before.

'It dragged me out of being an actor who was quite nervous and frightened of audiences. I didn't want to look at the audience, I'd never seen them before, and suddenly I was in the room with them.'

Sitting across from an actor considered by many as among the greatest of his generation, it was difficult to imagine Mark as being frightened of anyone.

'Though when I did look at them, I saw that they were not the enemy at all. You could see most of them really wanted it to be good. And if you told the story well – if you didn't get too much ahead of them or too much behind them – they were complete. You can be very quiet in there if the story warrants it, then the whole audience is quiet because they want so keenly to hear what the next thing is.'

Jon nodded. 'It's vital that the actors don't use sound reinforcement because it's a craft building with craftspeople on the stage, who are working their art. The moment you can dominate it by just turning the volume up, you've lost all the wonderful subtleties.'

Mark and Jon broke off to discuss a newly built theatre in New York, one in which the space can be configured and reconfigured to whatever shape the director requires, a technical marvel of a building, reliant on hydraulics and lifts.

Jon commented to me that this was exactly what the Globe was not, before turning back to Mark: 'Other, modern theatres have lights, revolving stages, sound and all sorts of things, but here you're just saying, Mark, tell me a story and that works here in a way that doesn't work anywhere else. I want to go somewhere that is something, that is somewhere, a place that's got a *genius loci*.'

Mark nodded. 'It's hard for the younger directors to know this but the star of the show *is* the building here. You will never dominate it so you have to learn to work with it and then it will really be a great friend to you. But if you try and dominate it or cover it, or pretend that you are more important than it, you're not going to get anywhere.'

The way he described it made the experience of appearing on stage at the Globe a kind of symbiotic relationship between the actors and the wood of these thousand trees, a kind of joint endeavor. Before I left, Mark recounted for me the first moments of that first performance of *Henry V* in 1997, in which he played the lead role. There were sixteen cast members crammed into a tiny, walled space behind the scenery, he recalled, and he opened the play by banging a stick on the floor, starting a kind of heartbeat, before the cast spread out onto the stage, and, as he talked, Mark tapped out a pulsating rhythm on the table, evoking for us the feeling of that play. Now, as I recall that moment, it seems appropriate for a play so full of war to start with a martial drumbeat, but I wonder whether it was also a sign of respect to a building made of living things. The restarting of a wooden heart that had been silent for 360 years. A kind of reanimating rhythm.

'We know sound penetrates matter, so all the sound that we've made in there across these twenty-five years has gone into that wood,' he commented. 'Some of it has come out the other side and some of it's still travelling through it very slowly, or is stuck in the wood. The energy is there. So, when I go into the Globe, I know that all those performances I was part of and all the performances that other people were involved with are all in there. All those nights of great roars of laughter, they're all in there. It's all in the building.'

I walked across the footbridge over the Thames, away from the wooden O, past the stone O of St Pauls, and only stopped at Denmark Street, where guitars have been sold and music recorded since the 1960s. There, I spent a few hours playing guitars that were far outside my price range.

To look at some of them, battered and worn, their bindings glued and reglued, you would think they would be worth far less than the shinier, newer models, but these instruments had been 'played in', the tone of the woods developing over years of being plucked and strummed.

As I picked out a tune on a vintage Martin guitar, constructed in the early 1970s, complete with nicks and dents, its body polished by the guitarists who had made it sing for half a century, I thought on Mark's words about sound entering wood. The thought followed me the rest of the journey through London and on that long train leg home. All those words, the roaring of the cast and crowd, the wailing and laughter, the beat of wood hitting wood like a pulsing heart, all working their way through the thousand trees that make up the Globe. All those words, music, and songs, working their way through the wood of the guitars too. The spirits in the wood. The ways in which we shape wood and are shaped by it. A relationship that stretches back into a past the details of which have long been forgotten, but the feeling of which is still very much present within us when we make contact with wood and with trees.

Back in the marquee in St Day, children took swift gulps from their parents' drinks when their backs were turned, and small groups huddled in different parts of the marquee. A guitarist and singer competed with the noise of the temporary room and when they gave way, the makers of speeches, blessing the new orchard, did the same. There would still be a wassail, a woman

Apple Day at Kehelland Trust, Cornwall. Image by Sharon Aston.

announced, over the sound of the billowing walls of the marquee. The children in the room would stand in for trees and we would wassail them instead.

If I was of more imaginative frame of mind, I might have said there was something almost folk horrorish about getting the children to gather in the centre of the tent and pretend to be apple trees. Certainly, it might make for a better story. Yet there was nothing dark about this celebration – it was all light and laughter, beer swilled and songs sung. The audience gathered in a human O around the child players on stage, standing in for trees, and the wassail songs were sung, imaginary birds shot out of imaginary branches with imaginary guns.

Several researchers of folk traditions have suggested that the trees are incidental to the tradition. The great commentator of all things folkloric Ronald Hutton suggested that wassailing could have come about simply as an excuse to drink and shout in the dark night – in some areas of the country, wassailing is known as howling.

I have been to several wassails now, some rowdy, some tame. In some, I have seen people overtaken by the howling, letting rip the sort of primal scream that comes of having sat at a desk in an office for most of the year; in others, it seemed simply an excuse for a community to gather at a time when most people might be tempted to stay in. Whatever the reason, it seems like a good idea to celebrate a new orchard.

Aside from the ones symbolized by the children at the centre of the circle, there were no trees at my first wassail, yet the ceremony felt both distinctly tree-like and particularly human. I wondered if anyone else in the marquee was struck by the resonance of this impassioned shouting by one generation to the next, whether anyone else felt a link between the shouting at the apple trees, the importuning of these tree spirits that the trees should grow strong, that they should bear healthy fruit and sustain us in years to come and the often silent wishes we have for our children, that they too should grow strong and healthy.

The singing was still going strong as I slipped out through the tent flap, back into the gale and I could hear shouts and cheers over the wind as I made my way back up the high street in the rain, a collective sound made against the dark of midwinter, or full of hope for the coming year, depending on which way you looked at it. It was a solemn ritual or a barnstorm, I couldn't decide which.

Whatever the intention, woodlands and forests are present in our minds even when there are not present. We willingly conjure up an orchard for wassailing and an Arden from the wooden O of the Globe and lose ourselves in fictional woods in a marquee behind a pub, where there are no trees in sight.

14

Tree Worshipper

An ancient yew grove on the border between England and Wales

I t is just over a year on, and Tom and I are back at my father's woodland again, on the border between England and Wales. We sit in the kitchen and watch the birds at the feeders, the protected pheasants and the vole engaged in his death-defying sprints along the gauntlet of the low wall, collecting dropped seed. The trees on the scalped hillside opposite are taking further, small steps towards recovery. Some small, shrublike willows and hazels are making their presence known among the fallen trees, though the bone-white trunks of those that were stripped and left by the heavy machinery still appear spectral. In contrast, the trees in my father's woodland-in-making are showing improbable green, as though they are rushing towards their summer state. The fields, in this state of greenery, the trees in new leaf, look lush and thick, ragged and scruffy. It is beginning to look more like a woodland, less like something planted.

There's a Welsh phrase, *dod ynôl at fy nghoed,* which relates to a return to a balanced state of mind after a period of turbulence, though a more literal translation would be 'coming home to my trees'. It makes sense that this should be the case. Compared to

My father's woodland in spring.

trees, we are flighty things, always on the move. We have always been inspired by the steadfastness of trees, by their immovability. Perhaps, when we commit to them, they offer us a sense of balance in an uncertain world.

Living at the far end of the country, in Cornwall, it gives me some comfort that my father has his trees to come home to, when he spends much of his time caring for his father, who is fast approaching a hundred and who needs more support each day. My father tells me being among the trees he planted grounds him.

On occasion, my father has called me to let me know if I should receive a call from a police station, it will be because he has been arrested for campaigning or some direct action he has been involved in with Extinction Rebellion. I think, secretly, he hopes he will be, but it has not happened yet.

The woodland is another of his environmental statements, an action where others might be content with words. There is more to it than that though. I think he wanted to create something that would outlast him, a canopy beneath which his children and grandchildren could sit and rest, though there has been little rest for him in getting the woodland growing.

Tom borrows my father's hazel walking stick again when we head out to walk the trees. The walking stick is shorter on him this year, though the trees continue to outpace him. We stomp our way into the heart of the small wood, where we are shaded by green, though to say that is to do the colours a disservice. In the thirteen species of trees, their trunks and leaves, the grasses and plants that have grown between them, the leaf litter and branches on the floor, there are more colours than it would be possible to count in a lifetime.

My father had originally planted the trees in rows, a condition of the grant he received, though as he takes more and more out to make way for those that are thriving most to spread their canopy, the grid is dissolving. I don't like to ask him about the taking down of trees he has nurtured for years, though it is making a difference.

He has stopped scything between the trunks now too. He is leaving branches and leaves in the spaces.

Tom has, in the intervening year, become interested in wizards and magic, much as I was at his age. He wanders off between the trees and I see him spread his arms, the walking stick held out in front of him like a mage's staff, as though he is casting a spell. He still has the concept of the woods as a magical place. I hope it remains that way. The books he reads are full of wizards and magic, though I do not think he has come across the idea of their forebearers, historical druids, yet, nor does he know that there were once druids here, in these valleys, and in those closer to our home in Cornwall too, perhaps the closest thing to wizards to walk these parts. Like those labelled witches, I suspect that although they were not persecuted in the same way; druids have, perhaps, been misunderstood by history, for their knowledge of the natural world, their understanding of the woodlands made into something rebellious and non-conforming.

To a dominant religion in which wisdom is imparted from above, the idea that one might find knowledge in the trees – or anywhere in the physical world – growing in front of us, is heretical. We have always feared that which sits outside our frames of reference, the structure we have imposed on the world. Perhaps, I wonder, as I press one of the newly opened leaves of a hornbeam gently between my finger and thumb, and then the same with the silver birch, the wild service and cherry, we are still living the legacy of that understanding of the world.

'I don't know whether it's pheromones or hormones or whatever, but every time I'm among the trees, I just get this lovely feeling,' my father says as we are making our way back up towards the house. 'It makes you feel good, there's no doubt about that, especially when you're down among trees you've planted in the dappled sunlight. It's just beautiful.'

In the afternoon, we left my father's woodland, one of the youngest in the area, in search of more ancient trees in another

One of the ancient yews at Llangadwaladr.

hidden pocket of this corner of North Wales among the sheep-grazed deserts. At Llangadwaladr, just a couple of miles from my father's house, stands a grove of nine ancient yews in the graveyard of a medieval church. They are enormous, gnarled things, their actual age a matter of debate, as it is notoriously difficult to age an ancient yew. Regardless of whether the oldest yews growing on these islands is 2,000 or 5,000 years, they are among the oldest living things here.

However old these trees are, they almost certainly predate the church that stands here, and the positioning of the grove is suggestive of deliberate planting. It has been suggested too, by scholars and amateur historians, that this was once a meeting place and a site of worship and of communion for Celts about whose lives we know almost nothing save what we think we know from the fanciful imaginings of our Victorian forebears. Whatever those beliefs were, they must have been powerful, as the Church chose to assimilate yews into the language of the churchyard rather than stamp out their significance as they did with the druids themselves.

What the druids knew of yew trees is lost to time, though we have rediscovered their power for our own age. Since the 1990s, alkaloid compounds from yew, poisonous on account of their property of preventing cell division and lethal at high doses, have been used to create drugs to treat cancerous growths in humans, preventing abnormal cell division. New compounds are being discovered in trees each year. In 2023, scientists at the University of Bath discovered a way of creating both the pain-killers paracetamol and ibuprofen from an extract in pine trees, where both are currently made using crude oil, a gentler way of producing the medications.

This is not what I imagined I would be getting excited about as an adult, the prospect of being able to create a painkiller from a tree rather than oil. The television programmes that stood out from my childhood in the 1980s were the ones that promised a radical vision for the future that was all glass, plastic and steel. *Tomorrow's World* predicted hoverboards and flying cars, and reruns of the 1960s' cartoon *The Jetsons* seemed to promise a future in which we were done with the need of nature to support us. The society of *The Jetsons*, who lived in the impossibly distant year of 2062, had conquered nature in favour of convenience, and the cartoon portrayed a life that was almost entirely anthropocentric. The only people who still lived on the ground were hobos; those who could afford to lived in the upper atmosphere. And what green space remained was confined to parks and mowed to within an inch of its life.

The Jetsons seemed like a logical conclusion for a generation whose parents and grandparents grew up in the hope of realizing John Maynard Keynes's promise of the golden era of leisure, a decade-and-a-half after the end of the Second World War. We were a society promised limitless abundance, convenience and man-made products in clear, shiny packaging. And small details aside – I am still waiting for my flying car and hoverboard – it is the future we got. I don't recall any talk in it of the downsides of wanting this future, the toll it might take, though that is the power of the law of unintended consequences. Which is, perhaps, one of the things that left us where we are – looking down the barrel of climate change, biodiversity loss, denuded seas and forests. It was thinking that only we mattered, that our feelings and desires somehow trumped the reality of our interconnectedness with the world around us. It seems no real wonder that so many people are rediscovering 'old ways' on one hand, and looking to the trees for solutions.

I wonder if it's time for a new *Tomorrow's World*, which imagines a regreened planet and the ways in which we might live on it. And perhaps a new *Jetsons* too, with the straight lines and flat, microbially cleansed, pure surfaces, replaced by living, breathing materials, which biodegrade and leave not so much as a trace they were ever used for anything other than their original state.

A new *Tomorrow's World* would have much to say on the topic of wood. As we were marvelling at the complexity of the ancient yew grove, standing among some of the oldest living beings on these islands, Japanese scientists were busy making satellites out of wood and, in other laboratories in the United States and Israel, scientists and designers were 3D-printing with wood, exploring its possibilities as a nano-composite that might offer solutions to our reliance on plastics, making phone screens from wood-based nano cellulose, ballistic glass, replacement tendons, body armour, purification filters, ultra-absorbent aerogels and bendable batteries.

'Wood is a new metal, a new plastic, a new concrete,' Liangbing (Bing) Hu, one of the world's leading researchers into new uses for wood, was recently quoted as saying. Hu is creating 'super woods' with strengths similar to that of metals or rubber. Breaking wood down into a nano material,

Nano-engineered wood.

he recomposes it, developing wood that bounces, squishes like rubber, transparent woods in place of glass, or in a form that is lighter and stronger than steel, offering the possibility of using it in buildings in place of metal struts and girders, saving on the carbon emissions associated with metal. Not only that, but Hu argues that developing these technologies may have a role to play in decarbonization. Using wood, you remove almost the same amount of carbon dioxide as steel emits, and at the end of its life, it is then itself biodegradable.

Trees and woodlands are our past, though they may be our future too. There is no return to some prelapsarian state, though looking forward to a new way of being – with and alongside, rich, fertile, abundant – in which, druid-like, we learn from the trees again, offers glimmers of hope.

The largest of the yews at Llangadwaladr is some 25 feet around though each of these trees is enormous, with spiralling branches,

huge burls and valleys that disappear into the black hollows and caves within their trunks. When we peered into them, we found these ravines were stuffed with small branches, wool, scraps of synthetic twine, small avian skulls, evidence of the rooks that make their home in these trees.

It is unsurprising that ancient yews hold such sway in our imaginations. They are perhaps the only other tree that approaches the iconic nature of the oak, in the UK in any case. Being almost entirely poisonous, to humans at least, the yew has a slightly edgier, wilder reputation, less friendly and wholesome, though powerful all the same. Yew, of all the trees that are native to Britain, are the only ones to retain their Old English name, the rest mostly having taken on the names they were given by the Saxons. Yews are less comforting than oaks. They are less huggable. They command respect and quiet reverence and we wandered among them silently. The ground beneath the yews was bare – little if anything will grow beneath a yew – they hold their own space. As we stood beneath them, the light shifted and, filtered down through the yews' branches, became a haze and the whole place took on a magical air.

Each of these trees is a woodland in itself. With their ability to live to a great age – some of the yews in the UK are among the oldest living things in Europe – they regenerate themselves through producing clones from the points at which their lower branches touch the ground. The poison that is present in all parts of the tree, save the flesh of its seeds, the powerful medicines these poisons represent, contribute to the yew's long history of being at once a symbol of life, death and rebirth, so it is unsurprising we still revere them, that we leave them be and allow them to live out their lives in sacred places.

There is another similar yew grove not far from here, at Pennant Melangell, another church that was built on a far more ancient site, this one Bronze Age. The legend associated with this yew-bound church, the story of Melangell, patron saint of hares, reminds me of my father and Alison's protection of the pheasants in their woodland from the organized shoots, and the small oasis they have created in which hares have taken up residence.

The story goes that Melangell was an Irish princess, the daughter of King Jowchell, who fled from an arranged marriage in Ireland in a coracle and ended up taking refuge in a remote wooded valley in the Berwyn Mountains where she lived alone, wild and untamed.

Some years later, Brochfael Ysgithrog, Lord of Powys, was chasing a hare through the woods at Llangynog, when he came across a woman standing in the path of his hunting dogs. The hare took refuge beneath Melangell's skirts and when Brochfael demanded she should hand it over – it was, after all, his rightful quarry and he the lord of the land – she refused. Brochfael became enraged and told Melangell that as Lord of Powys, owner of the woods, he was entitled to hunt there, to which she replied that it was not possible to own a forest and that she would protect the hare with her life. At this, Brochfael's dogs lay down at Melangell's feet, the hunt entirely gone from them, and Brochfael, moved by Melangell's courage and conviction, backed down, too. Further, he gifted her the land as a sanctuary for humans and animals. Melangell established a community of women on the site and became known as a protector of the natural world. According to some retellings of the legend, she lived in the hollows of the yews that grew there and cared for the trees and animals in the woods until she died.

Hares become known as Melangell's lambs locally and for several centuries it was illegal to kill a hare around Llangynog, and even beyond that, local superstition had it that hares here were both protected and symbols of protection, though in recent years there has been a regular hunt in the area.

My father calls the seasonal hunters the oil men – wealthy, tweed-suited visitors to the area who come to let off steam by shooting and hunting their way through the Welsh hills. The point, as with most of the commercial hunts, is not to hunt for food: the majority of the pheasants end up in landfill once shot. It makes me proud of the small rebellion taking place in my father's woods where the pheasants are protected. One cock pheasant, who Alison christened Finn, has been living there with a small harem for the last three years. Finn struts around by the bird feeders or around the edge of the trees. He is tame enough to feed by hand. The image I have in my head of Melangell is not dissimilar to the scene I watched from the breakfast table that morning as my father and Tom fed Finn by hand. They keep the birdfeeders full here and, as a result, the garden is always full of woodland birds. I'm sure it does not feel like an education when Tom listens as my father recounts the names of the various birds and as he starts to recognize them by sight and song, though in these moments I see again in him the seeds of someone who might grow to love deeply the trees and the birds found there, the oak galls and the tadpoles in the pond, someone who might provide refuge, and resist on their behalf, as Melangell did. As my father and Alison do.

Following her death, Melangell was named the patron saint of hares, though, like the yews that predate the churches in whose yards they sit, her story most likely has much older roots. It has many of the hallmarks of a goddess of the woods' story, or perhaps of one of the tales of the Welsh giants of the borders. In all likelihood, it was one of the church's many appropriations, part of a broader gathering up of traditions, symbols and stories that took place as Christianity spread across the country.

When I imagine Melangell, I find it hard to picture her as she is in many of the retellings of the story. I find I cannot imagine her as the meek but strong-willed woman who inspires the Lord of Powys to back down, but as someone powerful, terrifying even, a match for the inherited titles and take-what's-mine entitlement that come with land ownership. She was wild, perhaps as a *wuduwasa*.

The reverence for, and protection of, hares is certainly pre-Christian, embedded deep within Celtic mythology, and they remain lodged in our imaginations as symbols of freedom. The site at Pennant Melangell, like the yew grove at Llangadwaladr, seems to me something akin to a thin place, where the boundary between the world we see and the world we imagine might lie just beyond, becomes slightly visible, a place towards which the spiritually minded are drawn. It is in no small part a result of these ancient trees with their hollow trunks that fold in on themselves decade upon decade, century upon century, which reach back, living, into deep time, which allow us a glimpse of something we feel in our bones but are unable to comprehend. And if we can imagine gatherings beneath these canopies two millennia gone, it is perhaps because we recognize in them the communities we long for. Perhaps, beneath these ancient canopies, we feel connections to our distant ancestors who enjoyed their shade and the soft light that fell between the branches, the protection they offered and the contemplation they enabled.

The story of Melangell seems to speak of our need for places of refuge, places that are protected from the worst of us. And though ancient yew groves sit at some far end of the spectrum of the age of living things from the trees my father planted just nine years ago, they are both refuges and places of what the former Archbishop of Canterbury, Rowan Williams, called in a commentary of

St Melangell, contemplative resistance, statements of wild, emphatic love for the natural world.

Melangell's story reminds us too that we can be powerful and no more so than when we use that power to protect. There is currently a global pledge to restore 865 million acres of degraded forest. Perhaps, at the same time, we need to renew our understanding of trees and woodlands, to redefine their importance, to protect the woodlands we still have, and create new sacred groves that will come to maturity in the time of our grandchildren's children and, like Melangell, protect that which lives within them. Perhaps, in doing so, we might redefine our relationship with wood, the part it plays in our lives, and our appreciation of it as a material for our future.

I suspect that regardless of how much we feel we appreciate them, we underestimate what trees do for us, the ways in which our lives and theirs are intertwined. Few of us see them in the way the science writer Colin Tudge does, viewing the debt we owe trees to be absolute. We still have much to learn from woodlands, and much to learn from wood too, as a material with which we may create our future.

I hold on to the hope that there is still, somewhere, a woodland that would not recognize us if we blundered into it. The wildwood might be a fantasy, but it is one I cling to – it seems important that we should leave some things alone, perhaps a lot of things, and not just for the creatures that live there, but for us too, for our sense of ourselves in the world.

We have a complex relationship with the woods. On one hand, we rely on them. Along with the seas, they operate as the planet's lungs. They quite literally sustain our life here. Yet, in terms of the language we use, to be in the woods is a negative. We hope to be out of them soon. Disaster stories are full of tales of people who have become turned around when leaving the path in the woods only to emerge mostly starved. If they emerge at all.

The heart of the woods is a terrifying place to be, elemental and disorienting.

In the heart of my father's woodland in summer.

The heart of the wildwood is a mystery. At times, it is where we keep our secrets, that which is subversive and dangerous and yet, at others, it is a place of refuge and safety.

We need the woods, both literally and as a symbol. We need their shade, their protection, their ability to produce oxygen, fuel. And we need them for our stories too. We need to walk in the fictional woods, that enduring symbol of our psyche – we need to become lost in them in order to find ourselves.

We look to trees to make sense of our lives perhaps because we share much with them. We both stand upright. Both humans and trees have limbs that stem from a central trunk. Both have a crown at the top. Yet they are strange to us. Our debt to them, if not complete, is extensive in the extreme, for the oxygen they provide, the shelter from storm, their near endless useful properties for construction of homes, boats, for the instruments we can craft from them, for the firewood that kept us warm across millennia, and the fires around which we developed the ability to tell each other stories. Yet, they are so often beyond us. As the great writer of the environment Barry Lopez said, woods 'defeat the viewfinder'.

They are complex, from the canopy (a mature oak may have over 200,000 leaves in midsummer), through to the complexities of their root structures, their interrelationships with fungal networks about which we know so little, the mysteries of which we are only just beginning to scratch the surface. They defeat us too in their longevity. As ecologist Oliver Rackham observed, trees have no predetermined lifespan as we do, and, as such, they are beyond our understanding.

We can look to them as markers of the passage of time, though. We read the seasons in their states of leaf or unleaf, of bud and sap, in the colour of leaf. We read the years in their growth rings, in the spread of their canopies or their reaching up into the sky. We draw religious and spiritual inspiration from them and some of our greatest philosophical thoughts too.

It is no surprise that we would build trees into our narratives, as we sat beneath them, warmed by the flames they provided us, watched over by the faces we saw hidden in their trunks. The image of the forest as magical and dangerous runs through our folk tales and who cannot say when standing alone in the forest at night, they, too, have not felt that primal fear?

Wood time is wild time. Spend enough time in the trees and you might see the wodewose staring back at you from between the leaves, as you might find the Green Man peering in at you in from some darkened corner of a church. Everyone has a theory on the Green Man, and mine is that he is there to remind us of our own wildness, that beneath the layers of civilization and society, taboo and law, that we are tree people, though many of us may have forgotten it. He is the untamed and untameable, a necessary reminder of our true natures, and it is likely he has been walking with us since we first came down from the trees to the savannah.

In the knowledge that many species of trees may outlive us by several centuries, millennia perhaps, they act too as *memento mori*. They are alive yet still, to our eyes at least, change little day to day. Trees are capable of slow magic and are deeply connected to deep time. If trees could perceive us as we perceived them, they might see our lives as unbearably fast, as brief flickers. In a time of fragmentation, in which our attention is being pulled in different directions, this relationship we have with trees is in essence a relationship with deep time, which allows us to slow ourselves down, momentarily at least.

It seems fitting that the end of each of my trips to woodlands across the country is marked by iconic trees. Driving back into Cornwall, I point out the stand of trees at Lifton, just over the border from Devon into Cornwall.

Cookworthy Knapp, more commonly known as the Nearly Home trees, is a woodland of 140 beech trees that, depending on where you are, as the Cornish would put it, mark a return home or the beginning of holidays. It is still an hour on both train and by road from there before we will come home to our trees, the cherry in the front garden, the hawthorn at the side of the house and the silver birch at the back.

Our relationships with trees root us. So we return home and check the tree at the end of the road is still there – *dod yn ôl at fy nghoed* – we return to our trees. We touch wood, and in the case of these most familiar of trees, it is like touching the arm of an old friend. When that tree falls in a storm or because the council determines that its canopy has become too broad or that it poses a threat, we feel its loss. It is one of the small tragedies of the discrepancy between our lives and theirs that we notice the sudden felling, but so much more rarely, their growth.

We are drawn by the stability of trees. They do not move or migrate, at least not in a way that makes sense in our view of time. Yet, they have allowed us to move through the world and to connect, for good or ill. They have unshackled us from our borders, and with their timbers we have created boats with which to go viking, to look outwards into the world before coming home to our trees, where we tell stories beneath the shade of the banyan.

So, it seems fitting that dendrolatry – a worship of trees – is built into many of our religious systems, and that arboreal symbolism is built into our major rituals and festivals. Wood is the bringer of death, in the form of the hanging tree, the cross, the gallows pole and the pyre, the longbow and the arrow's shaft, the club and the boomerang, though it also allows us to walk in sacred Shintō and Buddhist groves. And when we bury our dead, we do so in wood or we scatter their ashes beneath the broad canopies of trees. We bring Christmas trees into our homes and light slow-burning yule logs, plant trees at Tu BiShvat, worship the sacred fig, or bodhi, tree, sing or shout into the dark night as we wassail.

They are symbols of strength and growth, reminders of some prelapsarian past, some great garden from which we are barred entry. Woodlands are places of retreat and they bring us together – whether to gather their fruit or simply to benefit from being in their presence. And if we are wise, we treat our trees and woodlands with respect because those trees that have lived long lives are our elders and those that are in their infancy are our future. They have shaped us as much as we have shaped them, and, as our lives are interlocked with theirs, our future too may be found somewhere in the heart of the woods.

The Nearly Home Trees at Cookworthy Knapp.

A GLOSSARY OF TREE WORDS

afforestation   The establishment of woodland and forest cover where previously there was little or none. Many of the most recent afforestation projects.

anchorage   A description of the way in which a tree is tethered to the ground by the interrelation of the roots and soil. The effect of anchorage is to offset the effects of the wind and gravity on the tree's trunk and canopy.

bodger   A woodworker who works in the forest making chairs through felling trees and coppicing poles. The bodger's art is characterized by the use of the pole-lathe, hand tools and green wood.

bole   The main trunk or stem of a tree, and the part of the tree most often used for its timber.

bolling   A tree from which all the branches have been cropped.

broadleaf   Another name for deciduous trees, which shed their leaves in autumn and regrow them in spring. They are so named as they typically have larger, flat leaves, as opposed to evergreen trees, which often have needle-shaped leaves.

burl   (or burr) is a growth on a tree, a kind of scar tissue that can be caused by damage to a trunk or branch. In a burl, the grain direction is inconsistent, and when used in furniture or woodcarving, burls often have highly figured grain patterns. Burls are highly prized by the makers of *kuksas* – traditional wooden cups – as they are less prone to splitting when filled with hot water.

carrying capacity   The maximum amount of healthy wildlife a habitat can support without degradation of that habitat.

clearcut   Removing, or cutting down, all the trees in a given area.

coppice with standards   A woodland in which the majority of trees are managed for coppicing, with some trees allowed to grow to full height.

crank   The lowest part of a wooden spoon, usually in the bowl.

crown shyness   The tendency for tree canopies to avoid touching.

deadwood   Any part of a tree that is no longer living.

dendrochronology   The science of dating a tree using the patterns of growth rings in its trunk.

dendrology   The branch of botany that deals with trees and woody plants.

dendrolotry   The worship of trees.

duodji   The traditional crafts of the Sami people of Finland. *Duodji* incorporates many crafts from knife-making, bags, clothes and cups. One area of *duodji* is the making of *kuksa* (or *guksa*).

forest   A gathering of trees over 1.24 acres. In the Middle Ages, the meaning of forest was similar to a 'preserve', land kept for specific purposes, such as hunting. As such, forests often supported wolves, deer and other game for hunting, but might have incorporated habitats such as heaths and grasslands. In the UK, several 'tiny forests' about the size of a tennis court – based on the ideas of the 1970s' Japanese botanist Akira Miyawaki – are being planted, the first in Bristol, with others planned in Birmingham, Wolverhampton, Leicester and Glasgow.

froe   A tool for cleaving wood with the handle and blade at right angles to one another. Froes are most often used to split the staves for casks or to cleave a block of wood into shingles.

Greenwood   A forest in full leaf. More specifically, the Greenwood is used as a description for mythical home of Robin Hood and, more generally, as the refuge for outlaws. To 'go to the Greenwood' is to become an outlaw.

haar   A wet mist or fog, coming in off the sea. The word *haar* is used in many parts of the UK, including the north-east of England and across Scotland.

Heartwood   The inner part of a tree trunk, often harder than the outer layers of trunk, which is known as sapwood.

Hoppus Foot   A method of measuring the cubic content of round timber.

inosculation   A natural phenomenon in which the trunks, branches or roots of a tree grow together. When the cambium of two trees (or the branches or trunks of one tree) touch, they sometimes self-graft and grow together. A linked concept is conjoined (or married) trees, in which two trees growing adjacent join as adult trees. In some parts of the world, this process is harnessed for architecture, for example India's Meghalaya living root trees, in which the roots of Ficus elastic trees (the Indian rubber tree) on opposing sides of a river or valley, are trained to grow towards one another and eventually inosculate. According to researchers from the University of Munich, these living bridges, which can span 65 feet, prove stronger than steel structures, which rust in the constant humidity or bamboo, and which wash away in floods.

komorebi   A Japanese word that refers to the quality of light as it passes through the branches and leaves of trees.

Krummholz   Also referred to as *Kneiholz*, of elfin-wood, *Krummholz* are stunted growth trees, shaped by relentless exposure to wind. From the German 'knee timber'.

leader   The top stem of a tree.

lignin   The substance that gives trees their woody texture.

mensuration   The measurement of the total wood mass of a forest.

kikkaminumanosakura   A Japanese word for change that occurs suddenly, such as the change that cherry blossoms undergo from being in full bloom to shedding their petals.

Ogham   An early medieval (possibly earlier) writing system found in Britain and Ireland (though differing in terms of the number of characters – British Ogham consists of twenty characters, Irish twenty-five). Due to the relationship between the characters and trees, it is also commonly known as the 'tree alphabet'.

overstory   The highest layer of a woodland or forest, consisting of the canopies of its tallest trees.

pollarding   The cutting back of the upper branches of a tree, encouraging new growth. Pollarding is similar to ***coppicing***, though takes place higher up the tree.

psithurism   The sound of the wind whispering through the trees. (Pronounced *sutherizum*, it is rather wonderfully onomatopoeic.) The American poet Longfellow had it that the sound of the winds in the trees was a 'celestial symphony.'

sakura   Japanese for cherry blossom, though the word has a secondary meaning of to laugh or smile.

shinrin-yoku   Forest bathing. A term introduced by the Japanese Forest Association in 1982 following research about the effects of pollution and stress in increasingly urban populations. The birthplace of Forest Therapy is Akasawa National Recreation Forest, located in the Kiso Valley.

shivelight   The way in which poet Gerard Manley Hopkins described the light that filters through a canopy of trees onto a forest floor, a lance of well-defined sunlight set against the darker backdrop of the forest.

silviculture   The cultivation of woods and forests, involving the growing of and tending to trees.

sloyd   The Swedish system for teaching woodwork.

snag   Standing dead or dying trees, providing habitats for birds, mammals, invertebrates

snedding   To prune or cut branches.

suckering   A form of asexual reproduction involving the formation of a new stem from an existing root system. Some trees, such as elms, cherries, and aspen are able to create suckers, clones of the mother or father tree.

suthering   The word coined by poet John Clare for the noise of the wind in the treetops.

tanbark   The bark of trees that is used in the tanning of hides or leather.

treen   An old English word that means 'of trees'. Seen in inventories and wills, treen relates to small household items made of wood such as bowls and cups, boxes and plates.

understory   The shrubs and small trees that grow beneath the main canopy of a forest, but above the forest floor.

Waldeinsamkeit   A German word that relates to the feeling one may get when alone in the woods. There is no direct English translation for this word, and a literal translation might be 'forest loneliness' though the word can be used to describe a feeling of profound peace and sublimity among the trees.

woodkern A word from medieval Ireland meaning a bandit or outlaw, living in the forest.

woodwose The mythical wild man of the woods, the woodwose is a figure of ancient folklore, often related to a satyr or fawn. *Wuduwasa* in Anglo-Saxon.

zan'ou The Japanese term for the last remaining cherry blossom petal. When this petal falls, it marks the end of spring and the beginning of summer.

NOTES

EPIGRAPH

p.7. Dafydd ap Gwilym, born around 1320, is widely regarded as one of the greatest Welsh poets, though little is known about his life. In 'Offern y Llwyn', as with many of Gwilym's poems, a love of nature is one of the core themes and his 'mass' seems – to me at least – to celebrate the birds of the woodland, ending on lines that suggest his worship is offered to the birds as much as it is to God. The translation of the poem is taken from the dafyddapgwilym.net, published by the Welsh Department at Swansea University and the Centre for Advanced Welsh and Celtic Studies, where the poem may be read in full.

I. WOODLAND PLANTER

p.16. *...the nearest town in Shropshire, was blanketed in acorns...* The previous year had been a mast year for oaks, one in which they produce far more than their usual number of acorns. The term 'mast' comes from the Old English *mæst* and refers to the nuts of forest trees. No one really understands why oaks have mast years, nor the mechanism that causes them to synchronize this mass production of acorns, though researchers at Wytham Woods are currently engaged in a study of this exact question.

p.15. *...a ship like the 104-gun HMS* Victory... The planting of oaks for a future navy seems, perhaps, like a particularly British thing to do, though in the 1830s, following the Napoleonic Wars, the Swedish Navy planted about 300,000 oaks on the island of Visingsö, to be used for their future navy. As with Collingwood's oaks, by the time the Visingsö oaks grew to a size of which they could be of use, Sweden's ships, like Britain's, were no longer constructed of wood.

p.15. *...fashioned into the planks of a hull...* The stand of 200 oaks now known as Collingwood's Oaks – one for each of the ships in the Royal Navy at the time – were in fact planted by his wife, Sarah, at the estate in Hethpool, in Northumberland, in 1815, five years after Collingwood's death en route back to England .

p.15.   *'Blessed is he who plants trees under whose shade he will never sit.'* This quote, or ones similar, appear across India and Africa, in Turkey and the Americas, in the writings of Cicero (*serit arbores, quae alteri saeclo prosint*), in sermons and in philosophical and political treatises. It is as close to a universal saying as any that exist.

p.17.   *The woodland comprises sixteen species of native...* There are sixty or so native trees in Britain, species that have established themselves without our involvement. The time boundary used to define native is about 8,200 years, the point at which the land bridge between Britain and mainland Europe was cut. 'Native' is a freighted term, though the trees in my father's woodland are all native in this sense. There in the garden – the beech, chestnut, sycamore, which are not. Source: *The New Sylva*, p. 28.

p.17.   *...crab apple and alder...* These are bolstered by the sycamore and oaks, a variety of apples in the small orchard, copper beech, yew and rowans that were already growing in the garden.

p.19.   *...constructed almost entirely from coppiced wood...* The Sweet Track was constructed of a rather wonderful collection of woods including oak, ash, lime, hazel, alder, holly, willow, poplar, ivy, birch, dogwood and apple and demonstrates that by the early Neolithic, people had already begun to manage woodlands in the knowledge that a coppiced tree is more productive than one left to grow without intervention. In *Trees and Woodlands in the British Landscape*, Oliver Rackham details several other known ancient uses of wood in Britain, including the Bronze Age Brigg Logboat, made from a single oak trunk, 48 feet (14.6 metres) long, and an enormous artificial wooden island at Flag Fen, near Peterborough, covering about 4 acres, from the late Bronze Age.

p.22.   *...much of the area is given over to sheep farming...* Of note, just a stone's throw from here is the site of Sycharth Castle, which was, between 1400 and 1403, the home of the leader of the last great Welsh rebellion against English rule, Owain Glyndŵr, before it was torched in May of 1403 by the young Prince Hal (the future Henry V). There is little to draw attention to the site now; it's just a bare hillock amid woodland in the grounds of a farm, though at one time there was a motte and bailey castle here.

p.23.   *...lack of language about trees and woodlands...* This is no new phenomenon. In 1878, Francis George Heath bemoaned, in his book *Our Woodland Trees*, that most visitors to woodlands *'know, in a sort of general way, perhaps half-a-dozen species'*.

2. WILLOW WEAVER

p.29.   *... with a roundwood timber-frame infilled with straw bale walls...* Ele and Anthony learnt to build their roundwood house from Sussex woodsman Ben Law, with whom they lived for several months in what Ele described as a collapsing yurt, when they were volunteers at Law's wonderfully named Prickly Nut Wood. Ele's stories of her time there are full of washing her hair with water boiled in a Kelly Kettle, and eating squirrel cooked over campfires. The couple were inspired by Law's way of being in the woods, the principles of permaculture and the idea of making a living from coppicing and making charcoal and furniture from the trees on his land, and set about creating their own self-sustaining woodland twenty years ago.

p.30. *'We do this every Imbolc,'...* One of the traditions of Imbolc, which is linked to the Christian feast day of St Brigid, itself an echo of an older lambing festival, is to weave a Brigid's Cross, which is hung in the rafters of the house in order to protect it and its occupants throughout the year. In the Waters' home, the wreath is a living willow that is woven into a circle around a centrepiece on the table. There it will grow and later the willow will be planted on the land here.

p.31. *The Anglo-Saxons celebrated the solstices and the equinoxes, the Celts...* Source: R. Hutton, *The Stations of The Sun*, 1996, p. 409.

p.31. *...within these, traces of the older celebrations remain...* It is worth noting that others disagree. Alternative theories include that these festivals are debasements of Christian and pre-Christian practices.

p.31. *...is largely a mid-twentieth century reconstruction...* As far back as Julius Ceasar's 'Commentaries on the Gallic War', he noted *'The whole nation of the Gauls is greatly devoted to ritual observances.'*

p.31. *It is the work of neo-druids and Wiccans...* The rather wonderful – possibly apocryphal – origin story has it that the wheel, as it is today, was developed during a naturist retreat of a Wiccan coven in Hertfordshire.

p.32. *...a bringing together of folklores and traditions...* A favourite is found in Wiccan mythology, popularized (or perhaps mostly invented) by Robert Graves, in which the Wheel of the Year is overarched by another narrative, that of the Oak King and the Holly King. These two figures are locked in an endless battle, the balance of which tips at the equinoxes. At the winter solstice, the Oak King overthrows the Holly King, who begins to regain his strength at the spring equinox until he defeats the Oak King at the summer solstice, and so the battle continues, life and death intertwined.

p.32. *As a still and increasingly secular society...* The UK Census noted a fall of 5.3 million Christians in Britain between 2001 and 2011, and a report on the state of UK church life in *Church Statistics*, 2015, forecast that church membership would fall from the 30 per cent of the population recorded in 1930, which represented a peak, in the twentieth century at least, to 8.4 per cent by 2025.

p.35. *...play that person's favourite games...* There is another Māori death tradition, the *tangihanga* – often shortened to *tangi* – a ceremony specifically designed around the mourning of the dead, which includes the recital of ritualized *whakataukī* on hearing the news of a death, such as *'Kua hinga te tōtara i Te Waonui-a-Tāne'*, meaning 'the tōtara tree has fallen in Tāne'. The tree is tall and strong, denoting the place in society held by the deceased and Tāne is the great forest god's woodland. It feels fitting to grow trees in the place of the ones that have fallen.

p.38. *...the practice certainly ancient...* Willow coffins were first documented in Roman times though willow has a far longer association with death. Our word 'coffin' derives from the Ancient Greek, *kóphinos*, for basket, which speaks to the probability that early coffins were woven. In Greek myth, willow provided a gateway to the underworld and is associated with Hades, god of the realm of death, who taught people to use magic using willow, water and the moon, and Orpheus, when he went into the underworld, carried willow with him as protection. There are practical reasons to use willow for a coffin. It is quick to grow – a single rod can grow 8 feet in a season – and willow breaks down after six months to a year in the ground, making it far more ecologically friendly than the laminates used in standard coffins. In more recent years, seagrass, hyacinth, bamboo, banana leaf and wool have also been used.

3. WOODLORE GATHERER

p.43. ...*nor the birds we hear in their canopies*... One study, conducted by company NPower, in 2019, found six in ten adults in Britain could neither identify a maple or oak leaf. The same survey found 16 per cent of the 2,000 people surveyed believed Wi–Fi was more important than trees.

p.44. ...*expanding dendrometer bands*... Dendrometer bands are used to make repeated measurements of a tree's growth.

p.44. *Wytham is one of just seventy-seven Forest Global Earth Observatory health sites in the world*... The Forest Global Earth Observatory is a global network of forest research sites and scientists that comprises seventy-seven forest research sites across the world. Wytham Woods is the only site located in the UK. It monitors around seven million trees and 13,000 species, as well as changes in the climate, and carbon levels.

p.44. ... '*as a place of sustained, intensive ecological research*'... Source: the introduction to *Wytham Woods: Oxford's Ecological Laboratory* edited by Peter Savill, Christopher Perrins, Dr Keith Kirby and Nigel Fisher, 2011.

p.46. ...*with subcutaneous tags used to track their movements*... Incidentally, these sensors were also designed by the postdoctoral researcher Curt Lamberth, who developed the sensor for measuring moonlight.

p.46. ...*the Old Man of Wytham*... Keith Kirby is one of the most influential figures in British ecology. He undertook his doctorate on bramble ecology at Wytham in 1976 and went on to work as a woodland ecologist with the Nature Conservancy Council, English Nature and Natural England. He is Fellow in the department of plant sciences at the University of Oxford, where he continues to write about woodland conservation. The Old Man of Wytham is the name of Keith's blog in which he records thoughts on woodlands. See: theoldmanofwytham.com

p.47. ...*has had its genome sequenced for the Darwin Tree of Life project, the model*... Much of our knowledge about the DNA of woodland plants and animals is being gathered here. It is one of the key sites for the Darwin Tree of Life project, the aim of which is to sequence the genome of all 70,000 eukaryotic species in Britain and Ireland – in other words, all the animals, plants and fungi. Thousands of specimens for the project are being gathered at Wytham.

p.48. ...*so the policy of the first foresters and conservators*... Wytham is remarkable for many reasons, not least of which is that it has had only three conservators since the university took ownership of the woods in 1942.

p.52.   *One scheme, the Living Ash Project...* The Living Ash project suggests that 1 per cent of ash trees have high levels of tolerance to the disease, and 10 per cent has some tolerance, qualities that are heritable, and therefore reproducible. For more on the Living Ash Project, see: www.livingashproject.org.uk

p.52.   *Beyond the ash trees, we came to Radbrook Common...* Over time, Keith told me, the land had shifted between open commons and woodland. At this point in its history, it was wooded, though might at some point return to being open again.

p.53.   *...'I understand well under 1 per cent'...* One example of how little we really understand about woodlands, Nigel told me, made national news only a month before, with a headline that read: 'Trees store twice as much carbon as previously thought'. It was a result of new technologies challenging existing knowledge, in this case the calculation used to determine the weight of biomass in mature trees. Where the previous way of ascertaining a tree's mass – and therefore capacity for storing carbon – was based on measuring the circumference of the tree at various points and applying an equation, the new calculations were based on three-dimensional laser scans of whole trees. It was little surprise, after my dizzying introduction to the woodlands, to discover the research had been undertaken in a 15-acre plot at Wytham. The previous method involved measuring the diameter of the tree at a certain point and performing a series of allometric equations to work out the biomass. The equation that had been used was based on young trees from the Lake District. In short, no one had wanted to do the work to update these old equations and as a result, when the laser scans revealed they had previously been vastly underestimating the biomass of trees. The study demonstrated that the old measurements had been out by a 100 per cent, though more worrying, perhaps, was the way in which the media treated the study. 'The focus of the early headlines said, "Look! Trees are going to save us",' Nigel said. 'The reality is that it's twice as important not to cut down trees. And we know that trees aren't actually the key thing in terms of climate change. It's a part of the picture, though it's not the full picture.'

p.54.   *...a common trope was tales of natural abundance...* Source: 'The Value of Evidence About Past Abundance: Marine Fauna of the Gulf of California through the Eyes of 16th to 19th Century Travellers'. Andrea Sáenz-Arroyo *et al*, 2006. *Fish and fisheries* (Oxford, England) 7(2), 128–46.

p.57.   *...the stick making industry of the Stroud valleys...* Source: S. Mills, 'Stick Manufacture in the Stroud Valleys', Gloucestershire Society for Industrial Archaeology Journal, 1996, p. 35.

p.57.   *...thousands of walking sticks and umbrellas were turned out daily...* Notable customers of the Chalford Stick Company included Charlie Chaplin.

4. HEARTWOOD CARVER

p.71.   *...they will recall the love with which I made it...* One Christmas, a few years ago, when our children were still young enough to believe in magic, my father carved them both wands from wood in his nascent woodland. There are few things they now treasure above their phones and games consoles, though these wands are precious things, and have continued to be long after the obsessions with Harry Potter have faded. Occasionally, years later, they still take them out of their boxes and give them a wave as if to test whether their magic has come in yet.

p.73.   *In his preface to* Woodland Crafts in Britain, *Herbert L. Edlin...* Herbert L. Edlin, *Woodland Crafts in Britain.* Reprinted 1973.

p.73.   *And there are the Bodgers, of course...* While, as with the other terms, Bodger is used as a surname, its etymology does not seem to be related to the craft of bodging, but instead to an Anglo-Saxon term for travelling peddlars, or – according to some sources – badgers. As the Industrial Revolution took hold and the small and familial were replaced by the factory and the machine-driven, the definition of the term 'bodger' morphed to mean one who does things badly, as in a bodged job.

p.74.   *...past people with spills of beech in their hair...* I later found out these beech spills were part of a small intervention for the festival for anyone where was attending but who was shy or socially awkward, titled CASH, which stands for 'come and say hello'.

p.77.   *...the crack cocaine of the bodging world, bowl turning...* I experienced this rabbit hole for myself after I started to carve spoons. I found myself setting challenges, to use as many different woods as I could, to use only one particular tool, and then to make my own tools. Only a few months earlier, my father and I had spent a day at a woodland forge at the Small Woods Centre in Ironbridge, making our own knives from scratch.

p.78.   *...but people interested in the adjacent field of bushcraft...* Kuksas stand as a kind of symbol of self-reliance, and the Nordic tradition is also echoed in another, that of the noggin or canoe cup, that was popular at the height of the fur trade in the northern states of America in the 1600s. Scottish and French-Canadian fur traders travelling in the North American interior by canoe travelled light. Aside from their clothes, they might carry a knife, a cup and a spoon. The cup was both an eating and drinking vessel, and when the canoe needed to be bailed out, it would serve for that too. When it was not in use, the handle would be tucked into the trader's sash, which was worn to prevent hernias from the exertions of paddling. When the old noggin had reached the end of its useful life, it could be discarded and another one carved. On a long journey, a trader might make a second, sometimes highly decorated canoe cup as a gift or to trade with the indigenous peoples from whom they bought their furs.

5. BOAT BUILDER

p.87.   *...date back some 8,000 years...* The earliest known boat is the Pesse canoe in the Netherlands, a dugout canoe created from a single pine tree.

p.87.   *A faithful replica...* When I spoke with Luke Powell about building *Agnes*, he talked to me about the negative bias against the word 'replica', which he felt was unfair to the craft. 'Replicating is seen as not as real as something new. I'm trying to say what we're building is absolutely as was, and the word "replica" should maybe not be used, because it's a derogatory. It implies something inferior. Building within the space and rebuilding a boat from those bones, makes it much more real than starting with something new.'

p.99.   *...and manoeuvrable, clinker-built boats...* The alternative to clinker-built boats was usually carvel design, in which the planks lay alongside each other, which made for a faster boat, though not as strong as clinker-built vessels.

p.99.   *...the people known as the Gall-Ghàidheil...* The word *GalGael* refers the ethic mix – *Gall*, the foreigner, and *Gael*, those from the heartland.

p.99.   *...were erased from the waters of the Hebrides...* Unlike Viking longboats, birlinns were not preserved in graves. Timber was scarce on the islands, so it is likely that when a boat came to the end of its life on the water good timber was reused and anything that could not be saved was used for burning.

p.100. *...of other prominent clan chiefs on the Hebridean islands...* Coinciding with the demise of the birlinn, the Gaelic language went into sharp decline too. Although Gaelic was on the wane by the medieval period – it was overtaken by English sometime in the 1400s –it was not until the 1600s that there was a concerted effort to eradicate the language. The Statutes of Iona required that the clan chiefs should send their heirs to Lowland Scotland to be educated in English-speaking schools. By the time of the Jacobite uprising of 1745, English speakers held all the power in the Highlands and by the time of the 1921 census, fewer than 10,000 people were noted as Gaelic-only speakers, following the ravages of the war on the language and those of the First World War. Although Gaelic is now taught in Scottish schools, and actively promoted, it is still marginalized, listed as a 'definitely endangered' language by UNESCO. Source: 'The decade when Scotland lost half its Gaelic-speaking people', *The Scotsman*, 18 December 2022. See: https://www.scotsman.com/news/national/the-decade-when-scotland-lost-half-its-gaelic-speaking-people-3957569

p.102. *...from one of Govan's two short-lived periods of prosperity...* The other of Govan's periods of prosperity was in the Middle Ages, when it was, briefly, a powerbase for Kingdom of Strathclyde.

p.106. *The protest built up around around the charity's charismatic leader...* Colin, like many people in Glasgow, saw the country park as a right for the community as it had been gifted to the people of Glasgow by Sir John Stirling Maxwell in 1911, 'that the open spaces and woodlands within the area shall remain for the enhancement of beauty of the neighbourhood as well as the citizens of Glasgow'.. Source: N. Haynes, *Pollok Park Conservation Area Appraisal*, 2016.

p.106. *...who became a spokesman for a movement...* Source: Birdman of Pollok/ *Curaidh na Coille*, BBC Alba (2019) .

p.109. *Sailing* Orcuan *is a rite of passage, he told me...* Though the same might be true of one of the charity's other rituals – the lighting of a fire, or the creation of a wooden bench on which others might sit.

6. LANDSCAPE ROAMER

p.115. *...including the barbastelle bat...* The Woodland Trust estimates there are about 5,000 barbastelle bats (*Barbastella barbastellus*) left in the UK. A recent study found these bats have been endangered for hundreds of years, since the great oaks of England were felled to create its vast navy. Source: Razgour, et al. 'Applying genomic approaches to identify historic population declines in European forest bats', *Journal of Applied Ecology*. 13 December 2023.

p.115. *...and the blue ground beetle...* The blue ground beetle's Latin name is *Carabus intricatus*.

p.115. *...on the temperate rainforests of Britain and land ownership...* Guy Shrubsole is the author of *The Lost Rainforests of Britain*, and *Who Owns England?: How we lost our land and how we can get it back.*

p.115. *...as well as the threat to them posed by high numbers of pheasants...* Somewhere between 40 and 50 million game pheasants are released into the British countryside each year, over three quarters in England. Source: 'Ecological Consequences of Gamebird Releasing and Management on Lowland Shoots in England': A review by rapid evidence assessment for Natural England and the British Association of Shooting and Conservation, 1st ed., July 2020.

p.116. *...fewer than two-thirds had been assessed in the last decade...* Source: 'A Sight for Sore SSSIs'. See https://wildjustice.org.uk/sssis/a-sight-for-sore-sssis-a-wild-justice-report/

p.117. *...a steep wooded valley of beautifully inosculated beeches...* The word 'inosculation' comes from the Latin *osculum*, to kiss.

p.119. *... to graze livestock pigs in a forest on Common Land...* The Commons is a concept that dates back to the medieval period and refers to land to which local commoners have rights. It might be land that is owned privately though over which people who live locally have some rights, such as the right to dig turf (turbary), the right to graze (pasture), or estover (the right to gather underwood, fallen branches, bracken and gorse, mainly for burning).

p.119. *...have fallen out of use in much of England...* Pannage is no longer observed in most areas, aside from in the New Forest in the south of England. Here, it is referred to as 'common of mast' and there is a set amount of time in which pigs are allowed to roam the forest and eat the acorns which make up a large proportion of their diet at this time. Estovers is, similarly, practised in the New Forest, as an area of Commons, though many tenants sold their rights to gather fuelwood to the Forestry Commission. This right is now controlled strictly, the Forestry Commission providing an amount of wood for burning to eligible commoners, and the collection of fallen branches restricted to anyone living in a property that was build prior to 1950, so long as they are transported by hand rather than vehicle.

p.119. *...since the Winter Hill protests...* While the Kinder Scout mass trespass of 1932 is better known, the earlier trespasses on Winter Hill in 1896 that paved the way for that landmark protest. The Winter Hill trespasses took place after landowner Richard Ainsworth closed a path used by the residents of Bolton to escape the city's ceaseless industry and the grime of the mills in which they worked. He had a fence built and erected a sign stating that trespassers would be prosecuted. On 6 September 1896, 10,000 people gathered to walk on the hill, the first of several organized trespasses to demonstrate against the restrictions. The Winter Hill trespasses failed, with key players being fined heavily and the courts ruled in favour of Ainsworth, though it served as a precursor to the later, more symbolically important trespass at Kinder Scout in the Peak District

p.119. ...*'and his eyes as deep as peat water pools'*... Source: Sabine Barind-Gould, *A Book of The West*, 1899.

p.120. ...*the nineteenth-century Devonian priest and scholar Sabine Baring-Gould*... Source: Sabine Barind-Gould, *A Book of The West*, 1899.

p.120. ...*that campers were damaging the environment*... The argument offered was conspicuously similar to that given by the landowners around Kinder Scout, who argued the protesters were disturbing the natural habitat of the moorland.

p.120. ...*without having to ask permission of a landowner*... This partial access is enshrined in the 2000 Countryside & Rights of Way (CRoW) Act, whereas access on Dartmoor is covered by the Dartmoor Commons Act 1985, which designates large areas as common land, with fewer restrictions.

p.123. *The Gaelic word* fiadh... Source: https://scotlandsnature.blog/2022/08/05/a-gaelic-view-of-wild/

p.125. ...*and found myself among the giant conifers of the place*... Reelig Glen is home to some of the tallest trees in Britain including an over 200 feet Douglas Fir, planted in 1882, the tallest larch, at over 150 feet, and lime trees in a similar region.

p.125. ...*whose trunks shot straight up*... The firs of Reelig Glen are also known for the straightness of their trunks. The mast of the ship on which Scott travelled to the Antarctic, *The Discovery*, came from the woods here.

p.126. ...*the Scottish Land Reform Act of 2003*... The Scottish Outdoor Access Code gives advice on how best to make use of the guidance within the Land Reform Act. See https://www.outdooraccess-scotland.scot/

p.129. ...*Margaret Wheatley's book,* Turning to One Another... M. Turning Wheatley, *Turning to One Another: Simple Conversations To Restore Hope to the Future*, 2009.

p.129. ...*a mix of Scots pine, downy birch, rowan, oak, aspen, alder and larch*... Scotland has between fourteen and twenty-one native trees, depending on how you count them (Source: Alistair Scott, *A Pleasure in Scottish Trees,* 2002, p. 19), notably Scots Pine, silver birch and sessile oak. There is little native pinewood left as many of the old pine forests were destroyed after the 1745 rebellion, and in this area, there are none of what the Scots call big granny pines.

p.130. ...*precipitated by human interference*... Source: T.C. Smout, *People and Woods in Scotland*, p. 14.

p.130. ...*described as overheated nineteenth-century romanticism*... Source: John Fowler, *Landscapes and Lives: The Scottish Forest Through The Ages*, 2002.

p.130. ...*just 5 per cent of Scotland was wooded*... Source: NatureScot, Scotland's Nature Agency.

p.130. *...ushering in an era of over-grazing and depopulation...* There is much more information on this at Trees for Life. See https://treesforlife.org.uk/into-the-forest/habitats-and-ecology/human-impacts/deforestation. Sources include: T. Smout (ed.). *Scottish Woodland History*, 1997. John Fowler, *Landscapes and Lives*.

p.131. *...an object of worship well before the arrival of the church there...* Source: T. Smout (ed.), *Scottish Woodland History*, p. 20.

p.131. *...represented a disconnect between people and trees in Scotland...* A. Mather, 'The Future' in T. Smout, T (ed.), *Scottish Woodland History*, p. 241.

p.132. *... had not been managed in the intervening time...* The community buy-out at Abriachan could be seen as part of a movement that also involved the community buy-outs at Assynt, Knoydart, and the island of Eigg.

p.132. *...or sitka plantations used as tax dodges...* It is worth noting that while 98 per cent of Scotland is classed as rural, only 17 per cent of the population live in these areas.

p.132. *...McIntosh describes as having...* Source: Alastair McIntosh, 'The Cheviot, the Stag and the Black, Black Carbon: Nature Capital, the Private Finance Investment Pilot and Scotland's Land Reform'. *Community Land Scotland*, 2023, p. 8.

p.133. *...when the Caledonian forest was still more truth...* It is perhaps 5,000 years since most of Scotland, aside from its high peaks and wet marshes, was covered in woodland.

p.133. *...keeping them dry and preventing them from rotting...* This finding was made at Abriachan Forest Trust where there is a replica roundhouse and where the roof rotted due to the lack of a constant fire.

7. WISH WEARER

p.139. *... 'tied indiscriminately to the branches of fir, and spruce, and beech'...* Source: 'The Clootie Well: A Highland Tradition from long before Culloden', *The Times*, 25 May 1957.

p.140. *...belonging to someone who is afflicted...* Other traditions for clootie wells include the leaving of babies and small children who were unwell at the site overnight.

p.142. *in the text* Capitulatio de partibus Saxoniae... '*Si quis ad fonts aut arbores vel lucos votum fecerit aut aliquit more gentilium obtulerit et ad honorem daemonum commederet*', which translates as: 'Sacrifices at groves in a heathen fashion and the custom of making meals in honor of demons are rejected'. *Capitulatio de partibus Saxoniae.*

p.142. *...divided between local charities...* Source: *Aberdeen Press and Journal*, 3 May 1937.

p.142. *...and similar forms of tree worship stretch across the globe...* The worship of the well and the tree together is long enshrined in religion. According to Norse myths, the great ash tree of life and wisdom, *Yggdrasil* was cared for by the three fates of the past, present and future, Urd, Verdandi and Skuld, who cared for it with water from the well of wisdom.

p.143. ...*writing in the eleventh century*... *Gesta Hammaburgensis Ecclesiae Pontificum*, c.1075.

p.143. ...*the shrine itself sits within the trunk's huge hollow*... Perhaps most amazingly, in 2016, at team of researchers found what they suspect may be tree shrines created by chimpanzees in the Republic of Guinea. They discovered trees with hollows filled with rocks which, they said, were 'eerily similar' to man-made stone shrines at sacred trees in parts of West Africa. Source: H. Kühl, A. Kalan, M. Arandjelovic, et al. 'Chimpanzee Accumulative Stone Throwing.' *Sci Rep* 6, 22219 (2016). See https://doi.org/10.1038/srep22219

p.147. ...*so people could report problems connected to individual trees*... Source: 'Melbourne's trees bombarded with emailed love letters', the *Guardian*, 29 January 2015.

p.148. ...*in which the forestry sector trashed wholesale many of Britain's native woodlands*... These prints, however, were echoes of a much earlier one. In Jean Honore Frogonard's *The Souvenir*, painted in the 1770s, a girl carves the initials of her lover into a tree, watched over by her lapdog, a letter – presumably from her lover – cast aside on the ground. It is a startlingly similar image, though Frogonard's painting was itself an echo of Jean Jacques Rousseau's epistolary novel *Julie*, which charts an illicit love affair between the eponymous Julie and her tutor and former lover, Saint-Preux.

p.149. ...*and the story is, most likely, apocryphal*... The *Guardian* reported the story as fact in an article titled 'Gravestone-encircled "Hardy Tree" falls in London' on 27 December 2022, though an editorial piece a week later titled 'The *Guardian* view on the death of the Hardy Tree: a legend uprooted' fact-checked the tree's provenance and questioned the author's involvement.

p.149. *Amateur historian*... David Bingham runs the London Dead Blog at: thelondondead.blogspot.com

p.149. *What seems clear though is that trees accumulate myth*... It is worth noting that our myths about trees extend to forestry and woodland ecology, as well as the history of Britain's woodlands, something ecologist Oliver Rackham rails against in his epic work *Woodlands* (2006).

p.150. ...*Raheen Woods in East Clare, Ireland*... The legend of the Wallace Tree is thought to stem from the belief that William Wallace was chained to a tree when he was captured by the English, the chains left on the tree when he was taken to London to stand trial (or, in an alternative telling of the story, when he escaped). Source: BBC Alba article, 'Deep roots of William Wallace tree legend', 3 February 2017.

p.150. ...*in the same place as the tree in which the king hid*... The current Royal Oak is believed to be a descendent of the original tree, about 200 to 300 years old.

p.152. ...*passing the child from mother to father through the riven trunk*... In the Irish tradition, following the passing of the child through the trunk of the tree, the sapling would then be bound, and the riven section would heal.

p.155. ...*without quite knowing why we do so*... This sort of ritual, the passing of a child across or through a threshold, goes back far into the mists of time, small, solemn moments of import, blessings and hopes in an uncertain world.

p.157. ...*both 'comfort and sanctuary'*... Conversation, 15 January 2024.

p.157. *...are planted in the centre of a farmyard...* Source: Douglas Forell Hulmes
    'Sacred Trees of Norway and Sweden: A *Friluftsliv* Quest', Norwegian
    Journal of Frilutsliv, 2009.

p.158. *'The older I get, the more I think that, besides books and a few people, trees are
    the love of my life'...* Tweet by Sarah Crown, 2 September 2019.

p.159. *...the largest of which is more than 25 feet around...* It is worth noting that
    there is current concern that their attraction is impacting the trees at Chirk
    Woods, through people walking round and compacting the ground around
    them, an example of the law of unintended consequences in which we may
    be destroying the thing we venerate.

p.160. *...that a tree considered little more than a weed in most of the country...* Sycamores
    are fast-growing and grow easily in places where other trees struggle. This
    is one of the reasons offered for why it may have thrived at Sycamore Gap,
    where there are no other mature trees in the area. Common knowledge has
    it that the sycamore was introduced to the UK in the 1500s, though some
    sources suggest it was brought over from Central Europe by the Romans.

8. FOREST BATHER

pp.163–4. *...as they are often particularly beautiful...* Other examples include the
    Devil's Arse in the Peak District and the Devil's Cauldron in Devon.

p.164. *... 'is a source of the sublime'...* E. Burke, *A Philosophical Enquiry into the Origin
    of our Ideas of the Sublime and Beautiful*, 1757.

p.165. *...of Sequoia National Park in California...* We are drawn to the biggest, the
    tallest, the oldest. The tallest tree in the world is named Hyperion, a redwood
    in California that stands at 379 feet, literally towering high above the other
    trees in the forest. The oldest tree in the world is thought to be the Great Basin
    Bristlecone Pine, which is over 5,000 years old. General Sherman is the world's
    largest tree (when measured by volume, with a trunk volume of 52,500 cubic
    feet) in Sequoia National Park. However, these trees are nothing compared
    to the giant fungus, the fruits of which are only really ever seen in the form
    of mushrooms. In Oregon's Blue Mountains there is an *Armaillaria ostoyae*
    that may be as much as 8,650-years old, and which covers an area of about
    5,890 acres (the equivalent of just over 9 square miles). Source: https://www.
    scientificamerican.com/article/strange-but-true-largest-organism-is-fungus/

p.165. *...in both sleep quality and the immune system...* For more on this, see Qing Li's
    book, *Forest Bathing: How Trees Can Help You Find Health and Happiness*.

p.169. *We touch wood to ward off bad luck...* Like many superstitions, the origins of
    this habit, which is one I share, is unclear. It is variously claimed that it calls
    back to the height of medieval Christianity when people with a relic from
    the 'true cross' would touch it for protection, or that it is a sailing superstition,
    with sailors knocking on the deck of a boat as protection against heavy
    weather, or a mining superstition, as miners would touch the beams beneath
    which they passed in the hope they would stay strong. Nalini Nadkarni, in
    her book *Between Earth and Sky*, suggests the habit of knocking on wood
    is believed by some linguists as originating in a spiritual practice, in which

the speaker knocked on the trunk of a tree to invoke the help of a spirit, or that it relates to an old Norse belief that knocking on a tree while speaking meant the spirit of the tree was unable to listen in to the speaker's plans, meaning they would be unable to interfere with them.

p.170. ... *'cool, silent, intimate hours'*... M. Proust, *Pleasures and Regrets*, 1896.

p.173. ... *'here are flowers, here are shrubs, birds flit about among them'*... C. Diehm, 'Staying True to Trees: A Specific Look at Anthropocentrism and Non-Anthropocentrism' *Environmental Philosophy*, vol. 5, no. 2, (Fall 2008), pp. 3–16.

p.174. ... *'it makes some feel they are in the presence of God'*... C. Diehm, *op.cit.*

9. MYTH WALKER

p.179. *A noise you cannot place...* This experience recalled an experiment Nigel Fisher, the conservator at Wytham Woods told me about, in which a researcher, Liana Zanette, played the sounds of different predatory animals outside a badger set at night in the woods at Wytham. She wanted to know which sounds would scare the badgers most, and perhaps whether they retained any vestigial memories of the predators their ancestors faced. The recordings ranged from sheep to dogs, bears to wolves to humans, in the form of recordings from the BBC. While the badgers did not react negatively to the sheep or wolves, Zanette found they were wary of the sound of bears, an animal that has been extinct in the UK for a thousand years. Somewhat depressingly predictably, the sound of which they were most wary was that of humans, even the reassuring tones of the Beeb.

p.181. ...*what writer Sara Maitland calls 'forest fear'*... Sara Maitland, in *Arboreal*, p. 215.

p.182. ...*in terms of walking into imagined woods...* For example, Umberto Eco's *Six Walks in the Fictional Woods* , and John Yorke's *Into The Woods*.

p.184. ...*into which they stray against all advice...* Vladimir Propp, *Theory and History of Folklore*, translated by A. Martin and R. Martin, 1984, p. 116.

p.184. ...*the dark woods of the stories the Grimms collected provide the perfect setting...* The Brothers Grimm conjectured that the source of the word 'forest' comes from the Old High German, *forha*, a term which related specifically to fir trees, and it is clearly a coniferous forest they had in mind when they wrote of Hansel and Gretel being led into the woods by their starving parents. Similarly, the *selva oscura*, the twilight forest of Dante's 'Inferno', the confounding, intimidating, disorienting wood in which the poet finds himself at the beginning of the narrative, seem to echo a particular type of forest.

Neither the fairytales Jacob and Wilhelm Grimm collected in the early 1800s, nor the *selva oscura*, were the stories of this island though. They were inspired by the vast forests of Bavaria. They have become so much a part of our cultural landscape it would be easy enough to forget this. But we have been telling stories based on the woods and forests of Britain and Ireland for centuries.

p.185. *...the landscape that inspired legends that originated closer to home...* This may be reflected in the ways in which woodlands and forests are explored in the Germanic fairytales of the brothers Grimm and those from England such as the 'Forbidden Forest', a story from Warwickshire, which tells the story of a king who becomes obsessed with a girl he sees while out riding. The girl refuses his advances and the king enforces a reign of terror on the country: no young woman is safe. The grandmother of the girl falls ill and the girl has to take her goods to market. Before she leaves, her grandmother warns her about the king, and of the wood through which she must pass, particularly a great oak. The girl sets out and in the heart of the forest encounters the tree her grandmother has warned her of. There is no way around or past this tree. When the girl curtseys to the tree, a way through opens up to her. The king, having followed her into the forest also comes across the oak, but he treats it with disdain. As he makes to pass it, a great branch falls from it and kills him, drawing his men into the forest which closes around them, sealing their fate. Source: *English Fairy Tales and Legends*, R. Kerven, 2008, pp. 126–8. In this story, the heart of the forest, while somewhat ambiguous and capable of great violence, is essentially on the side of natural law, that the innocent should be protected, as with the stories of Robin Hood.

p.185 *Stories of Robin Hood begin to crop up in fourteenth-century England...* J.C. Holt, in *Robin Hood*, p. 187, suggests that the legend was already a national one in England by the second-half of the thirteenth century, based on the proliferation of the surname Robinhood..

p.186. *...a kind of mythic memory of the freedom the Greenwood offered...* S. Schama, *Landscape and Memory*, p. 140. And Oliver Rackham, *Trees and Woodlands in the British Landscape*, 1990.

p.186. *...an assertion bolstered by the great survey of 1086...* S. Schama, *op. cit.* p. 142.

p.186. *...Schama describes the Greenwood as a useful fantasy...* S. Schama, *op. cit.* p. 154.

p.187. *When I read the medieval epic poem, 'Sir Gawain and The Green Knight'...* Written in the late fourteenth century by a poet whose name is lost to time, he is now known as The Gawain Poet.

p.188. *...he found that the wilderness was already within him...* It is worth noting that William Woods in his article, 'Nature and the Inner Man in "Sir Gawain and the Green Knight"', comes to a similar conclusion. Source: *The Chaucer Review*. Vol. 36, No. 3, 209–27. 2002.

p.188. *Just as Robin Hood seems to have the Green Knight in his...* There are many crossovers between the two stories, not least the Green Chapel, which some scholars believe is based on Lud's Church, the natural stone chasm in England's Black Forest in Staffordshire, and which, in one telling of the Robin Hood stories, becomes a place of refuge for Robin and his Merry Men. Robin Hood, to me, however, seems a kind of crossover between the elemental Green Man, and the natural justice and goodness represented by Sir Gawain. And all these figures seem in some way to be extrapolations of the spirits of the forest that appear the world over. There are few traditions in which trees and woodlands are not the home to some sort of deity or spirit of place that might watch over or threaten the lone walker in the woods. For as long as we have told stories about them, we have populated our woods with fantastical creatures which walk this fine line between curiosity, joy and something edgier, something more wild. The woods have been variously full of spirits and gods: *hamadryads*, the wood spirits of Greek mythology; the Japanese *Kukunochi* tree spirit; the *salabhanjika*, the Hindu tree nymphs; *Nang Tani*, the ghostly spirit who haunts banana trees in Thai mythology; *Božalosć* of Wendish or Slavic mythology; and the *Mahomanay*, who, in the mythology of the Philippines, are kind spirits who protect the creatures of the forest; the Finnish god of the forest, *Tapio*. Some of these spirits are benevolent, others harbingers of death; some mischievous, some deadly serious. Many of them, like Pan, are capricious, capable of helping or hindering, of leading you back to the path or taking you so far from it you no longer have any sense of where it was you came from nor how you might find your way out of the tangle of branches and brambles.

p.188. *...so the Green Knight echoes the even older figure of the Green man...* Not everyone agrees that the Green Man is an ancient symbol. Some scholars assert that he is an invention of the twentieth century since the Green Man of medieval carvings in churches was only named as such from 1939 onwards by the folklorist Lady Raglan, who conflated him with the Green Man of folklore, Jack-in-the-Green, Robin Hood, the King of May. Previously these carvings were known as the foliate heads or *têtes de feuilles*. In her essay, 'Lords of the Wildwood', in Hahn's *Robin Hood in Popular Culture*, Lorraine Kochanscke Stock points out that this conflagration may have been somewhat lazy, with the foliate head, garlanded by leaves or spewing (or consuming, depending on your viewpoint) greenery, more obviously having a link with the Wild Man, who was often portrayed as a bearded figure. Some modern scholars assert that the Green Man is a distinctly Christian symbol, the foliate head being a Christlike figure, the leaves in his mouth and around his head symbols of rebirth. However, there are many theories in which he represents something much older, a symbol that was incorporated into medieval Christian architecture. As a figure often carved from wood, it seems conceivable that the Green Man was a pre-Christian icon of which no trace remains other than in traces in stories. One of the most compelling suggestions of this for me is the famous pediment at the temple of Sulis Minerva Roman Baths at Bath, in England, at the centre of which is a figure strikingly similar to a foliate head. Known as the Gorgon's head, it is uncannily similar to some of the medieval Green Man carvings in churches, dating from around the first century CE. It suggests the figure, perhaps as a pre-Roman god, or what might be considered a product of convergent evolution – a figure recognizable as the 'wild man' common to many cultures across the world. When we are looking at the Green Man, are we then looking at a Christian symbol, a Roman one, a god that predated the Romans and their predecessors? The folklorist Bob Pegg, at least, considered that foliate faces (among other folk symbols) were evidence of an international subculture. Sources: Lady Raglan, 'The "Green Man" in Church Architecture', *Folklore* 50 (1939),

50; Brandon S. Centerwall, 'The Name of The Green Man', *Folklore*, 108 (1997), 25–33.

p.188. *...and the* wudawasa... Similar to the Bigfoot or Sasquatch; it is different in that it is more human than ape in appearance. Although the character's origins may stretch much further back, beyond the Roman god of the woods Silvanus, there are specific references to *wuduwasa* dating back as far as thirteenth-century Norway, and the image has since persisted. German artist Albrecht Dürer incorporated *wuduwasa* into some of his paintings. It is also a feature of Slavic, Germanic, Italian, Norse and Celtic mythologies, among others. In Irish mythology, it is the Woodkern – outlaws and outcasts who live in the woods, those on the edge of society, such as *Na Fianna*, the group led by the mythical Fionn mac Cumhaill.

p.188. *...a hairy, human-like creature that inhabits the woods...* In churches, images of the wild man are often carved or painted roof bosses – such as the one at Canterbury Cathedral, similar positions in which Green Men are often found.

p.188. *...I might be tempted to side with writer A.S. Byatt...* See Byatt's introduction to *The Annotated Brothers Grimm*, ed. Maria Tatar, *xxix*.

p.188. *And the Robin Hood we think we know is a reinvention of a reinvention...* Source: 'Lords of the Wildwood: The Wild Man, the Green Man and Robin Hood' by Lorraine Kochanske Stock, in *Robin Hood in Popular Culture*, ed. Thomas Hahn, 2000, pp. 239–49.

p.188. *...any authentic sources almost entirely absent...* Even one of the key sources for the Robin Hood story, 'A Gest of Robyn Hode', which reflects a medieval story, comes from the 1500s, making it almost impossible to know how much of the story was an interpretation of earlier materials and how much a true representation of them.

p.189. *These stories are seeds carried across time and continents...* A Green Man figure appears in two of my favourite novels. The poet and novelist, Max Porter incorporated him into his short novel *Lanny*, in the form of a mysterious, foul-mouthed Dead Papa Toothwort. At an event Max and I did in Falmouth in 2022, one member of the audience asked Max how Dead Papa Toothwort would feel about the climate crisis. Max replied that he was probably crying, though laughing at the same time, laughing as he was choking on plastic, fumes and oil, because the joke was on us. This, for me at least, nails something right at the heart of that atavistic figure. You can imagine him cackling at you, standing in the dark, terrified, a few feet away from a couple who are standing in the dark, terrified. In Russell Hoban's post-apocalyptic novel *Riddley Walker*, he appears as Greanvine, a face with leaves and vines that emerge from its mouth. The eponymous Riddley encounters the Green Man in the crypt of Cambry Cathedral where he wonders, like most of the Green Men scholars still wonder, how far back did this character go. Like the characters in *Riddley Walker*, we have a cultural amnesia about this figure. As Riddley says, '*Never seen that face befor yet it wer a face I knowit*', p. 165. We have no idea of the origins of the Green Man. He may have been walking with us since we came down from the trees ourselves and left the branches for the savannah. I've been following him into the woods for years and I imagine I will continue to do so for as long as I walk in the woods.

p.190. *Maria Tatar...* Maria Tatar, *The Hard Facts of The Grimms' Fairy Tales*, x1v.

p.190. *...when we return home...* If, as many critics of fairytales suggest, they encode within them taboos such as infanticide, fratricide, cannibalism, incest, child abandonment, once we know of these things it is impossible to unknow them. It is also worth noting that the danger of these taboos comes not from the forest itself, but from the home, from the 'safe' domestic sphere.

10. WAY FOLLOWER

p.197. *...which the Japanese call* momiji... *Momijigari*, the viewing of the autumn leaves, has been practised here since at least the ninth century.

p.197. *...as do the sakura blossoms...* While spring is known as *Sakura* season after the emergence of the cherry blossoms, autumn is known as *Koto*, the season of red leaves, in particular, those of the maple and ginko. Both are considered so important that there is a daily forecast specifically for these times, a blossom forecast – *sakura-zensen* (桜前線) in spring and a leaf forecast in autumn.

p.197. *...of spring...* Just the day before, I had been eating sweets in the shapes of maple leaves and mushrooms, as part of an autumn tea ceremony, and I had come up into the forest to find signs of autumn there too and, more than that, the carpenters' graveyard.

p.200. *...a woodworker friend of a friend...* I owe much to the designer Roy Tam for putting me in touch with Masashi Kutsuwa, who is not only an authority in the traditional woodworking practices of Hida Province, but an excellent and sympathetic translator and a true gentleman. And I owe more to Masashi himself for his generosity and friendship, his expertise and patience. In discussing the difficulties of translating Kiyoki Seike's *The Art of Japanese Joinery*, Yuriko Yobuko and Rebecca Davis wrote that because Japanese carpentry is so different to anything found in the West, there are few direct translations for the technical terms used. I was doubly lucky to have found Masashi for his sensitive translations and knowledge of the traditional woodworking sector in Takayama.

p.201. *'It's just that 93 per cent of it is forest,'...* Takayama's 74,000 residents pale next to the 37 million or so residents of Tokyo, according to the World Population Review in January 2024.

p.201. *...which were used to erect buildings and roofs without the use of nails...* Traditional Japanese joinery is done entirely without the use of metal fasteners like nails or pins. This led to the development of complex joints. The practical reason for this is that wood is inherently flexible, and in an archipelago that sits on the point at which four of Earth's tectonic plates meet, an area known as the Pacific ring of fire, or the Circum-Pacific Belt, where about 90 per cent of all earthquakes occur. As a result, Japan experiences more earthquakes that almost anywhere else on the planet, in the region of 1,500 a year. Wooden buildings are relatively easy to repair and, in addition, the joints, which have more freedom to move and flex, sway with the movement of the earth, resisting earthquake damage. In addition, Japan is relatively poor in terms of mineral deposits, so iron was not readily available to early carpenters, meaning innovation was a necessity.

p.204. *...with a billet of wood held in the groove of a wooden block...* Many traditional Japanese carpenters work on the floor rather than at a bench.

p.204. *...which he had learnt by looking at the old shingles...* The nature of the job means the roof is almost constantly in the process of being retiled, or its shingles rotated. This practice reminds me of another quintessentially Japanese practice, perhaps the greatest example of which is the rebuilding of the central shrine building at Ise in Mie Prefecture, which is only open to the emperor and which is rebuilt every twenty years, as a way of keeping alive the traditional skills of shrine woodwork. Carpenters involved can participate three times in their life – once in their twenties, as a younger, apprentice carpenter, at forty as a master, and at the age of sixty as a supervisor. The *Miyadaiku*, the most experienced shrine carpenters, oversee the project, which is undertaken by practised carpenters, while apprentices learn the techniques. What is being preserved here is not the building, but the traditions and techniques. The Ise Shrine is a particular case – the most valuable in Japan. Most shrines and temples struggle, as there are not enough traditional workers and not enough budget to rebuild those.

p.206. *...with the* sumitsubo, *the carpenter's line...* The *sumitsubo* is seen as a symbol of the carpenter's craft, an example of *Dōgu*, the 'instruments of the Way [of carpentry]', which also includes the square and the pull saw. It speaks to an ancient tradition that stretches back hundreds of years.

p.208. *...the carvings drawing out the yew's natural beauty...* In particular, the *Ichii Ittōbori* carvers of Takayama are known for their use of end grain, showing off the rings of wood growth on the faces of carvings.

p.209. *...the planes...* Anyone interested in the refinement of Japanese tools might check out the *Kezurokai*, the annual hand tool event and celebration of hand-planing, in which competitors shave off insanely thin strips of wood, using planes.

p.209. *...a national shortage of materials such as the urushi lacquer...* Masashi was not an impartial to this, he told me. He had skin in the game, as a professor of woodworking in neighbouring Gifu, and having trained as a woodworker in Takayama, he saw it as a kind of duty to ensure these crafts continued in some form. There was a personal aspect to it too, though. Masashi worked as a furniture maker in England for several years and benefited from the reputation Japanese woodworkers had when he was here, he told me. He was seen as an expert, in part at least, by virtue of his nationality. It was this reputation and the fact he had trained in Takayama, the heart of woodworking in Japan, that made him thankful to his ancestors, he told me, the carpenters and woodworkers who went before him, and who forged this reputation. He is in the process of attempting to establish a support centre for traditional craftworkers, a one-stop support centre for apprentices, materials and tools, connecting traditional workers with toolmakers or forest managers who can provide material.

p.211. *That realization makes it truly precious each time I work with this material...* According to Shintōism, trees that reach one hundred are inhabited by spirits, *kodama*. Even after it has been cut down, according to Shintōism, wood retains its essential spirit.

p.211. *...of the soul of the wood itself...* Kiyosi Seike, *The Art of Japanese Joinery*, p. 13.

p.214. *...or to one of the area's...* When I met the director of the Oak Village school, he talked about his students, including graduates of Kyoto University, one of the most prestigious in Japan, and someone who had left the firm Suzuki to become a woodworker.

p.217. *...and one that provides money but little satisfaction...* It is not just the crafts that are at risk of dying out. Masashi drove me to a young urushi plantation to see the work of a collective of designers and woodworkers' efforts to save the nations lacquer trees. There is a national shortage of the iconic red lacquer, which is applied to wood to create hardwearing, beautiful products. In the past, trees were cultivated and protected, though in the past few decades, people had stopped caring for the trees and recently there was a small scandal when the Japanese Emperor's household was unable to source a kilogram of the lacquer from within the country. It is a delicate job – the urushi tree is toxic and it takes time to build up resistance to it. The collective of sixty woodworkers and students give up their weekends to plant and tend the new trees, which will take ten to fifteen years to mature enough to be harvested for their sap, which is used to create the lacquer. It takes fifteen years to grow an urushi tree to the size needed to collect sap. When the tree has matured, a groove is made in the bark with a special tool, and the sap oozes out and is collected with a spatula. The tree is then cut down, from where it coppices. The sap – about half a pint from each tree – is distilled and purified over six months, an expensive and time-intensive process.

p.219. *...or Meiji shrine...* At almost 40 feet high, with each column the trunk of an enormous cypress tree, the *torii* at the Meiji Jingu is one of the largest temple gates in Japan.

p.221. *The UK has a paltry 13 per cent woodland cover...* Source: https://www.forestresearch.gov.uk/tools-and-resources/statistics/statistics-by-topic/woodland-statistics/#:~:text=Key%20findings,and%209%25%20in%20Northern%20Ireland.

p.221. *...yet almost 70 per cent of Japan is forested...* While Japan has a good level of woodland cover now, the country was almost entirely deforested in the 1600s.

p.221. *...'And the oak tree and the cypress grow not in each other's shadow'...* Source: K. Gibran, *The Prophet*, Alfred A. Knopf, 1923.

p.222. *...'the cherry blossoms have all fallen since I took my eyes off them three days ago'...* With thanks to Masashi Kutsuwa for his translation of *Mikkaminumanosakura*. *Mikka* is three days, *minu* is not looking, *ma* is space or period, and *sakura* is cherry.

11. SEED COLLECTOR

p.229. *The limestone pavement of the Burren, one of the largest expanses of karst in Europe...* The Burren National Park covers about 77 square miles.

p.229. *...such as those discovered at nearby Aillwee...* According to research led by Centre of Environmental Research Innovation and Sustainability in Sligo, the brown bear skull, discovered in the cave at Ailwee, in 1976, was radiocarbon dated to over 10,600 years old. Another brown bear bone, a patella, found in the Alice and Gwendoline Caves, showed cut marks that suggested it had been butchered. The findings prompted a rethink of the previously accepted dating of the first human habitation in Ireland by over 2,000 years. Brown bears went extinct in Ireland around 1,000 BCE.

p.229. *...land owned by Irish Catholics during the Plantations...* The Protestant English and Scottish settlers outlawed Catholicism, and a mark of the strength of feeling that continues about this time is reflected in an argument over a Mass Rock on the land at Hometree's base near Ennystimon. The rock, which was used for Catholic mass during the time of the Penal Laws, is now partly covered by a hawthorn bush – the charity has argued the bush ought to be allowed to continue to grow, though local landowners have argued the Mass Rock ought to be uncovered as a monument to the injustices of the Plantations.

p.231. *...that Oliver Rackham talked about...* Rackham made this remark in his lecture marking the 2011 UN International Year of Forests.

p.232. *In one project, Hare's Corner,...* Hare's Corner is run by the Burrenbeo Trust. See www.burrenbeo.com/thc/

p.235. *...many of which are associated with the native trees of Ireland...* The same is true of England. So *holm* stands for holly, as in Holmfirth. *Ac* stands for oak as in Accrington and Acton, and taking a different root, the River Dart comes from *Deruenta*, which translates as 'the river where oak trees grow'. Ashton is the town of ash, bex, as in Bexhill is the hill of the box tree. More generically, frith or firth denotes a woodland, so Holmfirth is the holly wood, Hurst is a wooded hill and *try* simply means tree, as in Oswestry, or Oswald's tree or cross. There are more obvious examples, Appledore, Woodeaton. In Scotland, *Eskedale* is Norse for Valley of The Ash Trees. Scots pine is indicated by *giuthas* in a name, e.g. Guisachan and *Coille Guibhas nan Saighaid* – The Scots Fir Wood of The Arrows. Source: The Place Names of Aire and Strathglass, Inverness-shire.

p.235. *...in the name are associated with oak woods...* The word 'oak' itself derives from the Anglo Saxon *ac* where the Irish word is derived from *daur* and the Welsh *dar*.

p.238. *...here fell victim to the furnaces of the Industrial Revolution...* More recently, the owner of the Raheen estate on which the Brian Boru oak stands, clear-felled 100 acres of spruce plantation to make way for a native woodland regeneration project.

p.238. *...the only Irish indigenous pine was found growing on the Burren...* Until recently, it was thought that the only *Sinus silvestrus* in Ireland was from Scotland, any indigenous pines having gone extinct over 1,500 years ago and replaced by imported Scots pine.

p.241. *...three of ash, one of oak and one yew...* Native Irish trees also feature heavily in the Irish Cycles and the Mythological Cycles, denoting their importance in the culture.

p.242. *...as a result of the fact they are dioecious...* Some trees, like holly and yew, are monoecious, bearing male and female flowers on the same tree. Aspen, on the other hand, is dioecious, each tree is either male or female.

12. FIRE LIGHTER

In the retelling of the story of Māui and Mahuika, I am indebted to several sources including: the 1910 volume *Legends of Maui*, by W.D. Westervelt; *Myths and Legends of the Polynesians*, by Johannes Anderson, 1928, and *The Handbook of Polynesian Mythology*, by Robert Craig, 2004.

p.249. *...the transformation of human life...* This is discussed in some depth in Dr Richard Wrangham's *Catching Fire: How Cooking Made Us Human*, 2009.

p.249. *...around the flames of the fire...* The British Exploring Society organizes its young people into 'Fires' rather than groups, a fire being the number of people who can comfortably sit around a campfire.

p.249. *...some of our greatest stories...* A portion of this chapter appeared in a different form in an essay I wrote, titled, 'The Heart of the Trees' for the journal *Elementum*, 5.

p.254. *... 'qualities like humour, congeniality, and innovation'...* Source: 'Embers of society: Firelight talk among the Ju/'hoansi Bushmen', Weissner, Proceedings of the National Academy of Sciences. Vol. 111, no. 39, Sept. 30, 2014.

13. APPLE WAILER

p.259. *...the first cultivated apple trees appeared in Kazakhstan...* Roger Deakin gives an excellent account of his journey to chart the origins of the domesticated apple in *Wildwood: A Journey Through Trees*.

p.259. *...some 4,000 to 10,000 years ago...* One way of measuring an uptick in interest in folk traditions is the way in which they are embraced by moneymaking outfits. Many of the major cider farms now run their own wassails. It has become quite a business, though across the south of England, there are still many smaller, community wassails. I chose the one closest to home, not a wassail claiming some ancient lineage, but one of the newest, set up to celebrate the community orchard that had been planted the year before.

p.259. *...7,500 or so heritage varieties...* Statistic from Common Ground. There are estimates that there have been over 17,000 varieties.

p.259. *...and Onion Redstreak...* Apples often have community names that mean the same variety might be known under different names in different counties, or even between different villages.

p.259. *Among the crowd, I found Sally Pyner...* Sally Pyner is currently the Horticulture and Project Manager at Kehelland Trust, Camborne, Cornwall.

p.259. *...lost 90 per cent of its orchards since the 1950s...* According to the People's Trust for Endangered Species, we have lost over 90 per cent of traditional orchards in the UK.

p.260. *...apples now grow in most places on Earth...* Michael Pollan, in his book, *The Botany of Desire*, proposes that the apple–human relationship is one defined by its mutually beneficial nature, with apple trees providing us with nutritious food, and us extending the apple tree's range extensively, doing much of the world of natural selection in order that it might survive in most conditions.

p.260. *...embedded in our oldest stories...* In Greek mythology, the golden apples of the garden of the Hesperides were guarded by the serpentine monster Ladon, since those who ate them gained immortality.

p.260. *...for its sweet fruit and its sheer cultural importance...* One alternative theory about the reason the tree of knowledge of good and evil is often portrayed as an apple is that it was a kind of medieval pun from the translating of the Bible from Greek to Latin. The Latin words for 'apple' and 'evil' are almost identical.

p.260. *...in which the same tree is often considered to be a fig...* Incidentally, apples are important in Jewish culture – at Rosh Hashanah, the Jewish New Year, one of the traditional dishes is apples dipped in honey.

p.260. *...and a decent contender for the title of the tree of immortality...* In the Quran, the tree is not referred to as the tree of the knowledge of good and evil, but as either simply 'the tree' or 'the tree of immortality'.

p.261. *...set amid the city's towers of steel and glass...* Although there are no wassails as a ritual in Shakespeare's plays, the word 'wassail' appears in several plays including *Antony and Cleopatra*, *Macbeth*, *Hamlet* and *Henry V*. It appears Shakespeare had a fairly dim view of the practice, as in most of these references, 'wassail' is used as a synonym for rowdy drunkenness.

p.262. *...put simply, all the world's a playhouse...* It is worth noting that the jury is out on whether this was the motto of the Globe or a fabulation of subsequent writers, though it was clearly the inspiration for the lines Shakespeare put in Jaques's mouth in *As You Like It*: 'All the world's a stage and all the men and women merely players' (Act II, Scene VII). In particular, Tiffany Stern questioned the veracity of the claim. Source: T. Stern (1997), 'Was Totus Mundus Agit Histrionem ever the Motto of the Globe Theatre?', *Theatre Notebook*, 51, 122–7.

p.263. *...shut as 'chapels of Satan'...* The phrase comes from a Puritan sermon of 1580, within a line that read, 'Whoever shall visit the chapel of Satan, I mean the theatre, shall find many young ruffians who are past all shame.'

p.263. *The Globe theatre now sits not far...* The modern Globe is less than a quarter of a mile from the original theatre, mostly due to changes in the width of the Thames.

p.263. *...many of which came from the Forest of Dean...* The wood used for the rebuilt Globe came from across the UK, a mark of the challenge posed by the requirement of straight timber that would stretch the required span of 32 feet.

p.264. *...'resonant music no living person has ever heard before'...* Source: R. Hornby in *The Hudson Review*, Vol. 50, No. 4 (Winter, 1998), 617.

14. TREE WORSHIPPER

p.278. *...as it is notoriously difficult to age an ancient yew...* Dating ancient yews is notoriously difficult – some sources suggest this tree may be as young as a thousand years, though the truth is no one really knows. Research by the Ancient Yew Group in 2019 found that yews grow more quickly than was previously thought, meaning even the largest yew trees may be younger than previously estimated. According to The Woodland Trust, though, over 500 churches in the UK have yew trees growing in their grounds which predate the building of the church itself.

p.279. *...creating both the painkillers paracetamol and ibuprofen from an extract in pine trees...* Source: J.D. Tibbetts, M. Hutchby, W.B. Cunningham, R.S.L. Chapman, G. Kociok-Köhn, M.G. Davidson, S.D. Bull, 'Sustainable Syntheses of Paracetamol and Ibuprofen from Biorenewable β-pinene', *ChemSusChem*, 2023, e202300670.

p.279. *...John Maynard Keynes's promise of the golden era of leisure...* Source: J. Maynard Keynes, 'The Economic Possibilities of Our Grandchildren', in *Essays in Persuasion*, W.W. Norton, 1963.

p.280. *...making satellites out of wood...* When satellites break up on re-entry, no one really knows what the effect of the metals in the atmosphere is. With wood, we do know, and it's not all that harmful. The satellites have to be recalibrated for the use of wood, as they interfere with the instruments, though this is, apparently, not an insurmountable problem.

p.280. *...and bendable batteries...* Source: K. Chapman, 'The Wonderful Wizards of Wood', *Chemistry World*, 20 February 2023.

p.281. *...it is then itself biodegradable...* Source: 'Liangbing Hu makes wood stronger than steel', *C&EN*, vol. 100, issue 7, 2022.

p.281. *...some 25 feet around...* A larger yew was reported to have stood on the same site until the mid-1800s at which time the tree was accidentally burnt down in an attempt to dislodge a swarm of bees from a hollow in the trunk by smoking them out.

p.285. *... it was one of the church's many appropriations...* One of the other (possible) appropriations, the Green Man, is visible on the fifteenth-century rood screen in the church at Melangell, which also depicts the story of the hare.

p.285. *...as Christianity spread across the country...* It is worth noting that there are several of these symbols in the grounds of the church at Llangadwaladr, notably the pagan sun disc in the church gate, as noted by Jim Perrin in his article on the church for the *Guardian* in 'Country Diary: A simple but fascinating church', 8 December 2018.

p.286. *...contemplative resistance...* In the Foreword he provided for the collection *The Hare That Hides Within: Poems about St Melangell*, edited by Anne Cluysenaar and Norman Schwenk.

p.286. *...no more so than when we use that power to protect...* There are other stories of the power of people and trees from this part of the world. '*Cad Goddeu*', a medieval Welsh poem by Taliesin tells of the druid Gwydion calling on the spirits of all the trees to fight for him. And in the Mabinogi story of the childhood of Lleu Llaw Gyffes, Gwydion makes a forest appear to be an invading army.

p.286. *...to restore 865 million acres of degraded forest...* The Bonn Challenge of 2014 led to political leaders across the world adopting ambitious targets to reforest 865 million acres of degraded forest and agricultural land by 2030, and area bigger than the whole of India.

p.286. *...the science writer Colin Tudge...* Source: C. Tudge, *The Tree: A Natural History of What Trees Are, How They Live and Why They Matter,* 2007.

p.288. *As ecologist Oliver Rackham observed...* Source: O. Rackham, *Trees and Woodlands in the British Landscape,* p. 11.

p.288. *We read the years in their growth rings...* Not all trees have growth rings. Many trees in the tropics, where growth is more regular, do not produce growth rings in the same way, and dendrochronologists – those who are concerned with trees and time – have a range of methods for ascertaining the age of a tree, from radioisotopes.

p.290. *...known as the Nearly Home Trees...* The Nearly Home Trees are known by many names, notably to holidaymakers as the Nearly There Trees.

p.290. *...worship the sacred fig...* One volume is too small a space to dedicate to trees. In *The Heart of The Woods*, the fig tree barely gets a mention though it is one of the most spiritually important trees, globally. The fig is thought to be the first fruit tree described in the Garden of Eden and, in both the Jewish and Islamic traditions, the fruit eaten by Adam and Eve is often considered to be a fig rather than an apple. The fig is the Bodhi tree beneath which Siddhartha Gautama attained Enlightenment, after which he became known as the Buddha. Perhaps unsurprisingly, given the links between Hinduism and Buddhism, the fig is marked as sacred within Hindusim too, the banyan – a species of fig – being the tree into which Brahma was transformed. What is notable about the fig tree is its near universal relevance – there are traditions spanning Asia, South America, Africa and Oceania – West Papua, Australia – China, Kenya, Tanzania, India, Bolivia, all relating to the spiritual relevance of the fig tree. Kikuyu women in Africa smear themselves with the sap of fig trees to ensure pregnancy. In Bolivia, soul-stealing spirits dwell in the canopy of figs and walking under or felling these trees can cause illness. In Papua New Guinea, figs are believed to be the haunt of evil spirits which are released if they are felled. The fig – of which there are 750 species – is nutritious for people and animals, and a source of paper, cloth and medicines. Sources include: D. Wilson and A. Wilson, 'Figs as a Global Spiritual and Material Resource for Humans', *Human Ecology*, 2013; DOI: 10.1007/s10745-013-9582-z

p.290. *...our future too may be found somewhere in the heart of the woods.* As a final note, the English word 'book' is related to the proto-Germanic word '*buch*', for 'beech', presumably because of the beechwood tablets on which runes were set down or for the beech bark bindings that protected manuscripts. So, in a sense, you have been reading a tree.

SELECT BIBLIOGRAPHY

Adams, M., *The Wisdom of Trees*, Head of Zeus, 2014.

Anderson, J., *Myths and Legends of the Polynesians*, Dover Publications, 1928.

Bramwell, M. (ed.), *The International Book of Wood*, Outlet, 1982.

Calvino, I., Introduction to *Italian Folktales*, translated by George Martin, Pantheon Books, 1980, xxi.

Copper, A., (ed.), *Arboreal: A Collection of New Woodland Writing*, Little Toller Books, 2016.

Cotterell, A., *Norse Mythology*, Lorenz Books, 2000.

Craig, R., *Handbook of Polynesian Mythology*, Bloomsbury Academic, 2004.

Deakin, R,. *Wildwood: A Journey Through Trees*, Free Press, 2009.

Edlin, H., *Woodland Crafts in Britain*, David and Charles, 1973.

Evelyn, J., *Sylva*, 1664.

Anon., 'The Gest of Robin Hood', *c*.1400.

Hahn, T. (ed.), *Robin Hood in Popular Culture: Violence, Transgression and Justice*, D.S. Brewer, 2000.

Hemery, G. and S. Simblet, *The New Sylva*, Bloomsbury, 2014.

Hoban, R., *Riddley Walker*, Thames and Hudson, 1980.

Holt, J.C., *Robin Hood*, Thames and Hudson, 1989.

Huisman, D., '"Hoap of a Tree" in Riddley Walker', *Christianity and Literature*, vol. 43, nos. 3–4 (Spring–Summer 1994), 347–69.

Hutton, R., *The Stations of The Sun: A History of the Ritual Year in Britain*, Oxford University Press, 1996.

Kerven, R., *English Fairy Tales and Legends*, National Trust Books, 2008.

Louv, R., *Last Child in the Woods*, Atlantic Books, 2013.

Maitland, S., *Gossip in the Forest*, Granta, 2012.

Nardizzi, V., *Wooden Os: Shakespeare's Theatres and England's Trees*, University of Toronto Press, 2013.

Pegg, B., *Rites and Riots: Folk Customs of Britain and Europe*, Blandford Press, 1981.

Phillips, R., *Trees in Britain*, Pan Books, 1983.

Powell, L., *Working Sail: A Life in Wooden Boats*, The Dovecote Press, 2012.

Propp, V., *Theory and History of Folklore*, Manchester University Press, 1984.

Rackham, O., *Trees and Woodlands in the British Landscape*, Phoenix Press, 1990.

Read, H. and M. Frater, *Woodland Habitats*, Routledge, 1999.

Richards, E., *The Highland Clearances*, Birlinn, 2005.

Schama, S., *Landscape and Memory*, A.A. Knopf, 2008.

Scott, A., *A Pleasure in Scottish Trees*, Mainstream, 2002.

Seike, K., *The Art of Japanese Joinery*, Weatherhill/Tankosha, 1979.

Smout, T. (ed.), *Scottish Woodland History*, Scottish Cultural Press, 1997.

Sheldrake, M., *Entangled Life*, Bodley Head, 2020.

Anon., 'Sir Gawain and The Green Knight', *c*.1400.

Tatar, M., *The Annotated Brothers Grimm*, W.W. Norton, 2002.

Tatar, M., *The Hard Facts of the Grimms' Fairy Tales*, expanded second edition, Princeton University Press, 2003.

Thoreau, H.D., *Walden, or Life in the Woods*, Tickner and Fields, 1854.

Tudge, C., *The Secret Life of Trees*, Penguin, 2006.

Westervelt, W.D., *Legends of Maui*, Pantianos Classics, 1910.

Weissner, P., 'Embers of Society: Firelight Talk among the Ju/"hoansi Bushmen"', *PNAS*, vol. 111, no. 39, Sept. 2014.

Woods, W., 'Nature and the Inner Man in "Sir Gawain and The Green Knight"', *The Chaucer Review*, vol. 36, no. 3, 2002, 209–27.

ACKNOWLEDGEMENTS

First and foremost, to the people who shared their stories with me and helped me to get closer to the heart of the woods.

To my agent, Peter Straus, my editors Richard Green, Phoebe Bath, Michael Brunström, Viviane Basset, Matthew Hopkins, Jasmine Brame, Aruna Vasudevan, and the teams at Aurum and Quarto.

To the kindness of funders at The Great Britain Sasakawa Foundation, in particular Rory Steele, and the Research Department at Falmouth University, who part-funded my research trip to Japan.

To the *Hida no takumi*, the master craftsmen and women of Takayama, above all 久津輪 雅, Masashi Kutsuwa, whose kindness and expertise floored me. Thank you, my friend – I owe you a great debt – 助けてくれてありがとう. To 蓑谷百合子, Minotani, Yuriko for introducing me to urushi forests and the Japanese tea ceremony. To 川上真司, Kawakami, Shinji, 松山義治, Matsuyama, Yoshiharu, 松山真也, Matsuyama, Shinya, 小坂礼之, Kosaka, Ayayuki, 川上憲一, Kawakami, Ken-ichi, 川上舟晴, Kawakami, Shusei, 西田恵一, Nishida, Keiichi, and 小木曽賢一, Kogiso, Ken-ichi. 本当にありがとうございます.

To Gabriel Hemery and Joe Bray at Sylva Foundation, Dorothy Graham, Alan Torrance and the community at GalGael. To Alastair McIntosh, Guy Shrubsole and the members of the Devon South Right to Roam group, Luke Powell, Felix and Gabe, Julie Fowlis, Will Gilchrist, Helen Reynolds, Hilary Coleman and Pol Jenkin, Ken and Ruth Powell, Nigel Fisher, conservator of Wytham Woods,

Professor Keith Kirby and Dr Cecelia Dahlsjö, Tom Ingate and Oli Udy, Ravi Bains, Andy Harbert and the workshop teams at Falmouth University, all at the Association of Pole-lathe Turners & Green Wood Workers, in particular Paul Adamson, Martin Hazell, Amy Leake, Maz and Fuzz Bown. To Suzann Barr at Abriachan Forest Trust. Rachel, Claire and the team at Moniack Mhor. To Tom Kemp at Working Woods Cornwall. To Jessie Carr, and Ele and Anthony Waters. To Nema Hart and Nick Hart for sharing their family tree with me, Sarah Crown, Jeremy Turkington, Matt Smith and Grace Wells at Hometree, Ireland. To Sarah Pyner and Jack Morrison. To Merlin Sheldrake and to Mark Rylance and Jon Greenfield. To Dad and Alison. To Mum and Maurice.

And, as always, to Emma, Tom and Alana.

INDEX

Page numbers in *italics* refer to captions.